Global Investment Competitiveness Report 2017/2018

Global Investment Competitiveness Report 2017/2018

Foreign Investor Perspectives and Policy Implications

WORLD BANK GROUP

ISBN (paper): 978-1-4648-1175-3
ISBN (electronic): 978-1-4648-1185-2
DOI: 10.1596/978-1-4648-1175-3

Cover design: Bill Pragluski, Critical Stages.

Library of Congress Cataloging-in-Publication Data has been requested.

Contents

Boxes

Figures

Maps

Tables

Foreword

This inaugural issue of the World Bank Group's *Global Investment Competitiveness Report* presents novel analytical insights and empirical evidence on foreign direct investment's (FDI) drivers and contributions to economic transformation. The report focuses on developing countries, given their growing role as both sources and recipients of FDI, and explores how policy makers and local companies can best harness FDI's potential benefits for inclusive and sustainable development.

Three key features distinguish this report from other leading FDI studies. First, its insights come from a variety of sources, including a new survey of investor perspectives, extensive analysis of available data and evidence, and a thorough review of international best practices in investment policy design and implementation. Second, the report provides targeted, in-depth analysis of FDI differentiated by motivation, sector, and geographic origin and destination of investment. Third, the report offers practical and actionable recommendations to developing country governments.

The report introduces a new concept of *investment competitiveness*, defined by the ability of countries to not only attract but also retain and integrate private investment into their respective economies. Enhancing investment competitiveness thus requires establishing a business environment in which both domestic and foreign companies can efficiently enter the market, expand operations, and develop more and better linkages with local, regional, and global economies. This report examines the key dimensions of investment competitiveness and highlights those that most commonly influence companies' investment decisions.

The report's groundbreaking survey of 754 executives of multinational corporations investing in developing countries finds that—in addition to political stability, security, and macroeconomic conditions—a business-friendly legal and regulatory environment is the key driver of investment decisions. The report also explores the potential of FDI to create new growth opportunities for local firms; assesses the effectiveness of fiscal incentives in attracting FDI; analyzes the characteristics of FDI originating in developing countries—so-called South–South and South–North FDI—and examines the experience of foreign investors in countries afflicted by conflict and fragility. Future editions of this biennial *Global Investment Competitiveness Report* will present findings on new sets of investment competitiveness topics high on the agendas of reform-oriented governments, complemented by an update of the survey.

We are confident this new report will bring value and a fresh perspective to a variety of audiences. For policy makers, the report offers clear insights into the role of policy and the decision-making processes of investors. For foreign investors and site location consultants, the report discusses relevant FDI developments and drivers across sectors and geographies. For academic audiences, the report's new datasets on investment incentives and FDI motivations offer scope for additional research and analysis. Last, for development assistance providers, the report highlights approaches for harnessing FDI's potential development benefits.

Above all, we recommend this report to all audiences interested in the central role that private investment can and must play in furthering sustainable and inclusive development.

Anabel Gonzalez
Senior Director
Trade and Competitiveness Global Practice
World Bank Group

Ted H. Chu
Chief Economist
International Finance Corporation
World Bank Group

Acknowledgments

This inaugural flagship report on global investment competitiveness was developed as a joint initiative of the Investment Climate team in the World Bank Group's Trade and Competitiveness Global Practice and the Economics and Private Sector Development Vice Presidency of the International Finance Corporation (IFC). The report's preparation was managed by Christine Zhenwei Qiang and Peter Kusek, under the general guidance of Anabel Gonzalez, World Bank Group Senior Director for Trade and Competitiveness, and Ted Chu, IFC Chief Economist. The report's authors comprised Maria R. Andersen, Benjamin R. Kett, Peter Kusek, Jose Ramon Perea, Alexandros Ragoussis, José-Daniel Reyes, Heba Shams, Andrea Silva, Matthew Stephenson, and Erik von Uexkull. The authors particularly appreciate the useful advice of Roberto Echandi.

The team would like to thank the following donors for making this report possible through their financial contributions: Prosperity Fund of the United Kingdom, the Department of Foreign Affairs and Trade (DFAT) of the Government of Australia, and the Federal Ministry of Finance of the Government of Austria.

The team is also grateful to the many internal and external reviewers who provided thoughtful insights and guidance throughout the process, including Cecile Fruman, Neil Gregory, Mary Hallward-Driemeier, Theodore Moran, Richard Newfarmer, Emanuel Salinas, and Pierre Sauvé. In April 2017, a consultative authors, workshop provided added feedback from Nabila Assaf, Sebastien Bradley, Marcio Cruz, Jan Loeprick, Ernesto Lopez-Cordova, Denis Medvedev, Sebastien Miroudot, and Gonzalo Varela. The authors are very grateful for the generous time and advice given at various stages of this report by external researchers, including Fritz Foley, Beata Javorcik, Michael Overesch, Karl Sauvant, and Charles Udomsaph.

The report's authors are grateful for the excellent research assistance and overall support of Laura Ardila, Abdullah Aswat, Angelina Yue Ben, Kunxiang Diao, Zhi Gan, Jingyu Gao, Daisy Claire Homolka, Xinyuan Huang, Salima Madhany, Jordan Pace, Martin Schmidt, and Xiaoxu Zhang.

The team would also like to recognize various World Bank Group and other colleagues for their helpful guidance and assistance—without them this report would not have been complete. These include

Daniela Gomez Altamirano, Gerlin Catangui, Laura Dachner, Wim Douw, Persephone Economou, Amr El Afifi, Francis Gagnon, Ulla Heher, Armando Heilbron, Sebastian James, Priyanka Kher, Kathy Khuu, Barbara Kotschwar, Jana Krajcovicova, Hania Kronfol, Veselin Kuntchev, Wim Naude, Ivan Nimac, Ngan Thuy Nguyen, Nadia Piffaretti, Yassin Sabha, Patricia Steele, Trang Tran, and Robert Whyte.

David M. Cheney was the principal editor of the report. Andrea Silva, Amanda L. Tan, and Edward Atkinson provided editorial assistance. Production and logistics support was provided by Aziz Gökdemir and Jewel McFadden. The communications efforts were led by John Diamond and included Egidio Germanetti, Amelia Kelly, Kristina Nwazota, and Madelynne Wager.

The *Global Investment Competitiveness Survey* analyzed in chapter 1 was undertaken on behalf of the World Bank Group by Kantar Public, a global survey firm. We are particularly grateful for the contributions of the following Kantar Public colleagues: Jamie Burnett, Lavinia Deaconu, Christopher Hanley, and Marco Pelucchi.

The team acknowledges the many formal and informal contributions of individuals, groups, and organizations that provided meaningful comments and inputs to enable the successful publication of this report. Keeping in mind these contributions, the team apologizes if it has inadvertently omitted formally acknowledging any such valuable contributions.

Abbreviations

BRICS	Brazil, the Russian Federation, India, China, South Africa
BIT	bilateral investment treaty
CATI	computer-assisted telephone interviews
CBA	cost–benefit analysis
CCSD	Center on Conflict, Security and Development
CIT	corporate income tax
CORFO	Chilean Economic Development Agency (Corporación de Fomento de la Producción de Chile)
CPIA	Country Policy and Institutional Assessment
EAP	East Asia and Pacific
ECA	Europe and Central Asia
EU	European Union
FCS	fragile and conflict-affected situations
FDI	foreign direct investment
FFP	The Fund for Peace
GDP	gross domestic product
GIC	Global Investment Competitiveness
GVC	global value chain
ICT	information and communications technology
IEG	Independent Evaluation Group
IFC	International Finance Corporation
IPA	investment promotion agency
ISIC	International Standard Industrial Classification
IT	information technology
LAC	Latin America and the Caribbean
M&A	mergers and acquisitions

MENA	Middle East and North Africa
MNC	multinational corporation
ODA	Official Development Assistance
OECD	Organisation for Economic Co-operation and Development
OFDI	outward foreign direct investment
POEs	privately owned enterprises
PPML	Poisson Pseudo-Maximum Likelihood
R&D	research and development
SAR	South Asia Region
SDGs	Sustainable Development Goals
SDP	Supplier Development Program
SEZ	special economic zone
SMEs	small and medium-size enterprises
SOEs	state-owned enterprises
SSA	Sub-Saharan Africa
UCC	user cost of capital
UNCTAD	United Nations Conference on Trade and Development
UNSD	United Nations Statistics Division
USAID	United States Agency for International Development
VAT	value added tax
WBG	The World Bank Group
WEF	World Economic Forum

Overview

Anabel Gonzalez, Christine Zhenwei Qiang,
and Peter Kusek

Foreign Investment Is a Major Contributor to Development

For many developing countries,[1] foreign direct investment (FDI) has become the largest source of external finance, surpassing official development assistance (ODA), remittances, or portfolio investment flows. In 2016, more than 40 percent of the nearly $1.75 trillion of global FDI flows was directed to developing countries, providing much-needed private capital (figure O.1). Yet the financing required to achieve the Sustainable Development Goals (SDGs)[2] remains prohibitively large and largely unmet by current FDI inflows—especially in fragile and conflict-affected situations (FCS) (map O.1). To maximize the development impact of FDI and thus help meet the SDGs, private investment will have to expand into areas where it has not yet ventured, notwithstanding the associated risks.

The benefits of FDI extend well beyond attracting needed capital. Foreign investment also confers technical know-how, managerial and organizational skills, and access to foreign markets. Furthermore, FDI has a significant potential to transform economies through innovation, enhancing productivity, and creating better-paying and more stable jobs in host countries, in sectors attracting FDI as well as in the supportive industries (Arnold, Javorcik, and Mattoo 2011; Bijsterbosch and Kolasa 2009; Echandi, Krajcovicova, and Qiang 2015; Rizvi and Nishat 2009; WEF 2013). Importantly, foreign investors are becoming increasingly prominent players in delivering global public goods, addressing climate change, improving labor conditions, setting global industry standards, and delivering infrastructure to local communities (IFC, forthcoming). This report builds on the literature in highlighting the role of FDI in upgrading growth and adding value to domestic firms, in filling the investment void in FCS, and more generally, in increasing competitiveness and stability.

FDI can accelerate productivity gains in host countries. It brings foreign technology and frontier knowledge that, if successfully absorbed by local firms, can improve their productivity directly. FDI can also increase

FIGURE O.1   FDI Inflows, Global and by Development Group, 2005–16

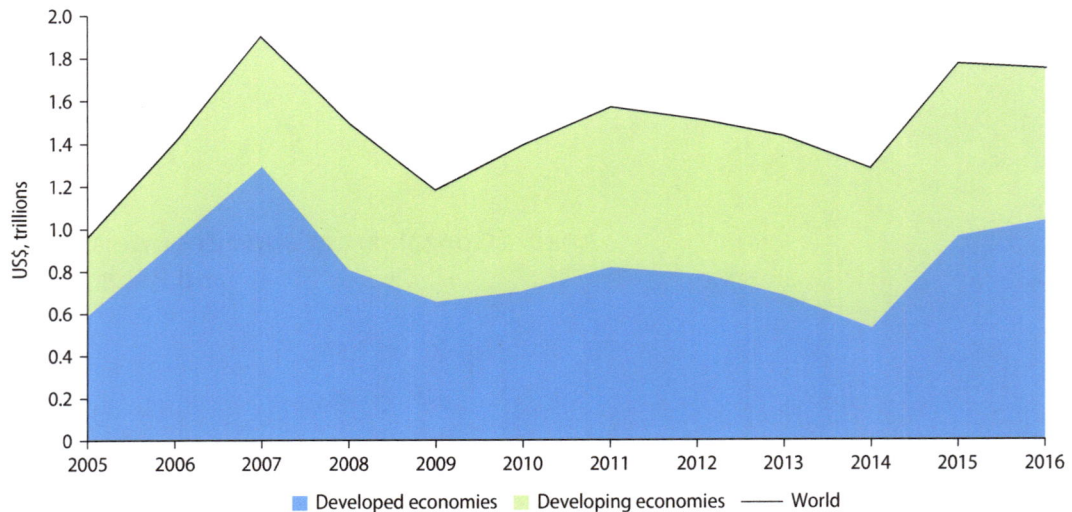

Source: Statistics and World Investment Report 2017, United Nations Conference on Trade and Development (UNCTAD).
Note: FDI = foreign direct investment.

MAP O.1   FDI Flows to FCS Remain below Potential, 2008–Present

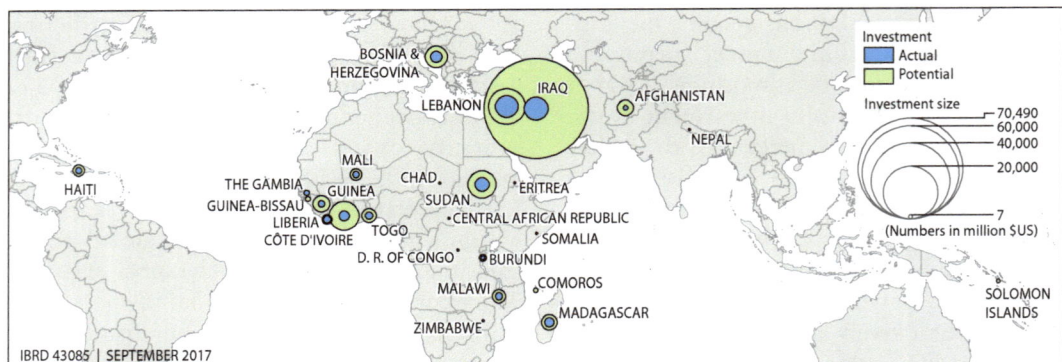

Source: Computation based on Investment Map Database, International Trade Centre; World Development Indicators, the World Bank; CEPII Database; Fragile States Index (2014), the Fund for Peace.
Note: Investment potential is calculated as foreign direct investment (FDI) inflow estimates without the negative effect of fragility. They are calculated for selected fragile and conflict-affected situations (FCS) based on countries' economic fundamentals (market size, growth, trade openness, savings), geographical remoteness, and abundance of natural resources, where the negative effect of fragility is removed.

competition among firms in the local market by leading to a reallocation of resources away from less productive to more productive firms, thereby increasing aggregate productivity over the long run. FDI can benefit domestic firms mainly through linkages and demonstration channels:

- *Linkages* between foreign firms and local partners or suppliers can promote

transmission of foreign firms' technology, knowledge, and practices, as well as requirements that may help domestic suppliers upgrade their technical and quality standards (Du, Harrison, and Jefferson 2011; Farole and Winkler 2014; Javorcik and Spatareanu 2009). A recent study in Turkey suggests that interactions between multinational corporations (MNCs) and their Turkish suppliers facilitate an upgrading of Turkish products (Javorcik, Lo Turco, and Maggioni 2017). Firm-level analyses from Lithuania and Vietnam present evidence that there are positive productivity spillovers from FDI through linkages between foreign affiliates and their local suppliers in the upstream sectors (Javorcik 2004; Newman and others 2015).

- The *demonstration effect*, in which domestic firms imitate foreign technologies and managerial practices either through observation or by hiring workers trained by foreign companies (Alfaro and Chen forthcoming; Alfaro and Rodriguez-Claire 2004; Alfaro and others 2006; Barba Navaretti and Venables 2004; Lipsey 2004), is another key channel benefitting firms in host countries. For example, the contribution of workers' mobility from MNCs to domestic firms in the Ghanaian manufacturing sectors has had a positive impact on the productivity of domestic enterprises. In Norway, workers with prior experience in MNCs contribute 20 to 25 percent more to productivity than workers without such experience (Balsvik 2006; Görg and Strobl 2005).

High-Growth Firms in Host Countries Benefit Most from FDI

This report analyzes the ability of domestic firms to benefit from the presence of MNCs, drawing on firm-level information across 50 manufacturing and services sectors and 121 economies in the developing world from the World Bank's Enterprise Surveys. It finds that local high-growth firms (defined as the subset of enterprises with the highest job creation rates) are most able to internalize FDI spillovers— through both linkages and demonstration channels. For the linkages channel, an increase of 1 percentage point in the share of inputs sourced domestically by foreign firms is correlated with a 0.6 unit rise in the measure of output growth of domestic high-growth firms. This result implies a 58 percent increase in sales over

two years for the average high-growth firm. For the demonstration channel, an increase of 1 percentage point in the share of foreign output in the sector is correlated with a 0.1 unit gain in output growth of high-growth firms, or 12 percent increase in sales over the two years for the average high-growth firm (figure O.2).

While high-growth firms usually account for only a small part of the private sector, they have a disproportionately large role in job creation and productivity gains. They are better able to maximize the benefits from FDI because of their higher absorptive capacities—their ability to recognize the value of, assimilate, and apply new information. Such abilities allow these firms to internalize foreign technologies and processes to improve their productivity, thereby dampening the competitive impact of rivalry with foreign-established firms. Furthermore, the demands of global brands, and their

FIGURE O.2 **High-Growth Firms Benefit from the Presence of Foreign Firms**

Average impact of FDI spillovers on firm growth, by firm type

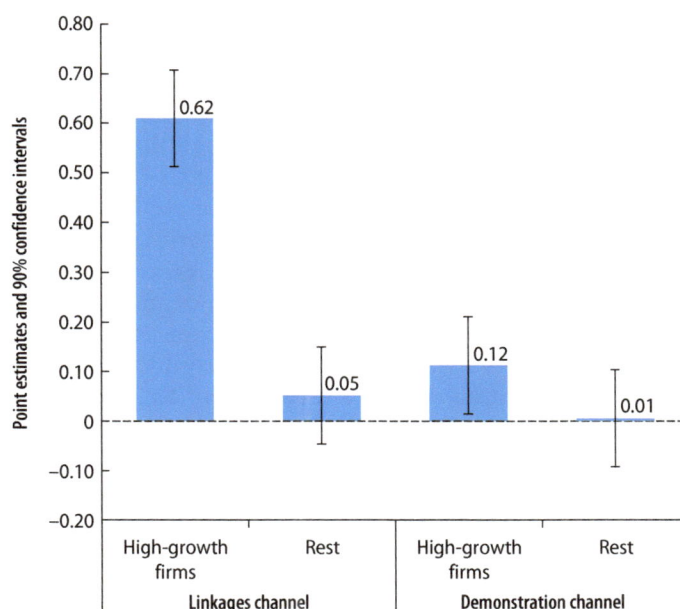

Source: Computation based on data from Enterprise Surveys, the World Bank.
Note: This figure shows the estimated coefficient and 90% confidence interval of the linkages and demonstration channels on high-growth firms and the rest of businesses in a sample of 121 economies. Vertical lines capture 90% confidence intervals. FDI = foreign direct investment.

commitment to their suppliers, create a strong incentive and impetus for suppliers to adopt new practices and invest in new technologies. From a policy perspective, identifying and targeting these firms, analyzing the constraints on their emergence, and deepening their absorptive capacities are all key to unleashing their full potential. The empirical evidence presented in this report indicates that policies that encourage FDI linkages as a way for high-potential indigenous firms to grow will enhance knowledge transmission between MNCs and domestic firms, and deliver strong development results.

Outward FDI Also Benefits Source Economies

FDI brings benefits not only to destination markets but also to source economies ("home country effects"). MNCs from developing countries use outward investment to strengthen their capabilities and competitiveness by entering new markets, importing intermediate inputs from foreign affiliates at lower prices, producing a larger volume of final goods and services abroad at lower cost, and accessing foreign technology (Herzer 2012). Some developing countries, instead of exploiting *existing* technological assets, aim to acquire *new* ones through outward FDI. Case studies of leading MNCs from BRICS countries (Brazil, the Russian Federation, India, China, and South Africa) show that they are disadvantaged in terms of patents, management know-how, or cutting-edge processes, which prompt them to acquire companies abroad to permit "late-comer catch-up" (Holtbrügge and Kreppel 2012; Rodriguez-Arango and Gonzalez-Perez 2016; UNCTAD 2005).

Outward FDI by developing countries can bring significant economic advantages back to source economies, especially enhanced innovation. While developed countries were once seen as the prime source of knowledge and technology—thus imparting a North–North or North–South bias to cross-border investment—a multipolar global technology network is now emerging, with growing South–South and South–North innovation-oriented interaction and collaboration (Nepelski and De Prato 2015). This may be partly because knowledge originating in developing countries may be better suited to other developing country settings, and because the level of complexity of that knowledge may be more easily absorbed by other economies at similar levels of development. This report highlights how the increased absorptive capacity of firms in source markets can promote a wide dispersion of outward FDI benefits in the home economy.

Despite abundant evidence on the development benefits of FDI, the global economic outlook remains uncertain, clouded by risks of trade and investment protectionism and geopolitical risk. While globalization brings aggregate productivity and economic growth, it may also bring hardship for low-productivity firms and low-skill workers. Slow public policy responses to rapidly evolving patterns of investment and economic activities contribute to misconceptions and oversimplification of features and potential effects of FDI. In certain countries, opponents of FDI-led integration further contend that its effects are often limited and, in some cases, detrimental—as it crowds out local competition, results in enclave production with limited linkages, and engenders a "race to the bottom" in labor or environment standards or in their enforcement.[3] Not surprisingly, policy discussions increasingly distinguish between "good" and "bad" FDI. Some argue that a foreign presence can lead to political grievances through its adverse effects on the distribution of income and opportunities, particularly concerning FDI in extractive industries (International Dialogue for Peace-Building and State-Building 2016). Others, however, find that trade and FDI complement each other in reducing the risk of conflict (Polachek and Sevastianova 2012). The truth is that there are different types of FDI, each with different potential social, economic, and environmental effects. Further, evidence shows that there is not intrinsic "good" or "bad" FDI. Rather, there are good or bad policies that can or cannot lead countries to fully reap the potential benefits of FDI for development (Echandi, Krajcovicova, and Qiang 2015).

On balance, the bulk of the research and empirical evidence finds that FDI helps to foster development in recipient economies. Though some of the above criticisms are warranted and the distributional effects of the different types of FDI merit closer study, evidence for such claims is often anecdotal and applicable to only a narrow subset of industries and economies. As this report shows, the benefits of FDI can be strongly magnified in economies with good governance, well-functioning institutions, and transparent and predictable legal environments. Moreover, not all types of FDI nor all stages in the investment life cycle[4] exert the same effects on host countries. Some countries may attract FDI yet not enable its entry and establishment, or enable its establishment yet not its expansion and "rooting" in the host economy through linkages and other spillovers. These point to the need for a more nuanced analysis of FDI impacts.

Investment Decisions Are Influenced by Risk–Return Calculations

Investors consider a broad range of factors in their decision to invest, including domestic market size, macroeconomic stability and a favorable exchange rate, labor force talent and skills, and physical infrastructure. According to the *Global Investment Competitiveness* (GIC) survey (box O.1),

---

BOX 0.1

Global Investment Competitiveness Survey

The Global Investment Competitiveness (GIC) survey was commissioned by the World Bank Group as a companion piece of the GIC report to bring data and information on the views and behavior of global investors that goes beyond anecdotal evidence. Phone interviews were conducted between February and June 2017 with 754 international business executives involved with the operations of their multinational corporation in developing countries. Respondents come from both developed and developing countries and represent a wide range of sectors.

The GIC survey captures perceptions of these investors on the role of investment climate factors in guiding their FDI decisions. It complements other existing investor surveys by focusing on variables such as administrative and legal barriers rather than broader economy-wide factors. These specific investment climate variables are areas that are actionable for policy makers.

The survey is composed of four sections:

1. *General information on the company and respondent*, including sector, number of employees, and position of the respondent in the company.

2. *Importance of factors in investing in a developing country*, where respondents rate the importance of country characteristics and investment policy factors on a scale from 1 to 4 from "not at all important" to "critically important." "Critically important" means it is a deal-breaker—by itself, it could change the company's decision about whether to invest or not in a country.

3. *Political risks and investment exit*, where respondents identify experiences of political risks and the company's course of action. They were also asked about experience of shutting down a foreign affiliate in a developing country and their reasons for doing so.

4. *Investment in a specific developing country*, where respondents select a specific developing country where they are most familiar with the operations of the affiliate. Questions on the specific investment included sector, activity, motivation, reinvested earnings, efficiency of government agencies, availing services of investment promotion agencies, incentives received, sources of inputs, and corporate programs for suppliers.

political stability and a business-friendly regulatory environment are most important in investors' decision making (figure O.3). Macroeconomic, political, and regulatory risks—whether actual or perceived—deter investors by raising their risk calculations. De-risking, or reducing project or country risk, can lead to the right risk–return profile and help attract private investment. Otherwise investments that are commercially profitable and economically attractive may simply not materialize.

Governments in both developing and developed countries use tax and other investment incentives to reduce the relative cost or risks to foreign investment so as to attract more FDI, often not distinguishing among the different types of FDI.[5] Given that most countries offer incentives, investment promotion agencies face pressure to match or even surpass offers by competing countries to compensate for adverse geography, small size, or distance to markets, in order to remain attractive for foreign investors.

Yet investment incentives become relevant only when investors waver between similar locations. Where FDI is motivated by access to domestic markets or natural resources, incentives are generally of limited value. However, in sectors where FDI is mainly efficiency-seeking in nature (for example, manufacturing of information technology [IT] and electronics, machinery and equipment, automotive, air- and spacecraft, and biotechnology and pharmaceuticals), competition for FDI is high and developing countries frequently offer incentives to compete. In these sectors, most FDI projects are clustered in a limited number of successful host countries. At the same time, the use of incentives is particularly prevalent in these sectors (figure O.4, upper right quadrant). This suggests that developing countries use incentives strategically in sectors with high shares of efficiency-seeking FDI where locational competition for FDI is particularly intense. It also reveals that, while incentives may be a more important part of the value proposition to efficiency-seeking investors,

FIGURE O.3   Factors Affecting Investment Decisions

Share of respondents (percent)

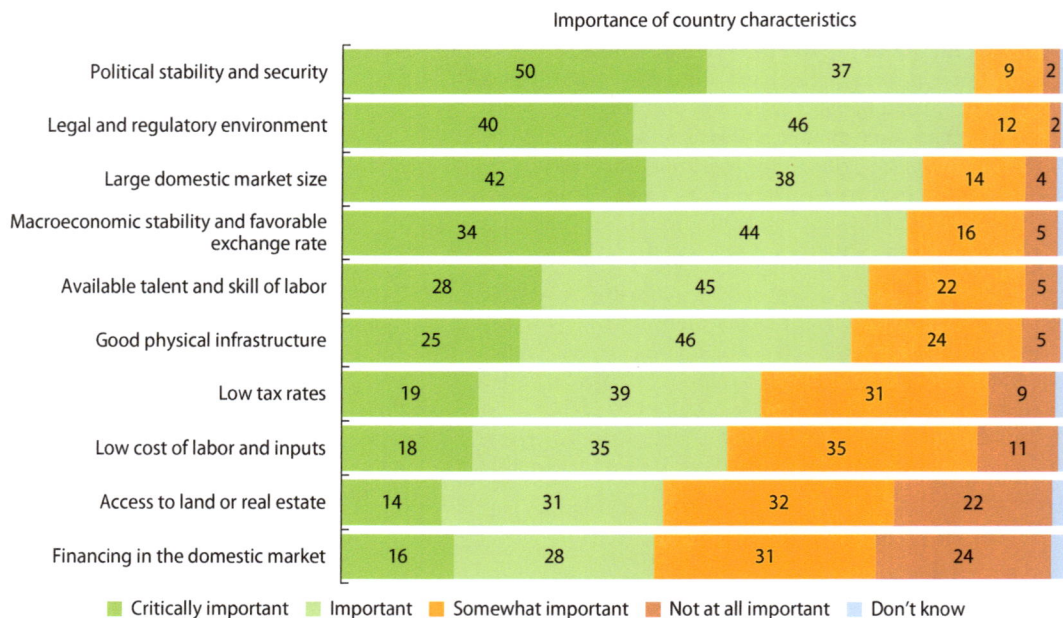

Importance of country characteristics

	Critically important	Important	Somewhat important	Not at all important	Don't know
Political stability and security	50	37	9	2	
Legal and regulatory environment	40	46	12	2	
Large domestic market size	42	38	14	4	
Macroeconomic stability and favorable exchange rate	34	44	16	5	
Available talent and skill of labor	28	45	22	5	
Good physical infrastructure	25	46	24	5	
Low tax rates	19	39	31	9	
Low cost of labor and inputs	18	35	35	11	
Access to land or real estate	14	31	32	22	
Financing in the domestic market	16	28	31	24	

■ Critically important ■ Important ■ Somewhat important ■ Not at all important ■ Don't know

Source: Computation based on the GIC Survey.
Note: Multinational corporation executives were asked how important these characteristics were in their decision to invest in developing countries.

FIGURE O.4   Prevalence of Incentives and FDI Concentration

(Incentives are used most in sectors with high competition for efficiency-seeking FDI)

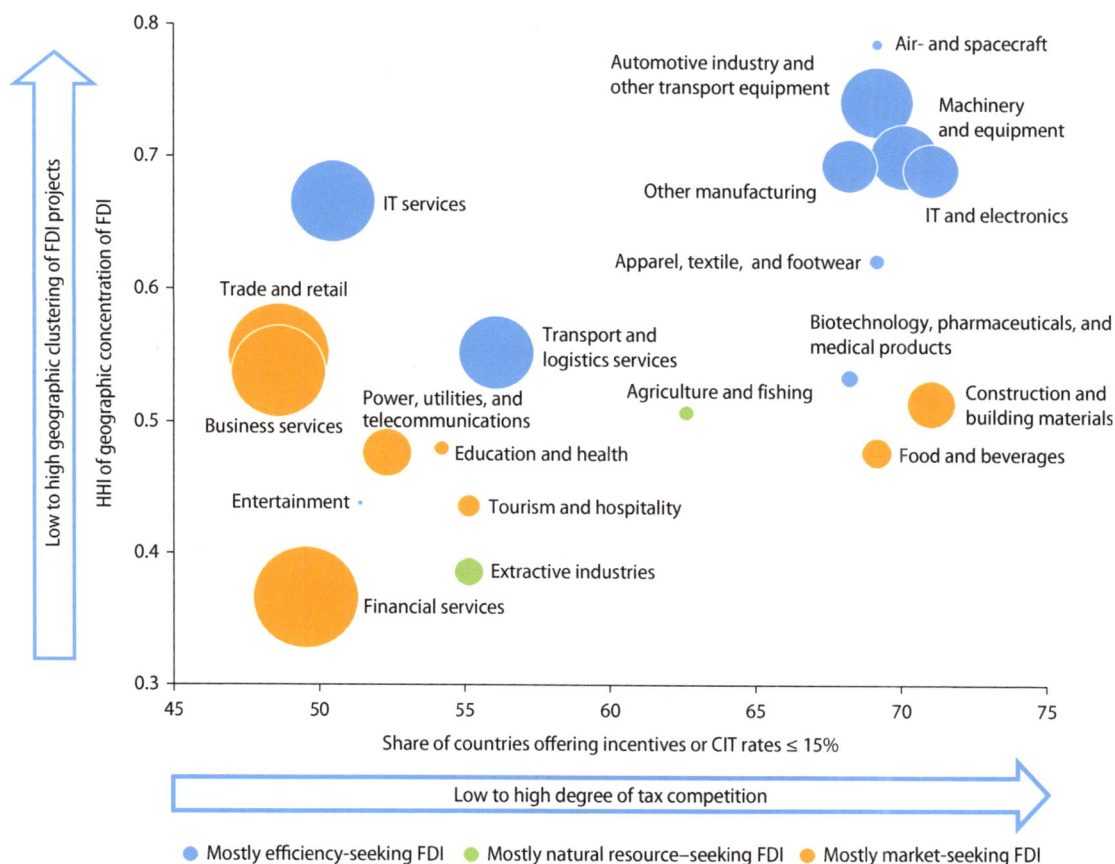

Source: Developing Country Tax Incentives database and FDI data from fDi Markets database, the Financial Times.
Note: The size of each bubble represents the number of FDI projects within the sector in developing countries. This was constructed based on information from the fDi Markets database. CIT = corporate income tax; FDI = foreign direct investment; HHI = Herfindahl-Hirschman Index; IT = information technology.

they are not a sufficient condition for FDI entry, as efficiency-seeking FDI tends to concentrate geographically in relatively few locations despite the broad availability of incentives.

More targeted, transparent, and cost-effective use of investment incentives can improve their impact. By targeting incentives toward those investors most likely to respond to them, developing countries can reduce unnecessary tax losses resulting from incentives granted to firms that would have invested anyway. This requires a thorough understanding of the type and motivation for FDI in the country, as well as measurable policy objectives. At the same time,

improvements in the design, transparency, and administration of incentives can help reduce indirect costs and unintended consequences including economic distortions, red tape, and corruption. Such policy reforms can greatly improve the cost–benefit ratio of incentives.

Governments Play a Key Role in De-Risking Private Investment

Reducing the risks of private investment at the project level does not compensate for failing to de-risk regulations and institutions at the country level. Investment incentives or investment guarantees are frequently used to bolster locational competitiveness or investment viability for specific projects or sectors, but investment climate weaknesses must be addressed first. If fundamental elements at the country level are lacking, investors are unlikely to respond to even the most generous incentive packages or such incentives may only attract unviable investments. Governments can reduce risks to private investors through a policy and institutional framework that supports an enabling business climate and ensures good governance. Since reliable regulations and institutions are key to de-risking private investment at the country level, they are an increasingly important element on the Maximizing Finance for Development agenda.

In this report, de-risking involves removing or reducing political and regulatory risks caused by government action, building on macroeconomic stability and good infrastructure in order to attract private investment.

Political risks are wide-ranging and include expropriation, transfer and convertibility restrictions, breach of contracts, unpredictable and arbitrary actions, discrimination, and the absence of regulatory transparency. Loss of investment and the associated damage to long-term harmonious relations with a promising investor can have a debilitating impact on a developing country. Political risk related to government conduct also sends negative signals to prospective investors, creating strong ripple effects.

More than three-quarters of investors surveyed in this report encountered some type of political risk in their investment projects in developing countries. In severe cases, such as expropriation, about half of the investors canceled a planned investment or withdrew an existing one (figure O.5). Legal protection to investors against such risk is usually provided by "investor protection guarantees" typically included in a country's domestic legal framework and its international investment agreements (IIAs). In this report's survey, 81 percent

FIGURE O.5   **Political Risks Are Prevalent and Discourage FDI**
Share of respondents (percent)

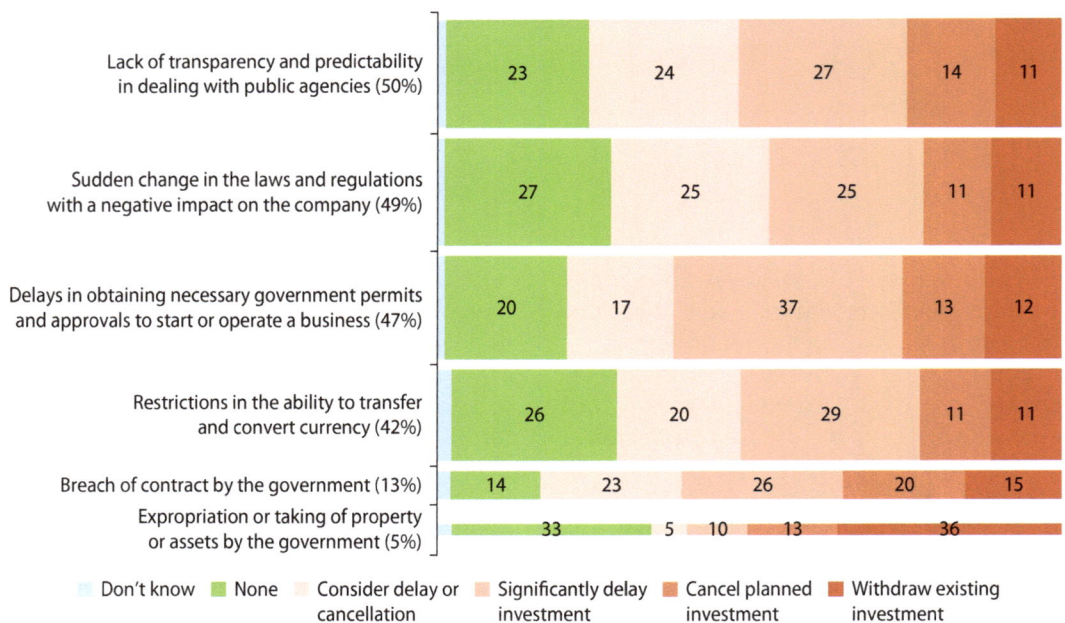

Source: Computation based on the GIC Survey.
Note: FDI = foreign direct investment.

FIGURE O.6   **Regulatory Predictability and Efficiency Are Critical**
Share of respondents (percent)

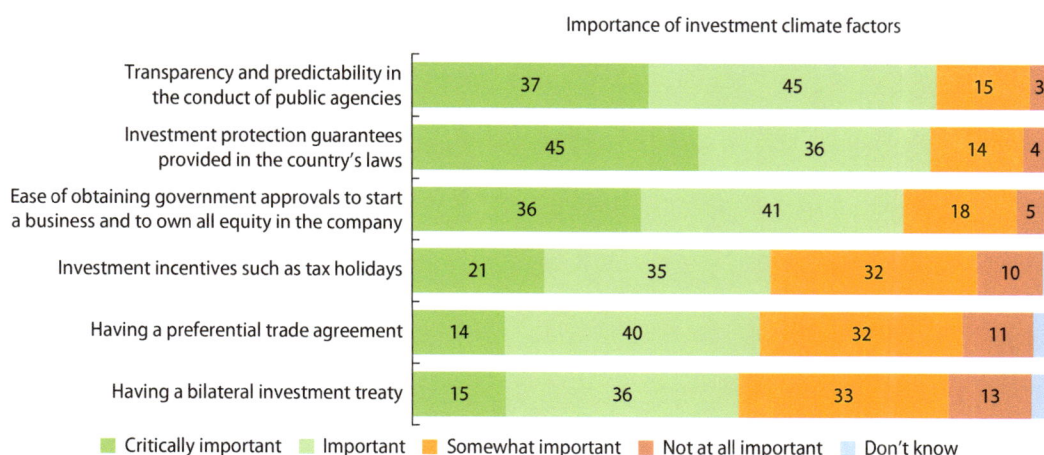

Importance of investment climate factors

	Critically important	Important	Somewhat important	Not at all important	Don't know
Transparency and predictability in the conduct of public agencies	37	45	15	3	
Investment protection guarantees provided in the country's laws	45	36	14	4	
Ease of obtaining government approvals to start a business and to own all equity in the company	36	41	18	5	
Investment incentives such as tax holidays	21	35	32	10	
Having a preferential trade agreement	14	40	32	11	
Having a bilateral investment treaty	15	36	33	13	

■ Critically important   ■ Important   ■ Somewhat important   ■ Not at all important   ■ Don't know

Source: Computation based on the GIC Survey

of investors rate country legal protections and 51 percent rate bilateral investment treaties as important or critically important in their investment decisions (figure O.6). Such findings echo the literature documenting the generally positive impacts of IIAs on FDI inflows (Echandi, Krajcovicova, and Qiang 2015).

Investors also seek predictability and efficiency in the implementation of laws and regulations (figure O.6). About four out of five investors surveyed rate the transparency and predictability of public agency conduct—and the ease of doing business—as important determinants of their locational decisions. This is not surprising, since many developing countries have inefficient bureaucracies, opaque regulations, complex procedures, and high transaction costs—all of which can undermine their competitiveness. More than one-third of investors rate these as critically important factors or potential deal-breakers. Predictability and efficiency are essential ingredients of sound and sustained interaction between MNCs and host governments, comprising both regulations themselves and their implementation.

Developing Country MNCs Are Today an Increasing Source of FDI

FDI from developing countries has increased twentyfold in the last two decades, accounting for nearly one-fifth of global FDI flows in 2015. As such, contribution of Southern MNCs to economic development of emerging markets is significant, especially given low investor confidence prevailing today among traditional Northern MNCs. Despite a fall in FDI from Organisation for Economic Co-operation and Development (OECD) countries by 57 percent below 2007 levels in 2012, FDI from developing countries rose by 19 percent (OECD 2014). While larger developing countries, especially the BRICS, are driving this phenomenon, about 90 percent of developing countries of all sizes and income levels are now undertaking outward foreign direct investment (OFDI) (map O.2). Both domestic policy choices in developing countries and global economic conditions have shaped changes in the investment landscape. Firms in Singapore and other high-growth economies embraced OFDI in the

MAP O.2   Growth of OFDI in Most Developing Countries

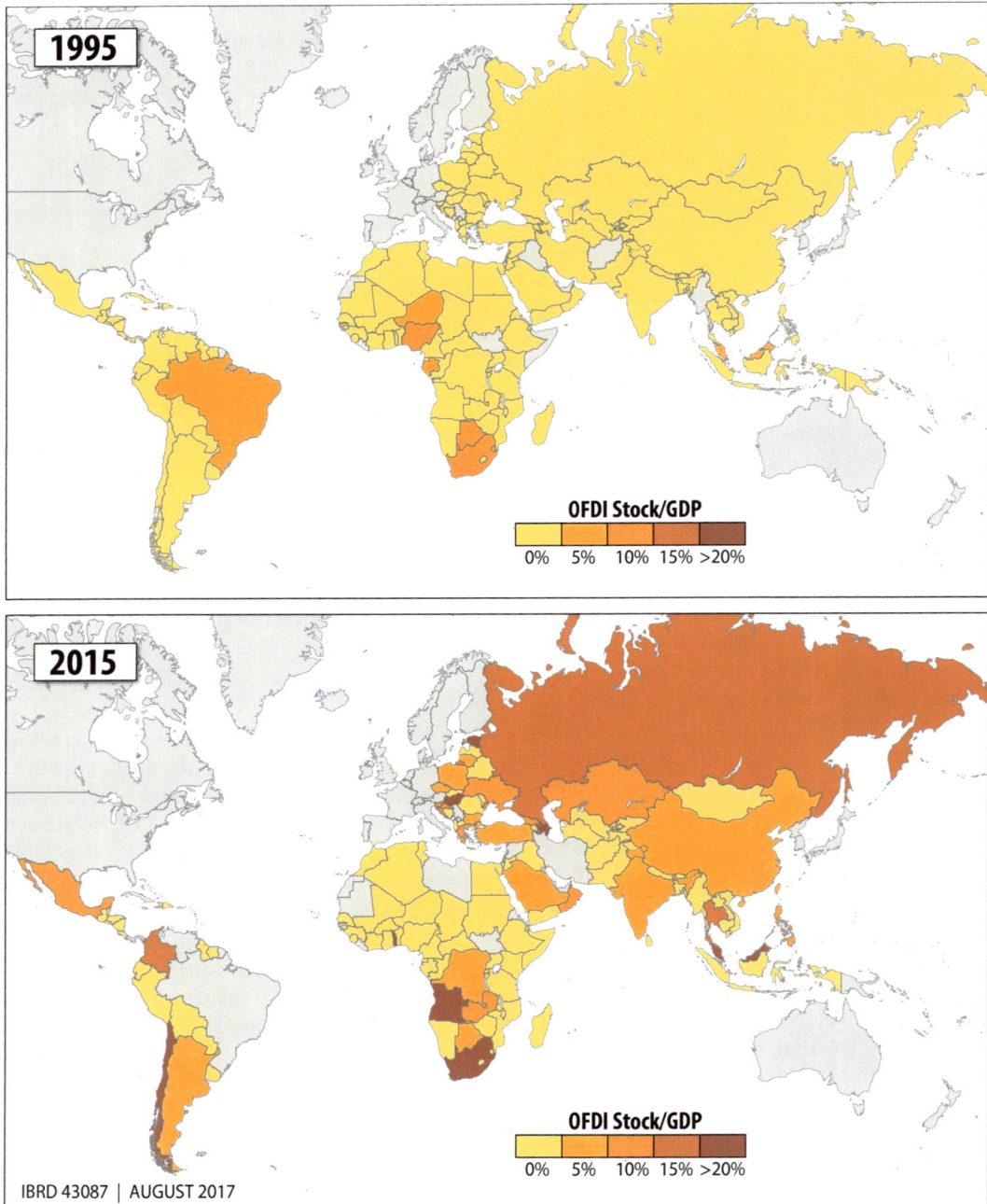

OFDI Stock/GDP

0%   5%   10%   15%   >20%

IBRD 43087 | AUGUST 2017

Source: UNCTAD and World Development Indicators, World Bank.
Note: GDP = gross domestic product; OFDI = outward foreign direct investment.

late 1990s and early 2000s as a development strategy to "achieve efficiency in resource allocation and diversify risks from economic shocks in any one region" (Lee, Lee, and Yeo 2016).

Firms in other developing economies soon emulated such efforts, with OFDI increasingly seen as a means to access markets, capital, technology, and knowledge in international markets—and thus boost firm-level and national competitiveness (Luo, Xu, and Han 2010). Global economic conditions also "pulled" developing-market firms into OFDI. First, rapid and sustained growth in much of the developing world during the last two decades helped firms to grow and prosper and, consequently, to internationalize. Second, the commodity super-cycle (until recently) gave some developing country exporters large windfalls, creating substantial liquidity that was used partly to finance OFDI.

The emergence of developing countries as a key source of FDI begs the question of whether they differ from developed countries in terms of the drivers and risk tolerance of their OFDI. Both the report's investor survey and data analysis suggest that developing country OFDI reacts to standard host economy locational determinants (for example, market size, income level, distance, common language, colonial links) in much the same way as developed country OFDI. Both are attracted to large and growing economies that are geographically close and culturally similar.

Developing country investors are more willing to target smaller and closer economies (Arita 2013) in a "stepping-stone" strategy. Evidence suggests that some of these firms find it difficult to compete in larger, more competitive, and more distant markets, not least because they often lack the networks and experience of developed country firms. Studies from Asia and Latin America find that regional investors usually expand into larger and more complex markets only after first successfully expanding in smaller, lower-income economies in the same region (Cuervo-Cazurra 2008; Gao 2005).

Developing Country and Regional Investors Target Higher-Risk Markets

Developing country investors may also be more willing to target higher-risk markets in host economies with weaker institutional quality.[6] In 2001, only 11 countries in the developing world (5 in Sub-Saharan Africa, 5 in Europe and Central Asia, and 1 in Latin America and the Caribbean) had half or more of their inward FDI stock coming from investors from other developing countries. In 2012, that number had risen to 55 countries. Developing countries are a particularly key source of FDI for countries in Sub-Saharan Africa, Europe and Central Asia, and South Asia. With many of these host economies characterized by low levels of economic development, such trends accord with the literature, which finds developing country OFDI to be less discouraged by weak institutional and economic host-country environments (Cuervo-Cazurra 2008; Dollar 2016; Ma and Assche 2011) owing to the "institutional advantage" argument (Cuervo-Cazurra and Genc 2008). This argument suggests that managers of developing country MNCs are more accustomed to uncertainty and may be more adept in dealing with unpredictable regulatory practices and less transparent administrative procedures. Several studies support this argument, finding that developing country OFDI investors are relatively more present in least developed countries. Some demonstrate an inverse relationship between host country political risk and, for example, Chinese OFDI (Cui and Jiang 2009; Duanmu and Guney 2009; Kang and Jiang 2012; Quer, Claver, and Rienda 2015).

Risks in FCS range from security and value-chain disruptions to regulatory, financial, and reputational uncertainty, all of which make foreign investors reluctant to engage. In many cases, governments lack the capacity and revenue base to perform basic functions. Often, informal and noninclusive institutions fill the governance vacuum, and their interaction with businesses is frequently motivated by rent-extraction. Firms also face an array of adverse market conditions similar to those in other low-income countries, such as weak macroeconomic and regulatory environments, infrastructure bottlenecks, and a limited supply of skilled labor, compounded by low demand. However, unlike in many developing countries, the destruction of physical and human capital and diminished state control result in highly risky business environments. As a result, FDI in FCS represents a mere 1 percent of global flows, more than five times lower than the world average. Despite having increased tenfold over the last two decades, the distribution of FDI directed to FCS is still mostly concentrated in a handful of middle-income or

resource-rich economies. Such FDI targets a handful of sectors, all of which are capital intensive and sustained mostly by foreign demand. Investors are more cautious when they enter FCS markets: they tend to commit to smaller projects that produce fewer jobs for every dollar invested and tend to concentrate their investment spatially in the most stable regions or cities in FCS.

Regional investors may have a comparative advantage in FCS contexts relative to global firms. A considerable amount of greenfield investment in FCS comes from regional firms (figure O.7). The investment footprint of France and the United Kingdom remains large in Africa and the Middle East, but greenfield investments (for example, from Russia to Uzbekistan, Malaysia to Cambodia, South Africa to Nigeria, Japan and Thailand to Myanmar, and the United Arab Emirates to Iraq) confirm that intraregional investment takes place in FCS on a large scale. Other regional investors include, for example, companies from Lebanon investing in neighboring Middle Eastern countries, companies from Morocco expanding into markets in North Africa, and Nigerian firms expanding into West Africa. These firms leverage their superior knowledge of the local context and their affinity with their target markets. As a result, such investors show greater resilience, take more risks (for example, committing to larger projects), and accept lower returns. This trend highlights once more the importance of regional sources of investment, and of regional integration schemes, in transitioning out of fragility.

First movers willing to make pioneer investments in challenging environments in FCS are critical for signaling the viability of business opportunities in these markets. MNCs operating in FCS often make strategic choices in terms of scale, staffing, and location that seek to address multiple challenges and risks simultaneously. Some of the response strategies documented by interviews with investors (IFC 2017) include integrated management and due diligence systems; strategically locating warehouses and production sites; staged investments; striving to meet

FIGURE O.7   Regional Investment Occurs on a Large Scale
Origins of greenfield FDI project announcements in FCS (2008–16)

FCS recipients

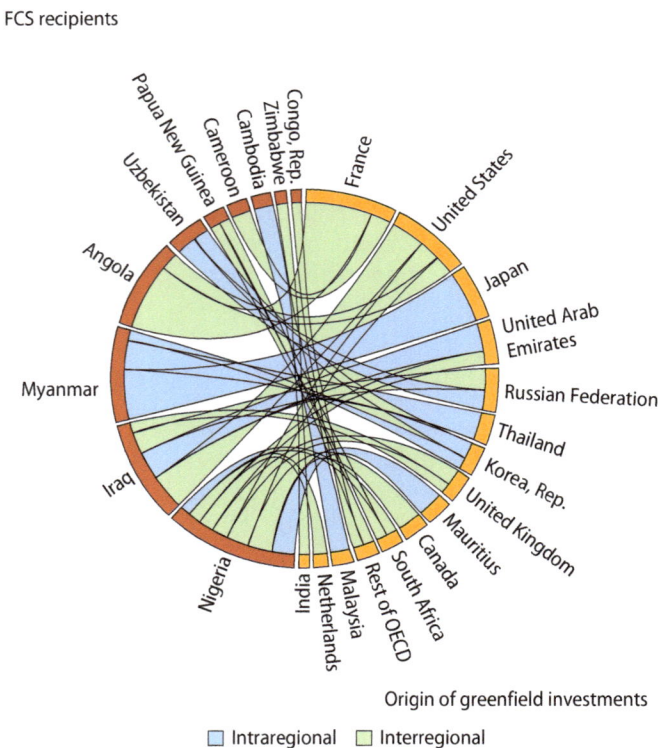

Origin of greenfield investments

□ Intraregional   □ Interregional

Source: Computation based on fDi Markets database, Financial Times.
Note: Origins (on the right side of the chord diagram, in orange) and FCS destinations (on the left side, in red) of greenfield projects exceeding US$3 billion since 2008. Blue chords indicate intraregional investment. FCS = fragile and conflict-affected situations; FDI = foreign direct investment; OECD = Organisation for Economic Co=operation and Development.

international standards; and flexibility in scale, supply, and business plans. Pioneering investments can help host-country governments develop regulations and support services, establish business and consumer markets, and generate positive externalities. They also offer a demonstration effect to other investors that the target countries and markets are open to financially viable investments despite high risk perceptions.

Investment Climate Reforms Reduce Uncertainty and Unpredictability

Investment climate reforms are necessary for markets to move from conflict to peace and from fragility to resilience. Firm-level responses are limited in what they can achieve—investors may strive to keep their companies out of harm's way, but they can only go so far in coping with them and cannot address these risks in a holistic and systemic way. Investment climate reforms tailored to the context of FCS, however, can go a long way toward reducing investors' risks and creating markets for viable investment. The limited capacity of many governments in FCS, combined with the urgency of positive returns on reform efforts, require the proper sequencing and prioritization of interventions. An investment climate engagement must be implemented in a balanced way by securing short-term gains while building the momentum for deeper institutional transformation over the longer term.

Regulatory simplification, removing barriers to investment entry, and addressing infrastructure constraints (for example, access to electricity and transit) rank among the most important confidence-building signals that can produce early results and trigger a private sector response. Value chain development through skills building, access to finance and technology, and connecting producers to markets can be second-stage interventions suitable for FCS (World Bank Group 2011). Deeper institutional reforms may take longer

to occur—it took the fastest-reforming countries in the 20th century two decades to achieve a functioning governance quality—and the scope and speed of reforms are themselves risk factors (World Bank Group 2011). But strengthening public institutions that provide citizens with security, justice, and jobs is crucial to breaking the cycle of violence.

The rest of this report is organized around five thematic chapters, each exploring a different dimension of FDI in developing countries:

The discussion of the findings from the GIC survey (chapter 1) aims to help policy makers design policies and prioritize reforms valued by foreign investors. Through some 750 interviews of executives of MNCs with investments in developing countries, the survey measures the role of investment climate variables (for example, investment incentives, investment promotion activities, FDI regulations, and administrative processes) in influencing FDI decisions. By identifying factors that are important to investors, reform-minded governments can leverage policy instruments that can most effectively attract, retain, and leverage FDI for development. Recognizing resource constraints faced by most governments, the authors of this chapter suggest where policy makers can focus their efforts to maximize impact.

FDI in developing countries benefits local high-growth firms the most (chapter 2). This is due likely to their higher absorptive capacity—that is, their ability to recognize the value of, assimilate, and apply new information to improve production processes. High-growth firms account for a sizable share of job creation and productivity gains in developing countries. The distinctive characteristics of these firms have been the subject of study from the perspective of both individual firms interested in sales and revenue growth and policy makers interested in job creation and economic growth. The findings discussed in this chapter have strong implications for programs aimed at facilitating the connection of domestic firms to established MNCs through government-supported linkage programs.

Tax incentives play a role in FDI in developing countries (chapter 3), and the authors of this chapter offer practical evidence to help developing country policy makers design and implement more effective incentives. Using a new dataset on tax incentives in developing countries compiled by the World Bank Group, the authors provide sector- and firm-level evidence to guide policy makers on how to target investment incentives more efficiently. The analysis assesses how developing countries use tax incentives by sector and over time, links the effectiveness of incentives to a simple framework of investor motivation to guide policy makers in these targeting questions, and presents new evidence on the relevance of tax incentives for investors. Tax incentives are found to be commonly used by developing countries, with some variation across sectors and regions, and tend to be more effective in attracting efficiency-seeking FDI. The authors also identify priorities for the design, transparency, and administration of incentive reforms.

Developing country OFDI has increased considerably in recent years (chapter 4), and the authors of this chapter explore its main drivers and offer policy proposals to maximize its development impact. They use several global data sources to assess changes over time in the investment patterns of developing country MNCs, particularly with regard to source and destination economies, target sectors, and modes of entry. The authors complement this information with findings from a gravity model to explain the influence on developing country OFDI behavior of several FDI location determinants, such as relative market size, geographical distance, common cultural and institutional features, and the existence of bilateral investment agreements. They also consider whether OFDI can foster the development of source economies and review the relevant literature. They offer evidence that OFDI increases home firm innovation and exports, but the literature on other aggregate benefits—such as productivity,

domestic investment, employment, and economic growth—is still nascent.

The discussion of FDI in fragile and conflict-affected situations (chapter 5) fills a gap in understanding the potential, patterns, and constraints of FDI in such states and explores ways to support investments that have a positive effect on peace and stability. The authors draw on original data and analysis of investment in high-risk environments to explain investment decision-making and coping mechanisms in such contexts. They propose an approach to investment climate reforms that aims at securing short-term gains while building the momentum for deep institutional transformation. Key elements of that strategy focus on reducing risks to investors as well as maximizing investment opportunities and rewards.

Notes

1. "Developing countries" in this report refer to low- and middle-income countries as defined by the World Bank. The full list of countries appears in the glossary. The list is based on income categories in fiscal year 2017 at http://databank.worldbank.org/data/download/site-content/OGHIST.xls.

2. The 17 SDGs of the 2030 Agenda for Sustainable Development were adopted by world leaders at a United Nations summit in September 2015 and are listed in http://www.un.org/sustainabledevelopment/sustainable-development-goals/.

3. According to work by Theodore Moran (2014), the evidence actually indicates that the entry of foreigners and their first-tier suppliers introduces *"Schumpeterian winds of creative destruction"* that may lead to beneficial restructuring of the entire industry, including opportunities for better-performing local companies in the same industry, and for suppliers in the vertical industries to emerge over time. Moran notes that the outcome to observe is the changing economic performance of the entire sector, as opposed to arbitrary measurement of the absolute amount of capital invested at any particular moment in the sector (as is often highlighted in the debates on crowding-in and crowding-out). The Czech Republic is a good

example of how acquisition of a dilapidated local carmaker Skoda by Volkswagen, one of the leading global firms, led to a successful transformation of the entire automotive industry in the country.

4. The FDI life cycle considers the relationship among foreign and domestic investors, governments, and civil society in various stages of investment. Based on the FDI vision and objectives of the host economy, the cycle begins with attraction of FDI into a country. It then moves into enabling investors to enter and establish presence in the domestic economy. Once operational, FDI is encouraged to stay in the long term, leading to expansion and "rooting" the FDI into the domestic economy through linkages and other spillover effects with the domestic private sector.

5. Other ways that help to de-risk private investment projects include blending grants or concessional funds with private finance to improve risk–return ratios; guarantees to, for example, large infrastructure projects to cover key noncommercial risks or sharing risks; partial credit guarantees that enhance the terms of commercial debt by extending maturity, lowering interest rates, or enabling access to financial markets.

6. The World Bank's World Governance Indicators (WGI) decompose institutional quality into six dimensions: Voice and Accountability; Political Stability and Absence of Violence; Government Effectiveness; Regulatory Quality; Rule of Law; and Control of Corruption. See http://info.worldbank.org/governance/wgi/#home.

Bibliography

Alfaro, L., A. Chanda, S. Kalemli-Ozcan, and S. Sayek. 2006. "How Does Foreign Direct Investment Promote Economic Growth? Exploring the Effects of Financial Markets on Linkages." NBER Working Paper 12522, National Bureau of Economic Research, Cambridge, MA.

Alfaro, L., and A. Rodriguez-Clare. 2004. "Multinationals and Linkages: Evidence from Latin America." *Economia* 4: 113–70.

Alfaro, L., and M. X. Chen. Forthcoming. "Selection and Market Reallocation: Productivity Gains from Multinational Production." *American Economic Journal: Economic Policy.*

Arita, S. 2013. "Do Emerging Multinational Enterprises Possess South-South FDI Advantages?" *International Journal of Emerging Markets* 8 (4): 329–53.

Arnold, J., B. S. Javorcik, and A. Mattoo. 2011. "Does Services Liberalization Benefit Manufacturing Firms? Evidence from the Czech Republic." *Journal of International Economics* 85 (1): 136–46.

Balsvik, R. 2006. "Is Mobility of Labour a Channel for Spillovers from Multinationals to Local Domestic Firms?" Mimeo. Norwegian School of Economics.

Barba Navaretti, G., and A. Venables. 2004. *Multinational Firms in the World Economy.* Princeton, NJ: Princeton University Press.

Barnard, R., M. de Bruyn, N. Kempson, and P. McLaren. 2014. "Sector Case Study: Mining." In *Making Foreign Direct Investment Work for Sub-Saharan Africa*, edited by T. Farole and D. Winkler, 117–62. Washington, DC: World Bank.

Bijsterbosch, M., and M. Kolasa. 2009. "FDI and Productivity Convergence in Central and Eastern Europe: An Industry-Level Investigation." ECB Working Paper 992, European Central Bank, Frankfurt.

Cuervo-Cazurra, A. 2008. "The Multinationalization of Developing Country MNEs: The Case of Multilatinas." *Journal of International Management* 14 (2): 138–54.

Cuervo-Cazurra, A., and M. Genc. 2008. "Transforming Disadvantages into Advantages: Developing-Country MNEs in the Least Developed Countries." *Journal of International Business Studies* 39 (6): 957–79.

Cui, L., and F. Jiang. 2009. "FDI Entry Mode Choice of Chinese Firms: A Strategic Behavior Perspective." *Journal of World Business* 44 (4): 434–44.

Dollar, D. 2016. "China as a Global Investor." In *China's New Sources of Economic Growth: Vol. 1: Reform, Resources and Climate Change*, edited by Ligang Song, Ross Garnaut, Cai Fang and Lauren Johnston. Australia National University Press, Acton.

Duanmu, J.-L., and Y. Guney. 2009. "A Panel Data Analysis of Locational Determinants of Chinese and Indian Outward Foreign Direct Investment." *Journal of Asia Business Studies* 3 (2): 1–15.

Du, L., A. Harrison, and G. Jefferson. 2011. "Do Institutions Matter for FDI Spillovers? The Implications of China's 'Special Characteristics.'"

NBER Working Paper 16767, National Bureau of Economic Research, Cambridge, MA.

Echandi, R., J. Krajcovicova, and C. Z. W. Qiang. 2015. "The Impact of Investment Policy in a Changing Global Economy: A Review of the Literature." Policy Research Working Paper 7437, World Bank, Washington, DC.

Farole, T., and D. Winkler, eds. 2014. *Making Foreign Direct Investment Work for Sub-Saharan Africa: Local Spillovers and Competitiveness in Global Value Chains.* Directions in Development. Washington, DC: World Bank.

Gao, T. 2005. "Foreign Direct Investment from Developing Asia: Some Distinctive Features." *Economics Letters* 86 (1): 29–35.

Görg, H., and E. Strobl. 2005. "Spillovers from Foreign Firms through Worker Mobility: An Empirical Investigation." *Scandinavian Journal of Economics* 107 (4): 693–709.

Herzer, D. 2012. "How Does Foreign Direct Investment Really Affect Developing Countries' Growth?" *Review of International Economics.* 20 (2): 396–414.

Holtbrügge, D., and H. Kreppel. 2012. "Determinants of Outward Foreign Direct Investment from BRIC Countries: An Explorative Study." *International Journal of Emerging Markets* 7 (1): 4–30. https://doi.org/10.1108/17468801211197897.

IFC (International Finance Corporation). 2017. *Private Enterprise in Fragile and Conflict Situations.* Washington, DC.

———. Forthcoming. *Multinational Corporations: Important Partners of IFC to Foster Global Economic Integration and Value Addition.* Washington, DC.

International Dialogue for Peace-Building and State-Building. 2016. *International Standards for Responsible Business in Conflict-Affected and Fragile Environment.* Paris: OECD.

Javorcik, B. S. 2004. "Does FDI Increase the Productivity of Domestic Firms? In Search of Spillovers through Backward Linkages." *American Economic Review* 94 (3): 605–27.

Javorcik, B. S., A. Lo Turco, and D. Maggioni. 2017. "New and Improved: Does FDI Boost Production Complexity in Host Countries?" CEPR Discussion Paper DP11942.

Javorcik, B. S., and M. Spatareanu. 2009. "Tough Love: Do Czech Suppliers Learn from Their Relationships with Multinationals?" *Scandinavian Journal of Economics* 111 (4): 811–33.

Kang, Y., and F. Jiang. 2012. "FDI Location Choice of Chinese Multinationals in East and Southeast Asia: Traditional Economic Factors and Institutional perspective." *Journal of World Business* 47: 45–53.

Lee, C., C. G. Lee, and M. Yeo. 2016. "Determinants of Singapore's Outward FDI." *Journal of Southeast Asian Economies* 33 (1): 23–40.

Lipsey, R. E. 2004. "Home- and Host-Country Effects of Foreign Direct Investment." In *Challenges to Globalization: Analyzing the Economics,* edited by Robert E. Baldwin and L. Alan Winters, 333–82. University of Chicago Press.

Luo, Y., Q. Z. Xu, and B. J. Han. 2010. "How Emerging Market Governments Promote Outward FDI: Experience from China." *Journal of World Business* 45 (1): 68–79.

Ma, A. C., and A. V. Assche. 2011. "Product Distance, Institutional Distance and FDI." Mimeo. University of San Diego, School of Business Administration.

Moran, T. 2014. "Foreign Investment and Supply Chains from Emerging Markets: Recurring Problems and Demonstrated Solutions." Working Paper Series 14-12, Peterson Institute for International Economics, Washington, DC.

Nepelski, D., and G. De Prato. 2015. "International Technology Sourcing between a Developing Country and the Rest of the World. A Case Study of China." *Technovation* 35: 12–21.

Newman, C., J. Rand, T. Talbot, and F. Tarp. 2015. "Technology Transfers, Foreign Investment and Productivity Spillovers." *European Economic Review* 76: 168–87.

OECD (Organisation for Economic Co-Operation and Development). 2014. *Development Co-operation Report 2014: Mobilising Resources for Sustainable Development.* Paris: OECD.

Polachek, S. W., and D. Sevastianova. 2012. "Does Conflict Disrupt Growth? Evidence of the Relationship between Political Instability and National Economic Performance." *The Journal of International Trade and Economic Development* 21 (3): 361–88.

Quer, D., E. Claver, and L. Rienda. 2015. "Chinese Outward Foreign Direct Investment: A Review of Empirical Research." *Frontiers of Business Research in China* 9 (3): 326–70.

Rizvi, S. Z. A., and M. Nishat. 2009. "The Impact of Foreign Direct Investment on Employment Opportunities: Panel Data Analysis: Empirical

Evidence from Pakistan, India and China." *The Pakistan Development Review* 48 (4): 841–51.

Rodriguez-Arango, L., and M. A. Gonzalez-Perez. 2016. "Giants from Emerging Markets: The Internationalization of BRIC Multinationals," in *The Challenge of BRIC Multinationals*, edited by Rob Van Tulder, Alain Verbeke, Jorge Carneiro, and Maria Alejandra Gonzalez-Perez, 195–226. Progress in International Business Research, Vol. 11. Emerald Group Publishing Limited. http://www.emeraldinsight.com/doi/full/10.1108/S1745-886220160000011011.

UNCTAD (United Nations Conference on Trade and Development). 2005. "Case Study on Outward Foreign Direct Investment by South African Enterprises." Geneva. http://unctad.org/en/Docs/c3em26d2a5_en.pdf.

World Bank Group. 2011. *World Development Report 2011: Conflict, Security and Development: 2011.* Washington, DC: World Bank.

WEF (World Economic Forum). 2013. *Manufacturing for Growth: Strategies for Driving Growth and Employment.* Geneva: WEF. http://www3.weforum.org/docs/WEF_ManufacturingForGrowth_ReportVol1_2013.pdf.

What Matters to Investors in Developing Countries: Findings from the Global Investment Competitiveness Survey

1

Peter Kusek and Andrea Silva

Developing countries compete to attract foreign direct investment (FDI) because of its potential benefits for the local economy, which include technology transfer, stronger managerial and organizational skills, increased access to foreign markets, and export diversification. FDI can enhance productivity, increase investment in research and development, and create better-paying and more stable jobs in host countries. But these benefits are not guaranteed, nor do all types of FDI have the same potential impact. Thus, host governments must adopt the right policies to maximize their gains from different types of FDI.

The *Global Investment Competitiveness Survey* (GIC Survey) offers practical evidence to help policy makers design policies and prioritize reforms that investors value. Through interviews with 754 executives of multinational corporations (MNCs) that have

investments in developing countries, the survey measures the role in influencing FDI decisions of such investment climate variables as investment incentives, promotion, FDI regulations, and administrative processes (see box 1.1 for key findings, annex 1A for survey methodology, and annex 1B for profile of respondents). By identifying variables that are most valued by investors, this chapter provides practical guidance to where policy makers in host countries can focus their efforts to attract and retain FDI, and maximize its gains for development.

Policy reform initiatives must consider that FDI is heterogeneous, driven by different motivations and having different economic, environmental, and social impact. MNCs possess different characteristics that influence their perspectives and decisions. This report is based on an FDI typology that builds on a framework proposed by Dunning and Lundan (2008) (see box 1.2). The framework

Top Five Findings of the Global Investment Competitiveness Survey

Through interviews with 754 executives of multinational corporations with investments in developing countries, the GIC survey finds the following:

1. Investors involved in export-oriented efficiency-seeking FDI that look for internationally cost-competitive destinations and potential export platforms value linkages, incentives, trade agreements, and investment promotion agency (IPA) services more than other investors. Incentives such as tax holidays are important for 64 percent of investors involved in efficiency-seeking FDI, compared to only 47 percent of their counterparts involved in other types of FDI. IPA services are rated important by about half of investors involved in efficiency-seeking FDI but by only about a third of those involved in other types of FDI.

2. More than a third of investors reinvest all of their profits into the host country. Investors value policies that help them expand their business more than just policies used by governments to attract them.

3. Investment protection guarantees are critical for retaining and expanding investments in the long term across all types of FDI. Over 90 percent of all investors rate various types of legal protections as important or critically important, the highest rating among all factors included in the survey. These guarantees include the ability to transfer currency in and out of the country, and existence of legal protections against expropriation, against breach of contract, and against nontransparent or arbitrary government conduct.

4. Investors strongly value the existing capacity and skills of local suppliers, but also find that government support, such as providing information on the availability of local suppliers, matters. With foreign investors sourcing about 43 percent of their production inputs locally, supplier contracts and linkages with local businesses have the potential to create significant benefits for the local private sector.

5. For close to 30 percent of investors that have experienced shutting down an affiliate in a developing country, some reasons for exiting the investment could have been avoided, such as unstable macroeconomic conditions and increased policy and regulatory uncertainty. Three-quarters of investors have experienced disruptions in their operations due to political risk forces and events. A quarter of investors that did experience disruptions canceled or withdrew their investment. Severe cases occur fairly infrequently—about 13 percent for breach of contract and 5 percent for expropriation—but when they do, the negative impact is strong. In cases of breach of contract, over a third of investors cancel or withdraw investments, and for expropriation almost half do so.

---

contends that MNCs are lured to a particular location with a predominant motivation in mind: accessing domestic markets, seeking increased efficiencies of production, taking advantage of natural resources, and acquiring strategic assets. This report extends the use of this typology to explore how various policy instruments influence investors differently depending on their FDI motivation, and how the impact of investment on the host economy varies by type of FDI. As a result, different types of FDI are based not only on investors' subjective motivation for cross-border investment, but also on the inherent objective characteristics of various investment projects, and their implications for developing countries.[1]

This chapter provides a corporate perspective on the investment decision making of MNCs across the stages of the investment cycle: attraction, entry and establishment, operations and expansion, linkages with the local economy, and in some cases, divestment and exit. The survey reveals how MNCs decide on FDI and how they identify and select a country for investment. It also looks at MNCs' operational, reinvestment, and expansion experiences, as well as their encounters with political risks and their decisions to shut down foreign affiliates.

While host-country policy makers listen to investor preferences, they must also consider the public interest. Although the survey focuses on MNC perspectives and preferences, this report does not necessarily recommend that governments simply yield to investors' wishes. Addressing investor concerns should be balanced with the public interest. For instance, low tax rates and incentives may be desirable from the perspective of MNCs, but governments should not simply lower tax rates and give more investment incentives, especially if these limit the country's gains from FDI. This chapter offers practical evidence on the relative importance of investment policies to guide policy makers in formulating and prioritizing reforms.

The following sections discuss the heterogeneity of FDI and how it affects MNCs' perceived importance of the legal and regulatory environment relative to other country characteristics, and of various investment policy–related factors. The chapter is organized according to the life cycle of investments—selecting a location, entering a country and establishing an investment, running and expanding operations, and considering divestment.

Foreign Investors Are Heterogeneous with Multiple Motivations

Investors with different motivations consider different factors in their decision to invest (box 1.2). MNCs that primarily seek access to natural resources—as in extractive industries—care more about such variables as access to land and resources they wish to exploit than other variables. Market-seeking FDI tends to prioritize the size of and purchasing power in the domestic market. Efficiency-seeking[2] FDI values policies that facilitate the import and export of goods and services, and lower production costs. Efficiency-seeking FDI also includes firms that participate in global value chains (GVCs), an important way for developing countries to integrate into the global economy. MNCs that seek strategic assets primarily pursue technologies and brands that can enhance their operations.

In addition to the subjective motivation of investors, the FDI typology considers FDI's objective impact on the host country—for example, increase in exports brought about by efficiency-seeking investments. The GIC survey focuses on the subjective motivation by asking investors to self-identify their company's motivations in a specific investment project in a developing country.

In this survey, close to 90 percent of investors said that accessing new markets or new customers was one of their motivations (figure 1.1). About half of respondents are motivated by lowering production costs or establishing a new base for exports. The motivation to coordinate a value chain occurs for two-fifths of respondents. For those investors that want to coordinate their companies' value chain, 70 percent are also motivated to cut production costs. Few respondents identify with the motivation to acquire strategic assets (15 percent) or access natural resources and raw materials (12 percent). Critically, almost two-thirds of investors selected multiple motivations and when asked about which motivation prevails, most investors (71 percent) say they are market-seeking.

Survey respondents represent a range of sectors with a combination of investor motivations (figure 1.2). They are in primary sectors (6 percent), manufacturing (47 percent), and services (45 percent), and other nonspecified sectors (2 percent). Although some sectors are naturally linked with specific motivations (for example, the primary sector being natural resource–seeking), motivations do not correlate strongly with sectors. While about 80 percent of services firms tend to be primarily market-seeking, some are also efficiency-seeking, such as services enabled by information technology (IT). Manufacturing firms are also mainly market-seeking but include a large concentration of efficiency-seeking firms and a handful of natural resource–seeking ones.

Investors involved in efficiency-seeking FDI, relative to investors involved in other types of FDI, are more sensitive to various host market characteristics, including investment climate factors. These host market

Investor Motivation Framework According to Dunning and Lundan

A well-known framework proposed by Dunning and Lundan (2008) differentiates four sources of foreign direct investment (FDI) motivation: natural resources in the host country, access to the host country market, strategic assets of firms in the host market, or cost savings through higher production efficiency (figure B1.2.1). The last type of investment is typically associated with offshoring production stages to the host country, and is thus export-oriented.

All four types of investment can have important, though varying, benefits for the host economy. For example, natural resource–seeking investment often generates sizable government revenues. Market-seeking FDI can be associated with availability of better and cheaper goods and services consumed by the population or used as inputs by other firms. Strategic asset–seeking investment allows domestic firms to expand their global networks. Efficiency-seeking investment is often seen as a means of job creation,

technology transfer, and integration of a country into global value chains. The levels of benefits vary, and some carry more risks than others.

From an investment policy and promotion perspective, it is important to note that the four types of investment can respond differently to policy measures and the overall investment climate. Efficiency-seeking investors—whose investment decisions are driven largely by the motive to save costs—tend to be highly sensitive to any variables that raise their cost of operation or hinder their free exchange of goods and services with the rest of the world as part of global production networks. Natural resource–, strategic asset–, and market-seeking investments tend to be less sensitive to investment climate variables if either the resource to be exploited or the firm that possesses competitive advantages can be found in the country or if the domestic market offers attractive opportunities.

FIGURE B1.2.1   Investor Motivation Framework According to Dunning and Lundan

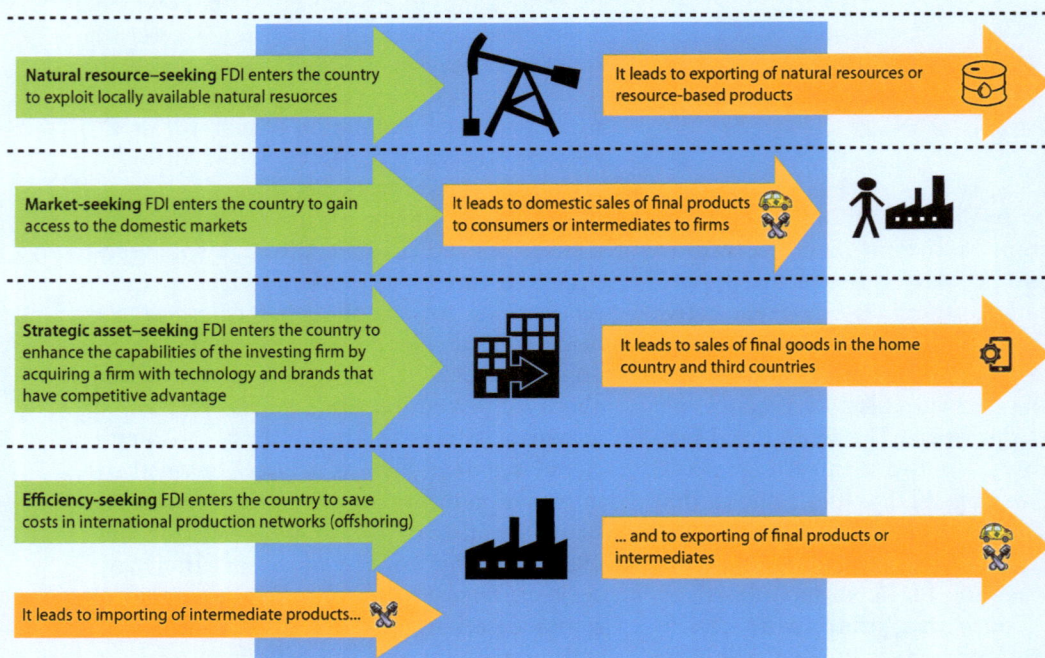

Natural resource–seeking FDI enters the country to exploit locally available natural resuorces

It leads to exporting of natural resources or resource-based products

Market-seeking FDI enters the country to gain access to the domestic markets

It leads to domestic sales of final products to consumers or intermediates to firms

Strategic asset–seeking FDI enters the country to enhance the capabilities of the investing firm by acquiring a firm with technology and brands that have competitive advantage

It leads to sales of final goods in the home country and third countries

Efficiency-seeking FDI enters the country to save costs in international production networks (offshoring)

... and to exporting of final products or intermediates

It leads to importing of intermediate products...

Source: Based on Dunning and Lundan 2008.

FIGURE 1.1   Most Investors Have Multiple Motivations and Are Market-Seeking
Share of respondents (percent)

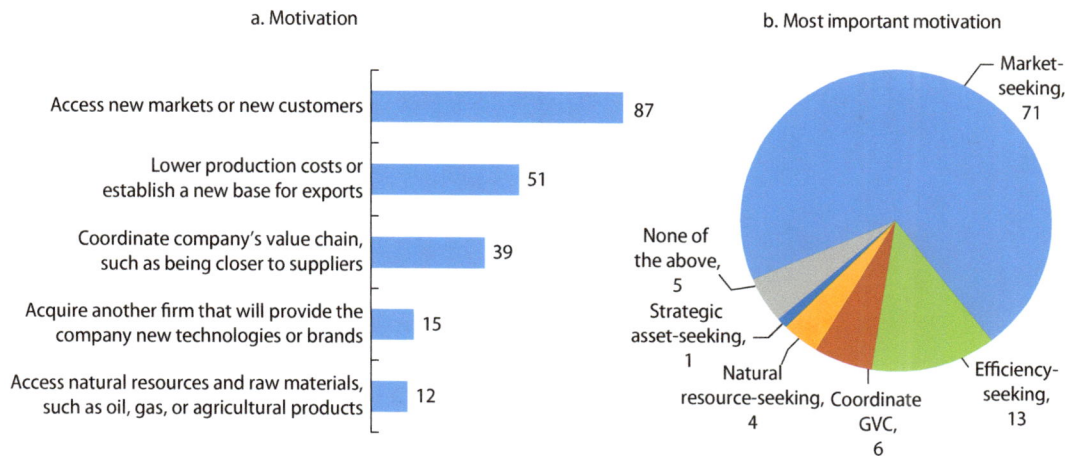

a. Motivation

Access new markets or new customers	87
Lower production costs or establish a new base for exports	51
Coordinate company's value chain, such as being closer to suppliers	39
Acquire another firm that will provide the company new technologies or brands	15
Access natural resources and raw materials, such as oil, gas, or agricultural products	12

b. Most important motivation

Market-seeking, 71
Efficiency-seeking, 13
Coordinate GVC, 6
Natural resource-seeking, 4
Strategic asset-seeking, 1
None of the above, 5

Source: Computation based on the GIC Survey.
Note: The numbers on the left do not add up to 100 percent because respondents are permitted to select multiple motivations: 62 percent of respondents selected two or more motivations. Many respondents may have understood the motivation to access new markets or new customers to apply not only to the domestic market in which they were investing, but also to the regional market. In fact, this motivation was commonly selected for investments in many small developing countries with an extensive network of trade and investment agreements with other economies, suggesting that the respondents were interested in accessing new regional markets or regional consumers, rather than just the small domestic market of the host country.

characteristics include macroeconomic stability and favorable exchange rate, labor pool, physical infrastructure, tax rates, access to land, and domestic financing sources. Among investment climate variables, MNCs involved in efficiency-seeking FDI assign a higher importance to investment protection guarantees, ease of entry, local suppliers, incentives, trade agreements, and bilateral investment treaties, compared with other investors. This suggests that firms involved in efficiency-seeking FDI may be more responsive to policies and reforms aimed at improving the business environment. This chapter thus explores the differences between MNCs involved in efficiency-seeking FDI and those that are involved in other types of FDI (box 1.3).

Host countries are also heterogeneous. A vast majority of survey respondents have operations in upper-middle-income countries (87 percent), about a third in lower-middle-income countries, and very few have foreign affiliates in low-income countries (8 percent). Thus, policy implications emanating from

the results of this survey are based on investors' responses mostly for middle-income developing countries, although they are likely relevant to low-income countries as well.

Investment Exploration and Location Decision: First Phase in the Investment Life Cycle

What Variables Determine MNC Investment Decisions?

Investors consider a broad range of factors in deciding to invest, the most important being political stability and security, as well as a business-friendly legal and regulatory environment. These top other variables such as infrastructure, labor talent and skill, and low costs of labor and inputs. Among survey respondents, 86 percent find the legal and regulatory environment important or critically important, suggesting that it weighs heavily in investors' decision to invest (figure 1.3).

FIGURE 1.2   Respondents Represent Firms across Various Sectors

Share of respondents per sector (percent)

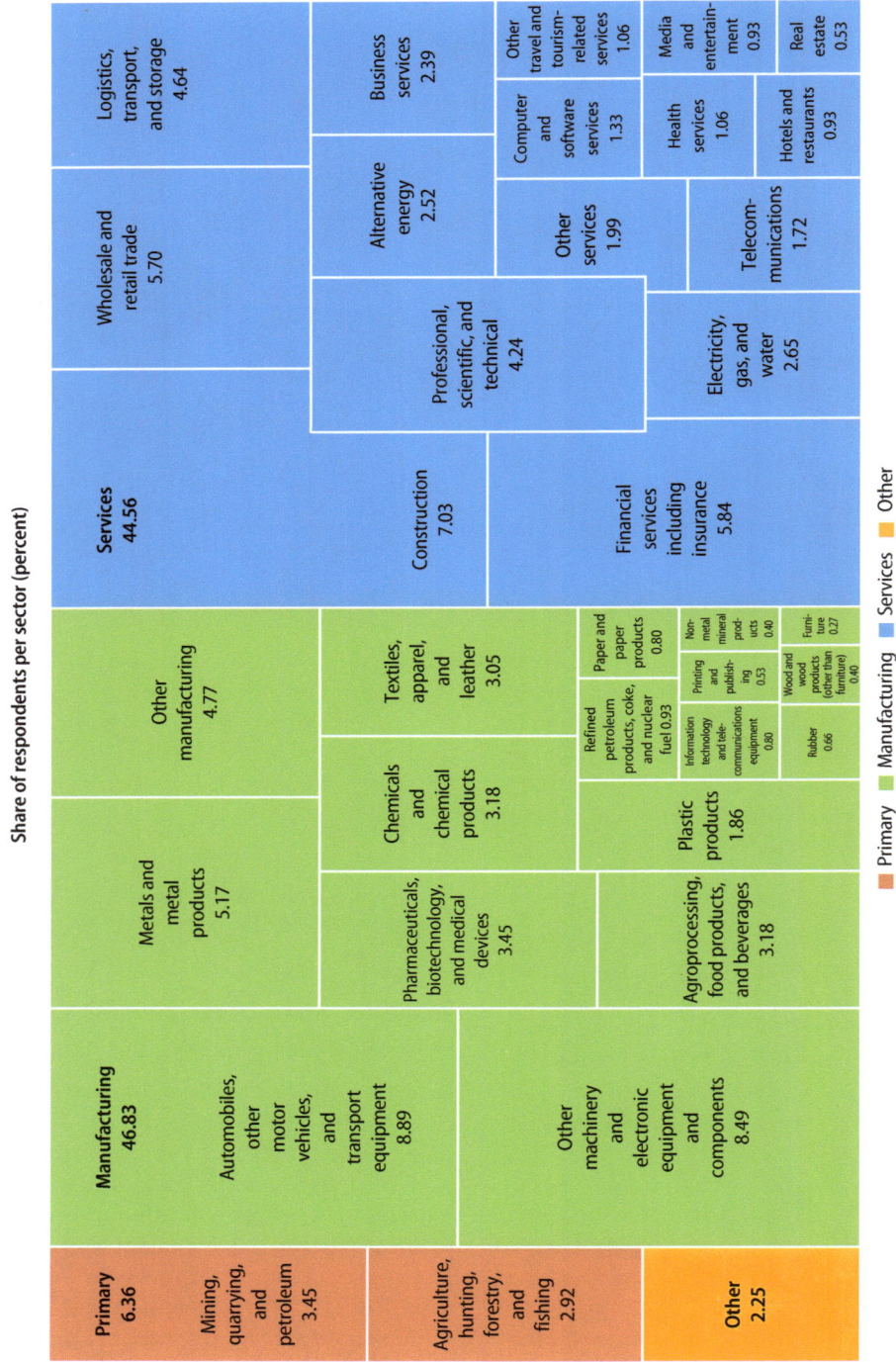

Primary
6.36

Mining, quarrying, and petroleum
3.45

Agriculture, hunting, forestry, and fishing
2.92

Other
2.25

Manufacturing
46.83

Automobiles, other motor vehicles, and transport equipment
8.89

Other machinery and electronic equipment and components
8.49

Metals and metal products
5.17

Pharmaceuticals, biotechnology, and medical devices
3.45

Agroprocessing, food products, and beverages
3.18

Other manufacturing
4.77

Chemicals and chemical products
3.18

Plastic products
1.86

Textiles, apparel, and leather
3.05

Refined petroleum products, coke, and nuclear fuel 0.93

Information technology and telecommunications equipment
0.80

Printing and publishing
0.53

Rubber
0.66

Paper and paper products
0.80

Non-metal mineral products
0.40

Wood and wood products (other than furniture)
0.40

Furniture
0.27

Services
44.56

Construction
7.03

Financial services including insurance
5.84

Wholesale and retail trade
5.70

Professional, scientific, and technical
4.24

Electricity, gas, and water
2.65

Logistics, transport, and storage
4.64

Alternative energy
2.52

Other services
1.99

Telecommunications
1.72

Business services
2.39

Computer and software services
1.33

Health services
1.06

Other travel and tourism-related services
1.06

Media and entertainment
0.93

Hotels and restaurants
0.93

Real estate
0.53

■ Primary   ■ Manufacturing   ■ Services   ■ Other

Source: Computation based on the GIC Survey.

Note: Respondents were asked to identify the main sector of their company globally, which may or may not reflect the sector of the affiliates in developing countries. About 10 percent of respondents noted that the sector in the foreign affiliate they are most familiar with is different from the main sector of the global company. See table 1B.4 for the complete list of sectors, distributional shares across respondents, and comparison with global FDI flows.

FIGURE 1.3   Business-Friendly Legal and Regulatory Environment Is Important for Investors
Share of respondents (percent)

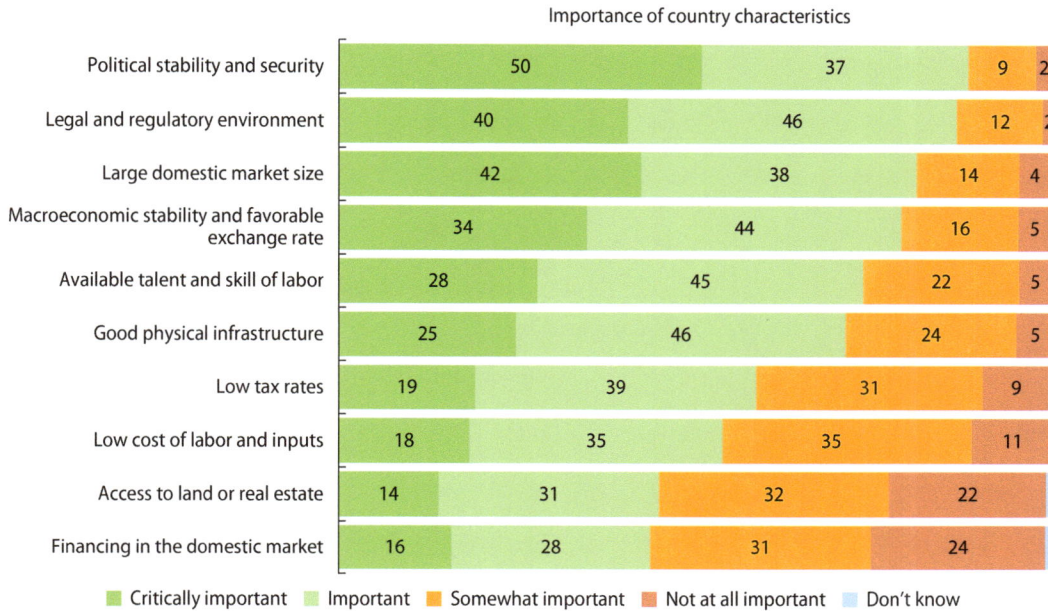

Importance of country characteristics

Characteristic	Critically important	Important	Somewhat important	Not at all important	Don't know
Political stability and security	50	37	9	2	
Legal and regulatory environment	40	46	12	2	
Large domestic market size	42	38	14	4	
Macroeconomic stability and favorable exchange rate	34	44	16	5	
Available talent and skill of labor	28	45	22	5	
Good physical infrastructure	25	46	24	5	
Low tax rates	19	39	31	9	
Low cost of labor and inputs	18	35	35	11	
Access to land or real estate	14	31	32	22	
Financing in the domestic market	16	28	31	24	

■ Critically important   ■ Important   ■ Somewhat important   ■ Not at all important   ■ Don't know

Source: Computation based on the GIC Survey.
Note: Respondents were asked, "How important are the following characteristics to your company's decision to invest in developing countries?" Factors were asked in random order. They are listed in the graph in descending order of importance, based on the combination of "critically important" and "important" in dark green and light green bars. Critically important means it is a deal-breaker; by itself this factor could change a company's decision to invest or not in a country.

FIGURE 1.4   MNCs Involved in Efficiency-Seeking FDI Are More Selective
Share of respondents (percent)

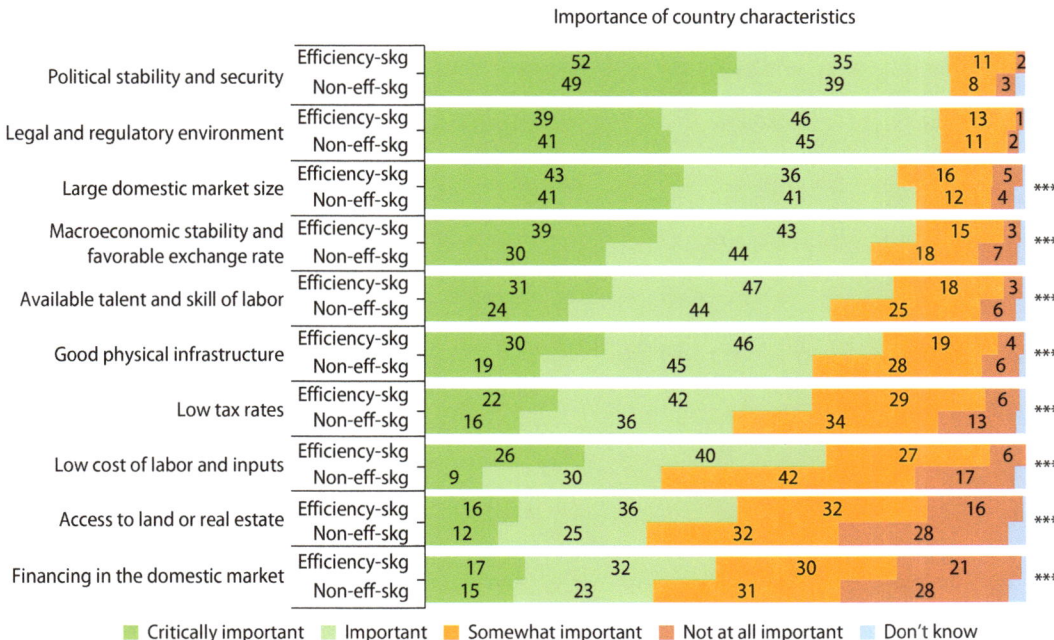

Importance of country characteristics

Characteristic	Group	Critically important	Important	Somewhat important	Not at all important	Don't know	Sig.
Political stability and security	Efficiency-skg	52	35	11	2		
	Non-eff-skg	49	39	8	3		
Legal and regulatory environment	Efficiency-skg	39	46	13	1		
	Non-eff-skg	41	45	11	2		
Large domestic market size	Efficiency-skg	43	36	16	5		***
	Non-eff-skg	41	41	12	4		
Macroeconomic stability and favorable exchange rate	Efficiency-skg	39	43	15	3		***
	Non-eff-skg	30	44	18	7		
Available talent and skill of labor	Efficiency-skg	31	47	18	3		***
	Non-eff-skg	24	44	25	6		
Good physical infrastructure	Efficiency-skg	30	46	19	4		***
	Non-eff-skg	19	45	28	6		
Low tax rates	Efficiency-skg	22	42	29	6		***
	Non-eff-skg	16	36	34	13		
Low cost of labor and inputs	Efficiency-skg	26	40	27	6		***
	Non-eff-skg	9	30	42	17		
Access to land or real estate	Efficiency-skg	16	36	32	16		***
	Non-eff-skg	12	25	32	28		
Financing in the domestic market	Efficiency-skg	17	32	30	21		***
	Non-eff-skg	15	23	31	28		

■ Critically important   ■ Important   ■ Somewhat important   ■ Not at all important   ■ Don't know

Source: Computation based on the GIC Survey.
Note: Country characteristics that have statistically significant differences between investors involved in efficiency-seeking FDI and investors involved in other types of FDI are marked on the right side of the graph. The differences between the two groups are significant at ***$p<0.01$, **$p<0.05$ and *$p<0.1$.

BOX 1.3

MNCs Involved in Efficiency-Seeking Investments Tend to Be More Selective

Investors' preferences and behavior differ depending on their motivation for investing in developing countries. In this survey, about half of respondents said that at least one of their motivations is to lower production costs or establish a new base for exports. Relative to investors with other motivations, these efficiency-seeking firms differ in the following ways:

1. MNCs involved in efficiency-seeking investments view most characteristics of host countries as more important than investors involved in other types of FDI. These characteristics include stable macroeconomic conditions and favorable exchange rate, available talent and skill of labor, good physical infrastructure, low tax rates, low cost of labor and inputs, access to land or real estate, and available financing in the domestic market. Among these, the difference is largest for low cost of labor and inputs, which 66 percent of firms involved in efficiency-seeking investment find important or critically important compared with only 39 percent of investors with other motivations.

2. Investors involved in efficiency-seeking FDI also rate most investment policy factors as more important than investors involved in other types of FDI. These include investment protection guarantees, ease of obtaining approvals, investment incentives, preferential trade agreements, and bilateral investment treaties. The difference is notable for preferential trade agreements, which 65 percent of firms involved in efficiency-seeking investment find important or critically important compared with only 45 percent of investors with other motivations.

3. Incentives also matter more for firms with efficiency-seeking investments. In this group, 63 percent find incentives important or critically important, in contrast with only 43 percent of investors with other motivations. Firms with efficiency-seeking investments rated eight different incentive instruments more highly than other investors with a difference of about 13 percentage points on average. They

also received incentives more often in a typical investment.

4. In terms of ease of entry, MNCs involved in efficiency-seeking FDI view efficiency of obtaining approvals, owning all equity, easily bringing in expatriate staff, and importing production inputs as more important compared with investors involved in other types of FDI. For firms with an efficiency-seeking motivation, the ability to import production inputs is rated slightly more important (73 percent) than the ability to bring in expatriate staff (71 percent) while the reverse is true for firms with other motivations (61 and 65 percent, respectively).

5. Capacity and skills of local suppliers are important or critically important for 77 percent of MNCs involved in efficiency-seeking FDI, compared with 70 percent of investors with other motivations. Government initiatives including information about availability of local suppliers, upgrading potential suppliers, and incentives to invest in supplier upgrading are rated more important by about 8 to 12 percentage points more by firms involved in efficiency-seeking FDI relative to firms involved in other types of FDI. To promote linkages, 55 percent of MNCs involved in efficiency-seeking FDI have internal "talent scouts" to find local suppliers, compared with only 45 percent of investors involved in other types of FDI.

6. MNCs involved in efficiency-seeking FDI value the services of investment promotion agencies (IPAs) more highly, with 52 percent of respondents identifying IPA services as important or critically important, compared with 37 percent of investors involved in other types of FDI. Specifically, meetings with agency officers to discuss investment opportunities, information and assistance in setting up an affiliate, and assistance in problem resolution are valued more by firms with efficiency-seeking investments, by about 9 to 12 percentage points, than by other investors.

Firms involved in efficiency-seeking FDI are more sensitive to a broad range of factors. MNCs seeking cost-competitive locations for their mostly export-oriented production value macroeconomic stability, labor skills, reliable infrastructure, low tax rates, low costs of labor and input, access to land, and domestic financing more than other investors. Because these investors are more sensitive to costs, they more carefully consider factors that directly affect their cost structure and productivity. The size of the domestic market is valued slightly more by investors without an efficiency-seeking motivation, which are predominantly motivated by accessing new markets. The two most important factors—political stability and security, and the legal and regulatory environment—are consistently valued highly across all types of investors (figure 1.4). (See figures 1C.1, 1C.2, and 1C.3 for differences in importance rating by manufacturing versus services firms, developed versus developing source countries, and parent company versus affiliate.)

Investors seek both strong legal protections and predictability and efficiency in implementing laws and regulations (figure 1.5). Many developing countries have inefficient bureaucracies, opaque regulations, complex procedures, and high transaction costs that undermine their competitiveness. Not surprisingly, four out of five surveyed investors rate transparency and predictability in the conduct of public agencies, investment protection guarantees provided in the country's laws, and the ease of starting a business as important in their decision on where to invest. Moreover, about a third of investors rate these as critically

important, or potential deal-breakers. Transparency and predictability may be interpreted as a reflection of the overall interaction between MNCs and host governments—comprising both regulations themselves and their implementation.

Investors value policies that help them expand their business more than policies to attract them. Forty-five percent of respondents rate investment protection guarantees as critically important or deal-breakers, highest among all investment climate factors. Over 90 percent of investors rate various types of legal protections as critical, including the ability to transfer currency in and out of the country as well as legal protections against expropriation, against breach of contract, and against nontransparent or arbitrary government conduct. All investors—regardless of sector, source country, or FDI motivation—find these guarantees of greatest value. These policies are bigger deal-breakers than investment incentives, preferential trade agreements, and bilateral investment treaties. These results suggest that host countries need to pay as much attention to investor aftercare as they do to attracting investors to their country. Given that respondents are investors that already

FIGURE 1.5 **Investors Seek Predictable, Transparent, and Efficient Conduct of Public Agencies**
Share of respondents (percent)

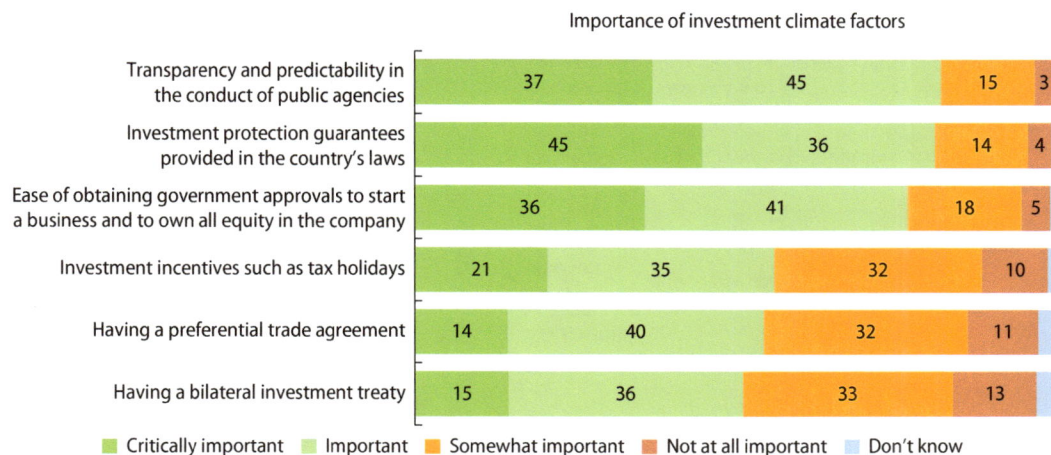

Source: Computation based on the GIC Survey.

have ongoing operations in developing countries and not prospective investors, this partly explains the emphasis on aftercare.

MNCs involved in efficiency-seeking FDI place more importance on investment climate factors compared to firms involved in other types of FDI. Except for transparency and predictability in the conduct of public agencies, which firms find most important regardless of motivation, firms involved in efficiency-seeking FDI value most investment policies more highly (figure 1.6). This suggests that MNCs involved in efficiency-seeking FDI may be more sensitive to these factors when deciding to invest. Such results are not surprising, given that most efficiency-seeking investment is export oriented and highly selective in where it locates, hence the importance of trade agreements and investment incentives. As such, policy makers in host countries should target their initiatives to attract these investors. (See figures 1C.4, 1C.5, and 1C.6 for differences in importance rating by manufacturing versus services firms, developed versus developing source economies, and parent company versus affiliate.)

How Critical Are Incentives in Attracting FDI?

Investment incentives to attract FDI are widespread and used by governments in both high-income and developing countries. Developing country policy makers often view incentives as necessary for their countries to compete for FDI. As discussed later in this report, incentives impose sizable costs on host countries through fiscal losses from non-collection of taxes, rent-seeking by firms, and associated tax evasion. Countries must thus walk a fine line between remaining competitive by offering incentives and ensuring that benefits outweigh their costs.

Investment incentives rank only fourth in importance to investors out of six investment climate characteristics listed in the GIC survey. They rank lower than transparent government conduct, investment protection guarantees, and ease of establishing a business (figure 1.5). Overall only one in five investors finds the absence of investment incentives as deal-breakers in deciding to invest. Another third of respondents find incentives to be important

FIGURE 1.6   **MNCs Involved in Efficiency-Seeking FDI Value Incentives, Trade Agreements, and Ease of Entry More than Other Investors**

Share of respondents (percent)

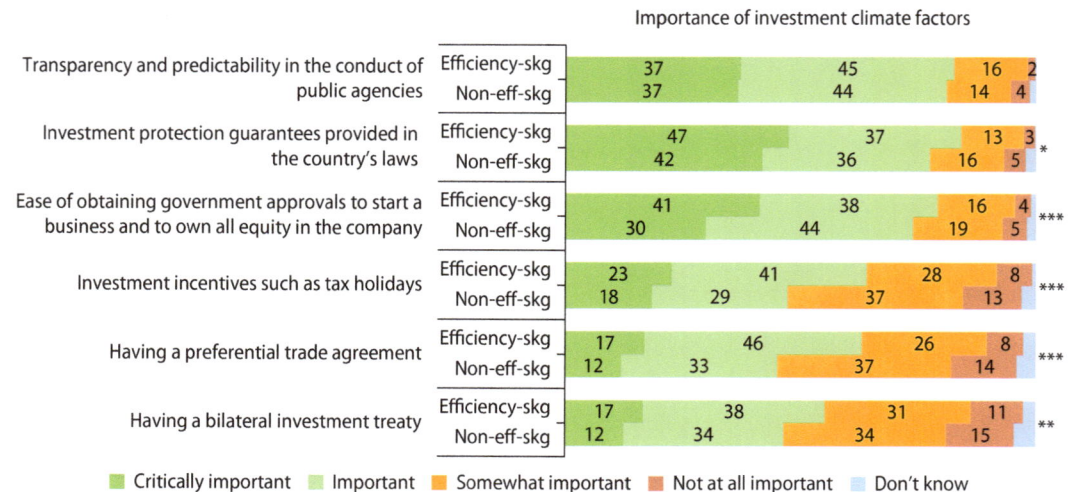

Importance of investment climate factors

		Critically important	Important	Somewhat important	Not at all important	Don't know
Transparency and predictability in the conduct of public agencies	Efficiency-skg	37	45		16	2
	Non-eff-skg	37	44		14	4
Investment protection guarantees provided in the country's laws	Efficiency-skg	47	37		13	3 *
	Non-eff-skg	42	36		16	5
Ease of obtaining government approvals to start a business and to own all equity in the company	Efficiency-skg	41	38		16	4 ***
	Non-eff-skg	30	44		19	5
Investment incentives such as tax holidays	Efficiency-skg	23	41	28	8 ***	
	Non-eff-skg	18	29	37	13	
Having a preferential trade agreement	Efficiency-skg	17	46	26	8 ***	
	Non-eff-skg	12	33	37	14	
Having a bilateral investment treaty	Efficiency-skg	17	38	31	11 **	
	Non-eff-skg	12	34	34	15	

■ Critically important ■ Important ■ Somewhat important ■ Not at all important ■ Don't know

Source: Computation based on the GIC Survey.
Note: Most investment climate factors in this graph have statistically significant differences between investors involved in efficiency-seeking FDI and investors involved in other types of FDI. The differences between the two groups are significant at ***p<0.01, **p<0.05 and *p<0.1.

but not deal-breakers. This does not necessarily suggest that incentives can be completely eliminated but that, by themselves, they are unlikely to convince investors to shift the location of their investment. The policy fundamentals of the investment climate must be addressed before policy makers resort to incentives as a means of attracting investors.

MNCs involved in efficiency-seeking FDI, however, value incentives more than investors with other motivations. Among investors motivated by cutting production costs and finding new export platforms, 64 percent find incentives important or critically important, in contrast with only 47 percent of investors with other motivations (figure 1.6). Investors involved in efficiency-seeking FDI are also granted certain incentives—duty-free imports, subsidized loans, and value added tax (VAT) exemption—more often than other investors. This suggests that they may be more responsive to incentives than investors with other motivations such as accessing new markets and natural resources.

Duty-free imports, tax holidays, and VAT exemptions are the top three most important incentives for investors (figure 1.7). About two-thirds of investors who said that incentives are at least somewhat important find these three instruments to be important or critically important. MNCs involved in efficiency-seeking FDI rated all types of incentives more highly compared with investors involved in other types of FDI, with a difference of about 13 percentage points on average. They also received incentives more often in a typical investment. When asked about the specific incentives that their companies have received, respondents identified the same three types of instruments—duty-free imports, tax holidays, and VAT exemption—as most frequently received. This suggests that the respondents' high rating of these types may owe to their familiarity with the specific instruments.

Obtaining fiscal and financial incentives typically takes three months but varies from about a week to over a year, depending on the

FIGURE 1.7   Duty-Free Imports, Tax Holidays, and VAT Exemptions Are the Most Attractive Investment Incentives

Share of respondents (percent)

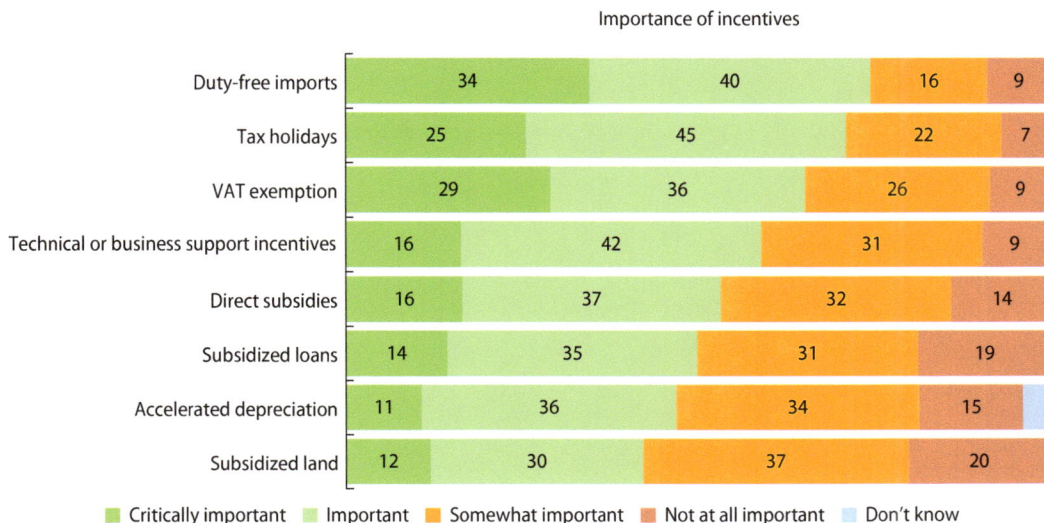

Importance of incentives

	Critically important	Important	Somewhat important	Not at all important	Don't know
Duty-free imports	34	40	16	9	
Tax holidays	25	45	22	7	
VAT exemption	29	36	26	9	
Technical or business support incentives	16	42	31	9	
Direct subsidies	16	37	32	14	
Subsidized loans	14	35	31	19	
Accelerated depreciation	11	36	34	15	
Subsidized land	12	30	37	20	

■ Critically important   ■ Important   ■ Somewhat important   ■ Not at all important   ■ Don't know

Source: Computation based on the GIC Survey.
Note: The question on incentives was answered by 663 respondents. These respondents answered somewhat important, important, or critically important on incentives in the question in figure 1.5. VAT = value added tax.

country and type of incentive. About one quarter of surveyed investors said obtaining incentives took less than one month, while about 6 percent noted it took more than a year.

Investment Entry and Establishment: Second Phase in the Investment Life Cycle

How Do Policies and Administrative Procedures for Business Establishment Affect FDI Decisions?

Investors strongly value business-friendly policies and efficient procedures related to business establishment. About four out of five respondents say that the ease of obtaining approvals for their investment is important or critically important, while only 2 percent say it is not at all important (figure 1.8). In fact, the speed of obtaining approvals and permits ranks even higher than investors' ability to own all equity in a project, to easily bring in expatriate staff, and to import production inputs. For MNCs involved in efficiency-seeking FDI, all these characteristics are rated as more important relative to investors involved in other types of FDI. For firms involved in efficiency-seeking

FDI, the ability to import production inputs is rated slightly more important (73 percent) than the ability to bring in expatriate staff (71 percent) while the reverse is true for firms involved in other types of FDI (61 and 65 percent respectively).

Although efficiency in obtaining permits is most important overall, restrictions on foreign equity ownership appear to be the biggest deal-breaker. Forty percent of respondents claim that owning all equity in their affiliate and not being required to share ownership with local firms or the government is critically important, highest among all policy factors considered. This result is significant in the context of foreign ownership restrictions still being relatively prevalent across developing countries, especially in services.

Obtaining investment approvals and permits to start a business typically takes three months, but varies by country and type of investment (figure 1.9). The variation is quite wide: on one end of the spectrum, about 10 percent of respondents say they waited less than a month while on the other end, another 10 percent of investors waited a year or longer. Respondents who value efficiency of government approvals encountered somewhat shorter waits. For this group, only 12 percent had processing times exceeding

FIGURE 1.8 Investors Strongly Value Business-Friendly Policies and Procedural Efficiency of Entry and Establishment of Affiliates

Share of respondents (percent)

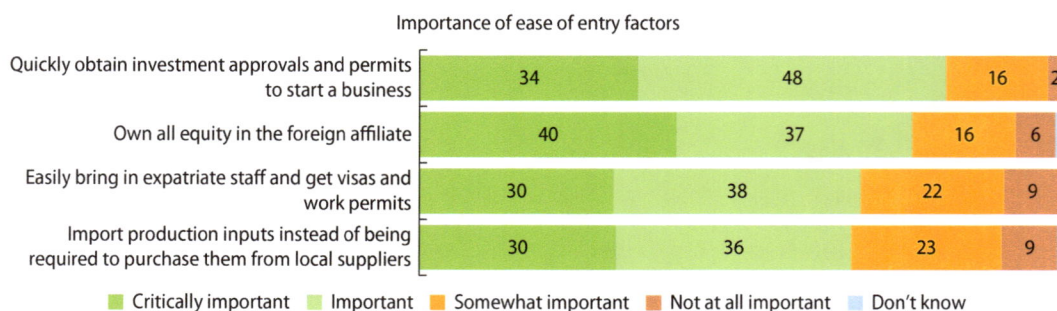

Source: Computation based on the GIC Survey.
Note: The questions on ease of entry were answered by 709 respondents. These respondents answered somewhat important, important, or critically important on ease of entry in the question in figure 1.5.

six months compared with 25 percent otherwise. This confirms that investors who value efficiency tend to favor destinations where approvals are quicker to obtain.

The median length of time for obtaining a land lease is two months, and for obtaining work permits is about 1.5 months. The dispersion of responses for both of these formalities also appears tighter than for obtaining initial investment approvals. Fewer respondents also experience wait times longer than six months—9 percent of respondents when obtaining a land lease and only 6 percent when obtaining work permits.

FIGURE 1.9 **Wait Times for Investment Approvals Vary but Typically Take Three Months**

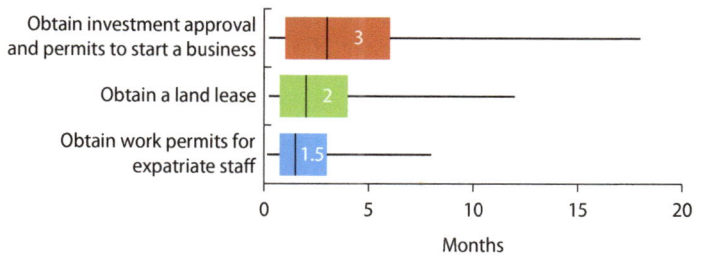

Source: Computation based on the GIC Survey.
Note: The boxplot shows the median point (with data label) as the middle bar. The ends of the boxes represent the 25th and 75th percentiles. The ends of the black lines show the 5th and 95th percentiles.

Investment Operations and Growth: Third Phase in the Investment Life Cycle

What Role Do Local Suppliers Play in MNCs' Operations?

FDI brings potential benefits to the host country through a variety of channels including linkages with the local private sector. Linkages between foreign firms and local suppliers enable knowledge and technology transfer, including know-how and practices that allow domestic suppliers to upgrade the quality and efficiency of their production. Linkages also expand the multiplier effect in the local economy. When foreign investors source inputs locally instead of importing them, they boost production of local firms and create jobs in the local economy. As such, policy makers try to promote linkages through various policies and programs. One such policy is local content requirements, where a certain percentage or absolute amount of local input is required of foreign firms. Research finds, however, that local content requirements and similar measures have a largely negative effect and discourage FDI.[3]

While investors resist being mandated to source their inputs locally, many of them prefer to do so if they are able to find in the local market the quality and quantity of the production inputs they need. On average, 43 percent of material inputs, supplies, and services are sourced locally, versus 34 percent of inputs sourced from another unit of the company and 23 percent of inputs imported (figure 1.10). The percentage of inputs sourced locally varies widely: about 13 percent of surveyed companies do not source any inputs locally, another 13 percent source all their inputs locally, and the rest of the firms (about 74 percent) source some portion of their inputs locally. Linkages are more prevalent for MNCs in service sectors compared with manufacturing firms.

Overall, 61 percent of MNCs consider linkages as important or critically important in their location decisions. Among those investors who identified linkages as at least somewhat important, 74 percent find that capacity and skills of local suppliers are important or critically important (figure 1.11). Local skills and capacity are valued even more by MNCs involved in efficiency-seeking FDI (77 percent). This suggests that government initiatives to promote linkages will only be effective if local companies can offer the capacity and skills expected by MNCs. At the same time, governments of host countries have the scope to facilitate linkages. Investors value information on the availability of local suppliers, rated as important or critically important by 68 percent of respondents. About 61 percent of respondents also rate supplier upgrading as important, whether in the form of direct financial incentives for companies to invest in supplier development or governments' own initiatives to upgrade suppliers. Only 42 percent of respondents value

FIGURE 1.10   Nearly Half of Material Inputs, Supplies, and Services Are Sourced Locally

Share of respondents (percent)

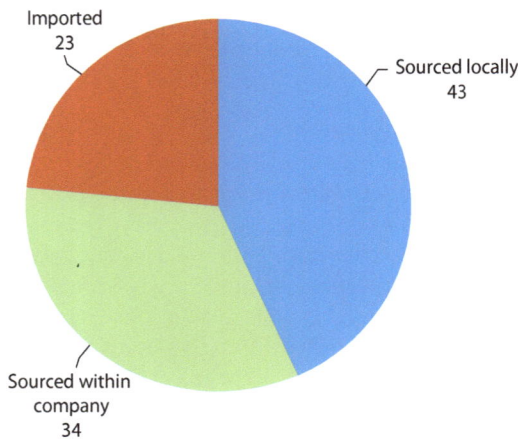

Source: Computation based on the GIC Survey.
Note: The number of respondents for each source vary and are fewer than 754 because some respondents answered "don't know."

matchmaking events with suppliers. These government initiatives are rated as important by about 8 to 12 percentage points more by firms involved in efficiency-seeking FDI relative to other investors.

When capacity and quality constraints in the local market prevent investors from finding appropriate suppliers, investors value being able to import inputs instead of being required to source them locally. This is especially true for MNCs involved in efficiency-seeking FDI and manufacturing firms. Many manufacturing MNCs invest in developing countries to reduce their cost of production. At the same time, to maintain a high quality of final products, which are often intended for export, foreign manufacturers appreciate the flexibility of importing their own inputs for production rather than sourcing them locally. Of the surveyed manufacturing firms, 68 percent rate the ability to import inputs as important or critically important, as opposed to only 56 percent of services companies. Among firms involved in efficiency-seeking FDI, 73 percent find this attribute important or critically important while only 61 percent of firms involved in other types of FDI consider it important.

FIGURE 1.11   Capacity and Skills of Suppliers Are Critical Linkages-Related Features

Share of respondents (percent)

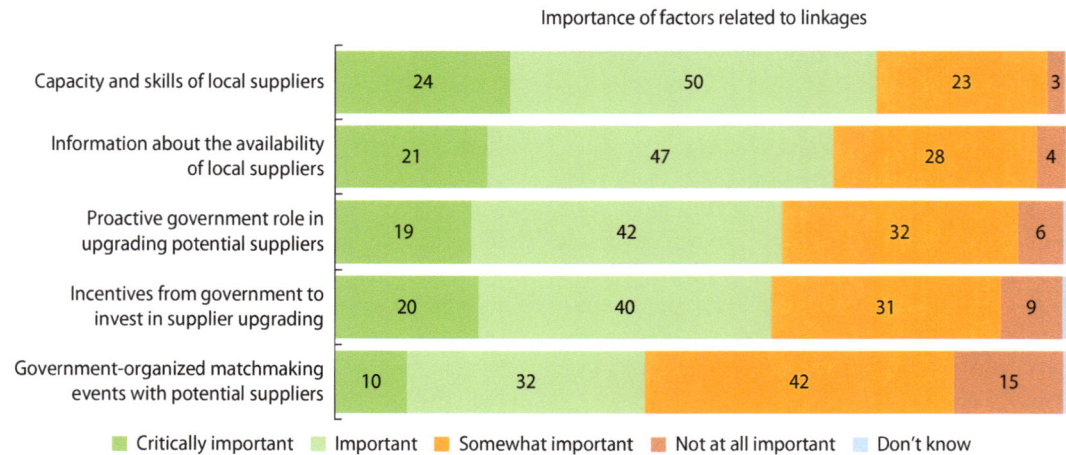

Source: Computation based on the GIC Survey.
Note: The questions on linkages were answered by 679 respondents who answered somewhat important, important, or critically important on the question, "How important are the capabilities of local firms to act as suppliers in your decision to invest in developing countries?"

Foreign investors themselves also have an interest in promoting linkages, but company-initiated programs are uncommon. Sourcing inputs, supplies, and services locally instead of importing them can reduce costs for foreign-owned firms. Some MNCs have their own programs to promote linkages, but these are not widespread. The survey finds that, among the foreign firms that do source locally, half use internal "talent scouts" to find local suppliers. Firms involved in efficiency-seeking FDI tend to have talent scouts more often (55 percent) than investors involved in other types of FDI (45 percent). Over 30 percent have vocational or training programs to upgrade local suppliers, and 11 percent have equipment-financing programs for local suppliers (figure 1.12). Among firms that have vocational or training programs, about a third sponsor certification programs and partner with local technical colleges and universities.

How Much Do MNCs Reinvest in Host Countries?

Host countries not only need to attract and retain FDI but also need to facilitate its growth to motivate investors to reinvest their earnings in the host country. Many variables may influence investors in deciding on the share of their profits to repatriate as dividends versus reinvest in growing their operations in the host country. These variables include taxation systems, transfer costs, investment opportunities in the ongoing business and elsewhere, relative costs of shifting financial resources out of the host country, and need to expand the ongoing business. Reinvested earnings are becoming an increasingly important source of FDI, growing from less than 30 percent of FDI flows in 2007 to about 50 percent in 2015 (UNCTAD 2016). This trend is confirmed by the survey results, where over a third of respondents say that they reinvest all their profits in the host country, and another 14 percent reinvests more than half (figure 1.13). This trend highlights the importance for host economies of retaining

FIGURE 1.12 **Corporate Programs to Promote Linkages Are Not Very Widespread**

Share of respondents (percent)

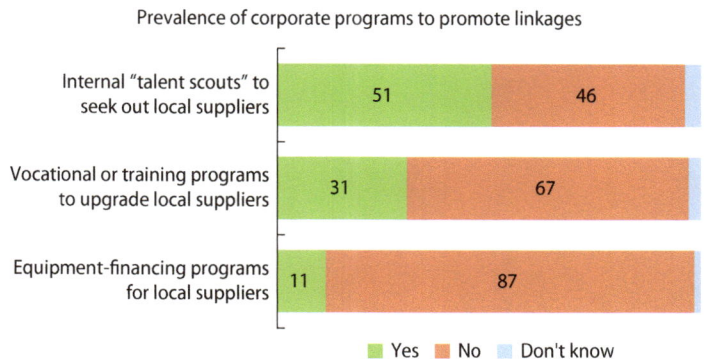

Prevalence of corporate programs to promote linkages

Source: Computation based on the GIC Survey.
Note: These questions on corporate programs to promote linkages were answered by 454 respondents. These respondents answered somewhat important, important, or critically important on the question "How important are the capabilities of local firms to act as suppliers in your decision to invest in developing countries?" and source some or all of their inputs locally.

and expanding existing investments in addition to attracting new ones.

How Do Investors Respond to Political Risks?

Among survey respondents, 76 percent experienced political risks in their investment projects. Political risk is the probability of disruption of business operations by political forces or events, and especially by government actions. About half of respondents experienced lack of transparency and predictability in dealing with developing country public agencies. Almost half encountered adverse regulatory changes and delays in obtaining necessary government permits and approvals to start or operate a business. Over 40 percent encountered restrictions in transferring and converting currency. In these cases, about one in four investors canceled a planned investment or withdrew an existing investment owing to political risks (figure 1.14).

More severe cases of political risk occur less frequently but with far worse impact. Only 13 percent of respondents experienced breach of contract by the government but

FIGURE 1.13   **More than a Third of Investors Reinvest All Their Affiliate-Generated Profits Back into the Affiliate**

Reinvested earnings

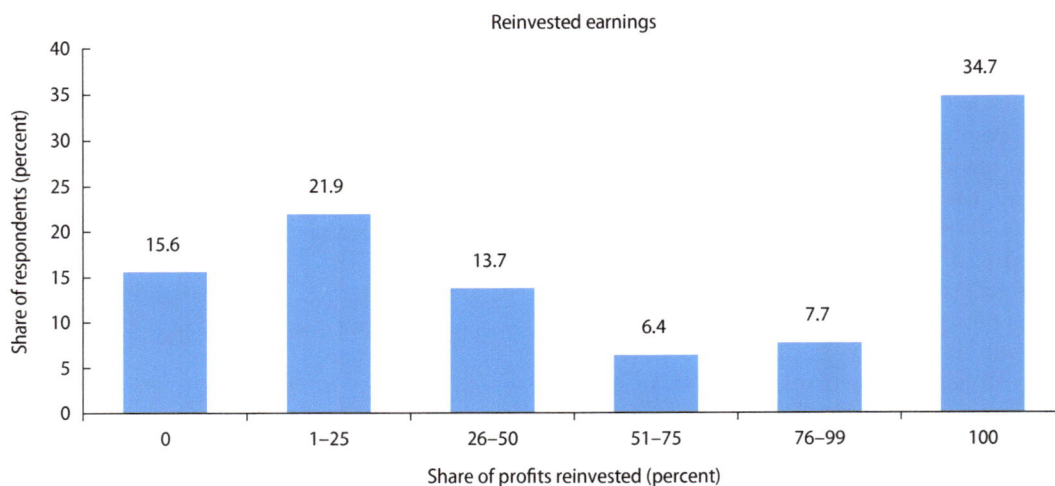

Source: Computation based on the GIC Survey.
Note: The question on reinvested earnings was answered by 597 respondents. The remaining 158 either refused, did not know the answer, or made the investment within the year. Respondents were asked about reinvested earnings in a specific developing country of their choice.

the impact was much greater—35 percent of those investors canceled a planned investment or withdrew an existing one. Expropriation was even more extreme: while only 5 percent of respondents experienced it, almost half of them canceled or withdrew an investment.

Investments in services tend to be more affected by political risk than manufacturing. Firms in the services sector experienced more disruptions related to political risk, particularly restrictions in transferring and converting currency, breach of contract by the government, and expropriation. Services—such as energy, telecommunications, or finance—are more tightly regulated than manufacturing, and thus more exposed to potential political interference. In particular, according to survey results, companies in the utilities sector—including electricity, gas, alternative energy, and telecommunications—experience more frequent adverse regulatory changes and expropriation and more delays in obtaining permits. Construction and business services

sectors report more frequent experiences of breach of contract by the government and lack of transparency and predictability in dealing with public agencies.

Governments should more adequately manage investor grievances. According to the survey, governments often do not effectively address grievances related to political risks. Only about one in five affected investors felt that their grievances were promptly resolved by the government, that the process of complaint was clear and efficient, or that the government introduced a systematic solution to address or prevent such grievances in the future.

Divestment: Fourth Phase in the Investment Life Cycle

Why Do MNCs Divest from Developing Countries?

Some 29 percent of investors surveyed had shut down at least one of their company's

FIGURE 1.14 **Severe Political Risks Are Infrequent but Can Have Highly Negative Effects on FDI**
Share of respondents (percent)

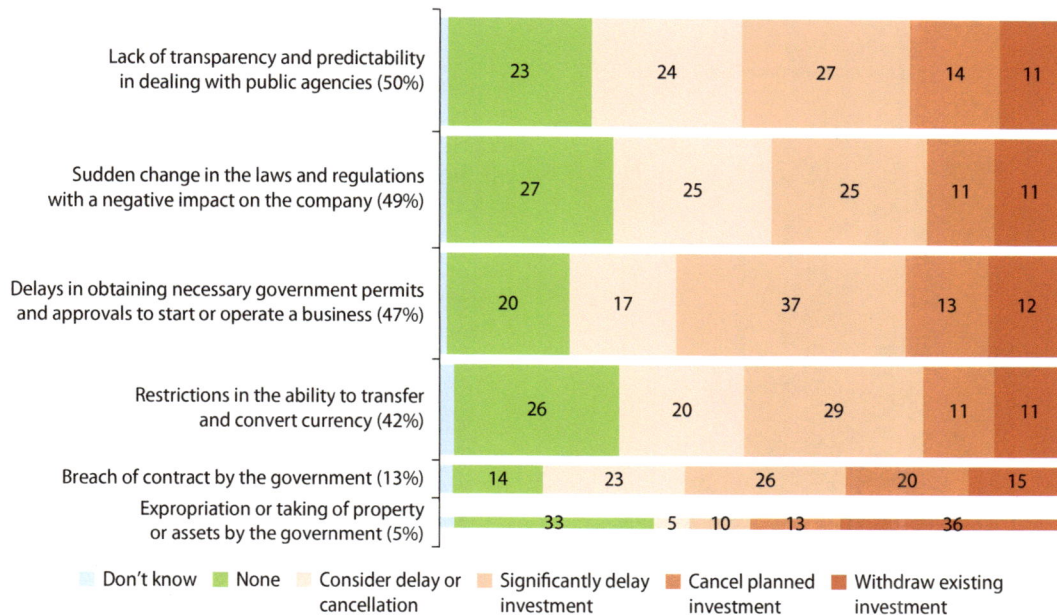

	Don't know	None	Consider delay or cancellation	Significantly delay investment	Cancel planned investment	Withdraw existing investment
Lack of transparency and predictability in dealing with public agencies (50%)		23	24	27	14	11
Sudden change in the laws and regulations with a negative impact on the company (49%)		27	25	25	11	11
Delays in obtaining necessary government permits and approvals to start or operate a business (47%)		20	17	37	13	12
Restrictions in the ability to transfer and convert currency (42%)		26	20	29	11	11
Breach of contract by the government (13%)		14	23	26	20	15
Expropriation or taking of property or assets by the government (5%)		33	5	10	13	36

Source: Computation based on the GIC Survey.
Note: The height of the bars reflects the percentage of respondents that experienced disruption in any of their investments owing to the political risk identified. The risks are arranged in descending order from most frequently experienced at the top, to least frequently experienced at the bottom. The numbers across rows do not add up to 100 percent because respondents could select multiple types of disruptions that their companies had experienced. The horizontal bars show the responses of companies, with the darker red bars reflecting more severe reactions. The bars reveal the most severe reactions of companies after experiencing the particular disruption. If, for example, a company experienced withdrawing an existing investment in one country, but only delaying in another, the most severe reaction was considered and the company was included in the *withdraw* bar.

affiliates in a developing country (figure 1.15). The most common reasons were changes in the company's strategy and unstable macroeconomic conditions, including an unfavorable exchange rate. Increased policy or regulatory uncertainty was the third most common reason, which occurred in about a third of the divestment cases (figure 1.16). Arbitrary government conduct, sudden restrictions on currency transfer, and breach of contract by governments are reported as factors by more than 20 percent of investors. These results confirm that companies value transparency and predictability in the conduct of public agencies, as well as investment protections. Foreign investors in services divest more frequently than manufacturing MNCs, possibly because they are

more highly regulated and thus vulnerable to political interference. Among the surveyed services companies, 35 percent had shut down an affiliate, versus just 23 percent of manufacturing firms.

Although some reasons for exiting investments are beyond the control of governments of host countries, many are avoidable. While governments cannot do much about changes in investor firms' corporate strategies or about global economic conditions, they can influence factors in their own countries. In particular, maintaining an appropriately valued exchange rate, managing macroeconomic stability, and ensuring transparent, consistent, and predictable policies and regulations are critical in keeping investors from exiting.

FIGURE 1.15   More than a Quarter of Respondents Had Shut Down an Affiliate in a Developing Country
Share of respondents (percent)

Shut down an affiliate in any developing country

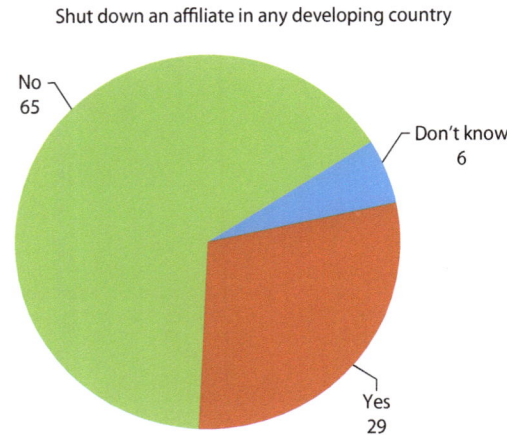

No
65

Don't know
6

Yes
29

Source: Computation based on the GIC Survey.

FIGURE 1.16   Reasons for Exiting an Investment Are Mixed, Some Controllable and Others Not
Share of respondents (percent)

Reasons for exiting an investment

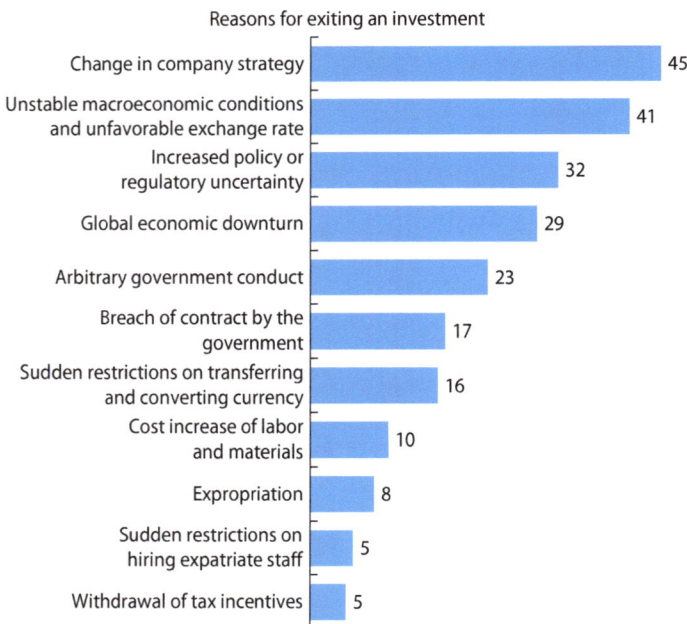

Change in company strategy	45
Unstable macroeconomic conditions and unfavorable exchange rate	41
Increased policy or regulatory uncertainty	32
Global economic downturn	29
Arbitrary government conduct	23
Breach of contract by the government	17
Sudden restrictions on transferring and converting currency	16
Cost increase of labor and materials	10
Expropriation	8
Sudden restrictions on hiring expatriate staff	5
Withdrawal of tax incentives	5

Source: Computation based on the GIC Survey.
Note: Results are based on 219 respondents that were aware that their companies had shut down an affiliate in a developing country. Shares do not add up to 100 because respondents could select up to five of the most relevant reasons.

What Role Do Investment Promotion Agencies Play across the Investment Life Cycle?

Although MNCs have their own strategic motivations for selecting specific investment locations, the quality of services provided by the host economies can play a key role in MNCs' corporate decisions. The role of investment promotion agencies (IPAs) in facilitating investments can be particularly important in countries with larger physical or cultural distance from the home economies of investors.

IPAs complement rather than substitute for a good investment climate and ecosystem for investment projects. Only 43 percent of the surveyed investors say that IPAs are important or critically important in their decision to invest, the lowest among investment climate variables queried in the survey. Only 12 percent consider quality of IPA services to be deal-breakers, while 14 percent rate IPAs as not at all important. These results suggest that other factors play a more prominent role in firms' decision making. Sound economic fundamentals need to prevail before the services delivered by IPAs become critical for investors.

IPA services thus have great scope for improvement. The relatively low rating of the importance of IPAs does not necessarily suggest that host countries should not strengthen them. The reverse could actually be true—that host countries currently offer poor-quality IPA services for investors, which is why investors' perceptions are not very positive. Only 11 percent of respondents use IPA services in their typical investment, despite 43 percent saying they are important. The proportion of users is somewhat greater for investments in low-income countries than in middle-income countries, suggesting that IPAs provide more value when the business environment is more difficult and information harder to obtain, as is often the case in low-income countries. MNCs involved in efficiency-seeking FDI value IPA services more highly, with 52 percent of respondents identifying IPA services as important or critically important, compared with 37 percent of investors involved in other types of FDI.

Among investors who do find IPAs to be important or somewhat important, two-thirds highly value help in handling issues and resolving grievances with government, information and assistance in setting up, and business advocacy efforts to improve the business environment. These services are rated more important than investment promotion activities (figure 1.17). Promotion efforts to attract investors—advertising online and in media, and exhibitions at trade shows, investment conferences, and events—are rated as relatively less important. Only about a third of investors find these services important or critically important, the lowest rated among the various factors considered.

Among the 11 percent of investors that did engage with IPAs, their services during entry and establishment were used most

frequently. Investors used IPA services for assistance in registering and obtaining permits for a new investment (76 percent), expanding investment (59 percent), exploring locations for a new investment (46 percent), helping address operational issues or problems (41 percent), and finding domestic suppliers (28 percent). These results likely reflect the availability of services offered by IPAs in the first place rather than investors' needs. IPAs often dedicate resources for investment promotion and facilitation, but not many offer additional services after the investment becomes operational. A potential mismatch is apparent—while investors would appreciate assistance with their operations (for example, in resolving issues or grievances with the government), the services they typically receive from IPAs are more focused on the start-up phase.

Some investors value IPA services more than others. In particular, investment promotion efforts—exhibitions, advertising,

FIGURE 1.17 **Investors Value IPA Help in Resolving Problems and Setting Up More than Promotion Efforts**
Share of respondents (percent)

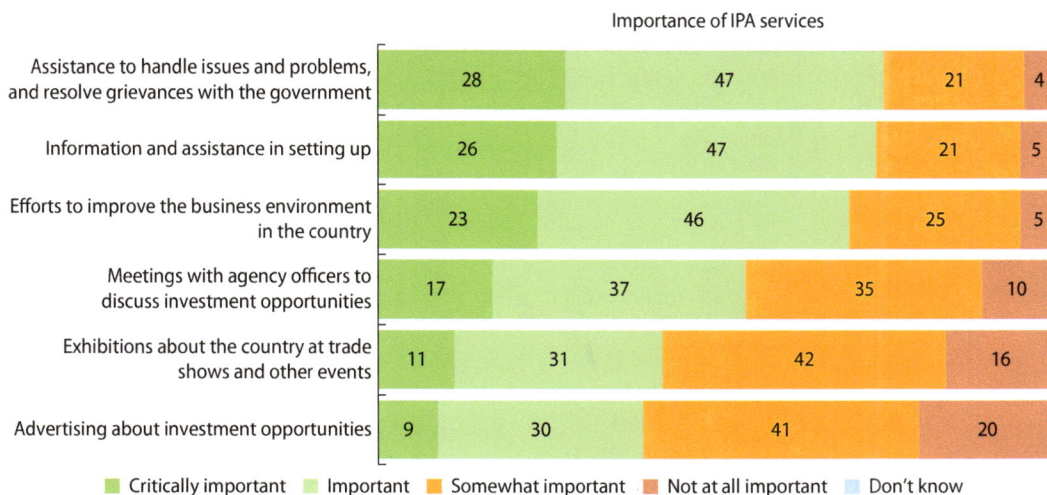

Importance of IPA services

	Critically important	Important	Somewhat important	Not at all important
Assistance to handle issues and problems, and resolve grievances with the government	28	47	21	4
Information and assistance in setting up	26	47	21	5
Efforts to improve the business environment in the country	23	46	25	5
Meetings with agency officers to discuss investment opportunities	17	37	35	10
Exhibitions about the country at trade shows and other events	11	31	42	16
Advertising about investment opportunities	9	30	41	20

■ Critically important ■ Important ■ Somewhat important ■ Not at all important ■ Don't know

Source: Computation based on the GIC Survey.
Note: The questions on IPA services were answered by 632 respondents. These respondents answered somewhat important, important, or critically important on the question, "How important are high-quality services and support from the country's IPA in your decision to invest in developing countries?". IPA = investment promotion agency.

and meetings with agency officers—resonate with investors from developing countries more than those from developed countries, and with investors in the services sector more than those in manufacturing. Meetings with agency officers to discuss investment opportunities, information and assistance in setting up an affiliate, and assistance in problem resolution are valued more by firms involved in efficiency-seeking FDI. In general, the ratings remain relatively low, but this suggests that IPA services in attracting investments can be better targeted to those companies that may be more responsive, whenever they align with the country's target sectors and target markets. IPAs often focus on traditional investors from industrialized economies, but as FDI increasingly originates from developing countries, IPAs may well benefit from redirecting their activities accordingly.

Policy Implications

To maximize the gains from foreign investments, developing country governments must adopt effective reform strategies, champion reform at the highest political levels, and strengthen interagency coordination. They must also balance the public interest with investor preferences to ensure that the host country truly benefits from FDI. The results of the survey of MNC executives highlight several priorities for policy makers in developing countries seeking to create a conducive business climate for FDI:

Predictable government conduct is at least as important to MNCs as countries' laws and regulations. Investors cited the importance of transparency and predictability in the conduct of government agencies as the most important among investment climate factors. Investors look not only at policies on paper but also at implementation and administration of those policies. Implementation weaknesses can include bureaucratic inefficiencies, complex regulations and procedures, and unpredictable or arbitrary government conduct. Addressing these weaknesses can not only attract new investments but also prevent divestments by existing investors.

Addressing policy reforms to attract FDI and offering aftercare services are equally important. Policy makers tend to focus on attracting FDI through investment incentives, facilitation, and proactive investment promotion. While these are important, investors say that investment protection is even more critical to them, suggesting that government efforts should also aim to encourage investors to stay in the country and expand their operations. Policy initiatives should include strengthening investor protection guarantees, providing proactive investor aftercare, managing grievances, and promoting linkages.

Targeting policies and reforms to relevant types of investors can maximize effectiveness and cost efficiency. While most investors value some characteristics across the board—such as investment protection guarantees and transparency and predictability—some policy variables are more important for certain investor types. Firms involved in efficiency-seeking FDI seem more responsive to incentives. Manufacturing firms may be more responsive to business-friendly policies on importing inputs, while services firms are more sensitive to adverse government conduct. MNCs from developing countries value IPA services and some types of incentives more than firms from developed economies. These results reinforce the need for targeted policy approaches by governments, keeping in mind the specific types of FDI they wish to attract, retain, and harness for development.

Annex 1A. Survey Methodology and Characteristics

Methodology

The GIC Survey captures perceptions of international business executives on the role of investment climate factors in their FDI decisions. The survey respondents were 754 business executives involved with the operations of their MNC in developing countries. The sample frame consisted of nearly 8,000 eligible companies in the commercially available Dunn and Bradstreet database. The 754 respondents were executives who were reached by telephone and agreed to participate in the survey. The sample included investors with existing investments in at least one developing country. Respondents were a combination of executives at the global headquarters and executives at a foreign affiliate. The characteristics of their firms are discussed below.

The World Bank Group commissioned a survey firm to conduct 30-minute computer-assisted telephone interviews. The interviews were conducted in 13 languages: Arabic, Bahasa Indonesia, Chinese, English, French, German, Italian, Japanese, Korean, Portuguese, Russian, Spanish, and Turkish. The interviews consisted of a screener phase, to ensure the eligibility of respondents. The interviews were conducted between February and June 2017.

Characteristics

The survey complemented other existing investor surveys by focusing on investment climate variables, such as administrative and legal barriers rather than broader economy-wide factors. These specific investment climate variables were areas actionable for policy makers.

The survey was intended to provide a broad understanding of corporate perspectives and investor behavior and is not intended as a benchmarking tool to compare countries.

The survey was composed of four sections:

1. *General information on the company and respondent*, including sector, number of employees, and position of the respondent in the company.

2. *Importance of factors in investing in a developing country*, where respondents rate the importance of country characteristics and investment policy factors on a scale from 1 to 4 from "not at all important" to "critically important." "Critically important" means it is a deal-breaker—by itself, it could change the company's decision about whether or not to invest in a country.

3. *Political risks and investment exit*, where respondents identify experiences of political risks and the company's course of action. They were also asked whether they had shut down a foreign affiliate in a developing country and their reasons for doing so.

4. *Investment in a specific developing country*, where respondents select a specific developing country where they are most familiar with the process of establishing an affiliate. Questions on the specific investment included sector, activity, motivation, reinvested earnings, efficiency of government agencies, IPA services used, incentives received, sources of inputs, and corporate programs for suppliers.

Annex 1B. Respondent Profile

1. *Location of company headquarters.* Among 754 respondents, 73 percent were headquartered in high-income countries and 27 percent in developing countries. Over half of respondents had headquarters in Western Europe (figure 1B.1).

The respondents were stratified by source economy of FDI. The sampling method considered whether the source economy was developed or developing but did not aim to make the composition of respondents representative at a country level. Practical considerations such as sample size and translations to local languages precluded the survey methodology from obtaining a representative sample of companies globally. The sampling method also considered that respondents should comprise a large enough sample of developing economies as source

FIGURE 1B.1   MNCs Come from Various Regions and Levels of Development

Share of respondents (percent)

Home economies of investors by region and income level

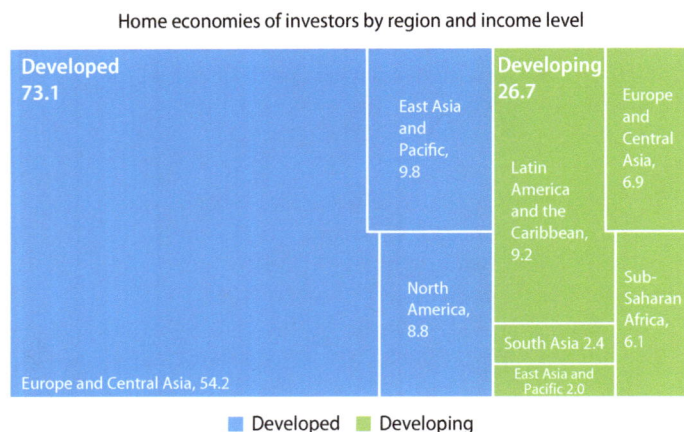

■ Developed ■ Developing

Source: Computation based on the GIC Survey.
Note: Respondents were asked to identify the location of their global headquarters. The classifications of developing and developed are based on the World Bank Group's income level classifications. High-income economies are considered developed economies, while low-, lower-middle-, and upper-middle-income economies are considered developing economies. The analysis for this report is unable to disaggregate into income groups owing to the small sample size. MNC = multinational corporation.

countries of FDI. Table 1B.2 compares the composition of respondents from developed and developing economies with global outward FDI stock in 2016.

2. *Location of respondent.* Of respondents, 401 (53 percent) were executives located at the global headquarters while 353 (47 percent) were executives of an MNC affiliate in a developing country.

3. *Position of respondent in the company.* A large majority of respondents were either the Chief Executive Officer (CEO) or Chief Finance Officer (CFO), or their equivalent (table 1B.3).

4. *Sectoral Distribution.* Some 47 percent of respondents were executives of manufacturing firms, 45 percent were from services, 6 percent were from extractives, and 2 percent were from "other" noncategorized sectors (table 1B.4).

Table 1B.5 compares the composition of survey respondents with global FDI flows for greenfield investments and mergers and acquisitions (M&A). Data on greenfield investments and M&A are based on data from UNCTAD's World Investment Report, based on the total number of investment projects (not value of investments) over the last five years (2012–16). During this period, there were 15,692 greenfield investment projects and 51,283 M&A purchases.

5. *Number of employees.* Large companies with 1,000+ employees constituted 40 percent of the sample. About one-third (32 percent) of the interviewed companies had fewer than 250 employees, and 26 percent had between 251 and 1,000 employees (figure 1B.2).

6. *Motivation.* Only about a third of companies (33 percent) had one dominant motivation for an investment in a specific developing country. A significant majority (62 percent) had two or more FDI motivations (table 1B.6).

TABLE 1B.1   **Location of Headquarters**

Developed economies	No. of respondents	Percentage of respondents	Developing economies	No. of respondents	Percentage of respondents
Germany	111	14.72	South Africa	35	4.64
Spain	80	10.61	Argentina	23	3.05
United States	60	7.96	Turkey	20	2.65
Italy	53	7.03	India	16	2.12
Korea, Rep.	37	4.91	Mexico	14	1.86
Austria	36	4.77	Bulgaria	10	1.33
Japan	32	4.24	Brazil	9	1.19
France	30	3.98	China	8	1.06
United Kingdom	28	3.71	Malaysia	6	0.80
Netherlands	22	2.92	Russian Federation	6	0.80
Sweden	20	2.65	Nigeria	4	0.53
Switzerland	20	2.65	Colombia	4	0.53
Canada	6	0.80	Peru	4	0.53
Belgium	5	0.66	Venezuela, RB	4	0.53
Australia	4	0.53	Belarus	3	0.40
United Arab Emirates	1	0.13	Bosnia and Herzegovina	3	0.40
Uruguay	1	0.13	Guatemala	3	0.40
Chile	1	0.13	Romania	3	0.40
Taiwan, China	1	0.13	Serbia	3	0.40
Iceland	1	0.13	Ukraine	3	0.40
Finland	1	0.13	Kenya	2	0.27
Estonia	1	0.13	Costa Rica	2	0.27
Denmark	1	0.13	Panama	2	0.27
			Egypt, Arab Rep.	1	0.13
			Bolivia	1	0.13
			Botswana	1	0.13
			Ecuador	1	0.13
			El Salvador	1	0.13
			Pakistan	1	0.13
			Saint Lucia	1	0.13
			Sri Lanka	1	0.13
			Swaziland	1	0.13
			Thailand	1	0.13
			Uzbekistan	1	0.13
			Djibouti	1	0.13
			Ghana	1	0.13
			Zambia	1	0.13
			Cameroon	1	0.13

TABLE 1B.2   Composition of Respondents Compared with Global FDI Stock
Percent

Location of headquarters	Percentage of respondents	Share of global FDI stock
Developed economies	73.21	76.31
Developing economies	26.79	23.69

Source: Computation based on the GIC Survey and UNCTAD.
Note: FDI = foreign direct investment.

TABLE 1B.3   Position of Respondents in the Company

Position	No. of respondents	Percentage of respondents
CFO/Finance director/Treasurer/Comptroller	336	44.6
CEO/President/Managing director	146	19.4
Head of business unit/Head of department	126	16.7
Other C-level executive	61	8.1
SVP/VP/Director	26	3.4
Board member	24	3.2
Director of global operations or global manufacturing	18	2.4
Other	12	1.6
CIO/Technology director	5	0.7
Total	754	100.0

TABLE 1B.4   Sectoral Distribution of Respondents

Sector	No. of respondents	Percentage of respondents
Primary		
Agriculture, hunting, forestry, and fishing	22	2.92
Mining, quarrying, and petroleum	26	3.45
Manufacturing		
Refined petroleum products, coke, and nuclear fuel	7	0.93
Agroprocessing, food products, and beverages	24	3.18
Textiles, apparel, and leather	23	3.05
Chemicals and chemical products	24	3.18
Rubber	5	0.66
Plastic products	14	1.86
Pharmaceuticals, biotechnology, and medical devices	26	3.45
Metals and metal products	39	5.17
Nonmetal mineral products	3	0.40
Wood and wood products (other than furniture)	3	0.40
Furniture	2	0.27
Paper and paper products	6	0.80
Printing and publishing	4	0.53
Automobiles, other motor vehicles, and transport equipment	67	8.89
Information technology and telecommunications equipment	6	0.80
Machinery, and electrical and electronic equipment and components	64	8.49
Other manufacturing	36	4.77

table continues next page

TABLE 1B.4 **Sectoral Distribution of Respondents** *(continued)*

Sector	No. of respondents	Percentage of respondents
Services		
Electricity, gas, and water	20	2.65
Alternative energy	19	2.52
Construction	53	7.03
Wholesale and retail trade	43	5.70
Hotels and restaurants	7	0.93
Other travel and tourism-related services	8	1.06
Logistics, transport, and storage	35	4.64
Telecommunications	13	1.72
Computer and software services	10	1.33
Financial services including insurance	44	5.84
Real estate	4	0.53
Business services	18	2.39
Professional, scientific, and technical services	32	4.24
Health services	8	1.06
Media and entertainment	7	0.93
Other services	15	1.99
Other	17	2.25
Total	754	100.00

TABLE 1B.5 **Sectoral Distribution of Respondents Compared with Global FDI Flows**
Percent

Sector	Share of global FDI flows for greenfield	Share of global FDI flows for M&A	Percentage of respondents
Primary	**0.5**	**4.7**	**6.4**
Agriculture, hunting, forestry and fisheries	0.0	0.5	2.9
Mining, quarrying and petroleum	0.5	4.1	3.5
Manufacturing	**47.3**	**22.2**	**46.8**
Food, beverages, and tobacco	3.6	2.8	3.2
Textiles, clothing, and leather	8.8	0.6	3.1
Wood and wood products	0.9	0.2	0.4
Paper and paper products	—	0.7	0.8
Publishing and printing	0.1	0.2	0.5
Coke, petroleum products, and nuclear fuel	0.5	0.2	0.9
Chemicals and chemical products	5.0	2.7	3.2
Pharmaceuticals, biotechnology, medical devices	—	1.6	3.5
Rubber and plastic products	2.5	0.5	2.5
Nonmetallic mineral products	1.0	0.8	0.4
Metals and metal products	2.2	1.9	5.2
Machinery and equipment, electrical and electronic equipment	12.4	7.0	8.5
Precision instruments	1.1	—	—
Motor vehicles and other transport equipment	6.7	1.5	8.9
Manufacturing of furniture	—	0.2	0.3
Other manufacturing	2.4	1.2	4.8

table continues next page

TABLE 1B.5   Sectoral Distribution of Respondents Compared with Global FDI Flows (continued)

Sector	Share of global FDI flows for greenfield	Share of global FDI flows for M&A	Percentage of respondents
Services	**52.2**	**73.2**	**44.6**
Electricity, gas, and water	2.2	1.9	5.1
Construction and real estate	1.6	1.1	7.6
Trade	5.3	4.5	5.7
Hotels and restaurants, travel and tourism-related	0.8	3.0	2.0
Transport, storage, and communications	6.4	49.1	6.4
Finance	7.2	11.1	5.8
Business services	26.2	—	2.4
Public administration and defense	—	0.7	—
Education	0.7	0.2	—
Health and social services	0.5	0.7	1.1
Arts, entertainment, and recreation	1.2	0.4	0.9
Other services	0.2	0.3	2.0
Other	—	—	2.3

Source: Computation based on UNCTAD World Investment Report 2017, which sourced its data from UNCTAD M&A database and fDi Markets database, the Financial Times, and based on the GIC Survey.
Note: Sector categories have been slightly adapted to harmonize across the three data sources. Sectors marked with "—" are not in the list of sectors from their original source. FDI = foreign direct investment; M&A = mergers and acquisitions.

FIGURE 1B.2   Size of MNCs by Number of Employees
Share of respondents (percent)

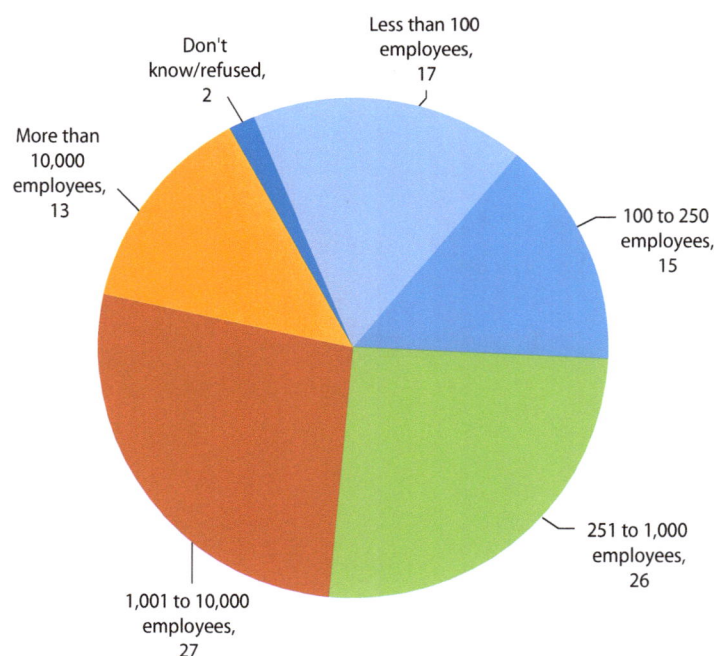

Source: Computation based on the GIC Survey.
Note: MNC = multinational corporation.

TABLE 1B.6   Number of Motivations

No. of motivations	No. of respondents	Percentage of respondents
0	34	4.51
1	249	33.02
2	227	30.11
3	159	21.09
4	64	8.49
5	21	2.79
Total	754	100.00

Annex 1C. Differences by Group

The importance of country characteristics varies by sector and source of FDI. Manufacturing firms find cost of labor and other inputs, and access to land or real estate, more important than services firms, probably because the efficiency-seeking motivation is more common in the manufacturing sector than in services. Services firms, on the other hand, are more sensitive to political stability and security,

FIGURE 1C.1   Importance of Country Characteristics by Manufacturing versus Services Firms
Share of respondents (percent)

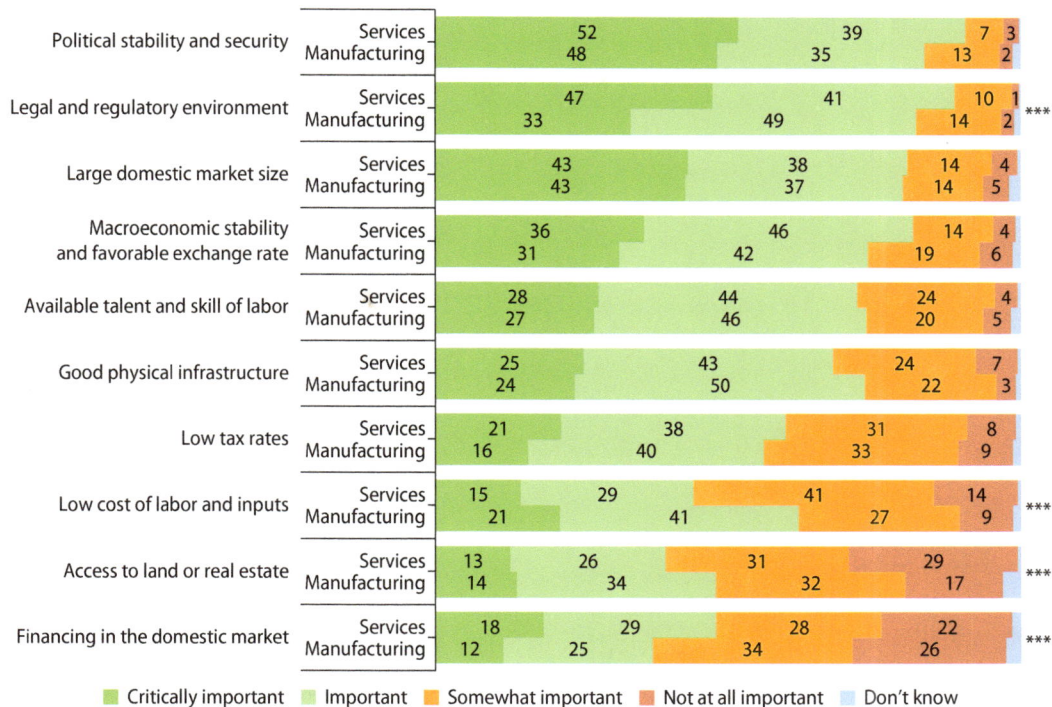

Critically important ■ Important ■ Somewhat important ■ Not at all important ■ Don't know

Source: Computation based on the GIC Survey.
Note: The differences between the two groups are significant at ***p<0.01, **p<0.05 and *p<0.1.

the legal and regulatory environment, macro-economic stability, and financing in the domestic market (figure 1C.1). Many of these services firms offer financial services, retail trade, energy, and telecommunications that are more highly regulated. Investors from developing countries also tend to value many of these factors highly, compared with their counterparts from developed economies—these characteristics include macroeconomic stability, low cost of labor and inputs, low tax rates, and availability of domestic financing (figure 1C.2). Respondents from affiliates located in developing countries tend to rate most characteristics as important compared with respondents based at the companies' global headquarters (figure 1C.3). This suggests that executives on the ground, who are more aware of the challenges in setting up and operating MNC affiliates in developing

countries, value more highly factors such as a business-friendly legal and regulatory environment; indeed, almost half said that the absence of such an environment was a deal-breaker, versus only 32 percent of respondents in parent companies.

The importance of investment climate factors also varies by sector. Services firms are more sensitive to transparency and predictability in the conduct of public agencies, investment protection guarantees, and ease of starting a business, likely owing to these industries being more highly regulated (figure 1C.4). Investors from developing countries also seem to value investment climate factors more highly than those from developed economies, but the differences are not statistically significant (figure 1C.5). Respondents from affiliates located in developing countries tend to rate investment

FIGURE 1C.2   **Importance of Country Characteristics by Developed versus Developing Source Countries**

Share of respondents (percent)

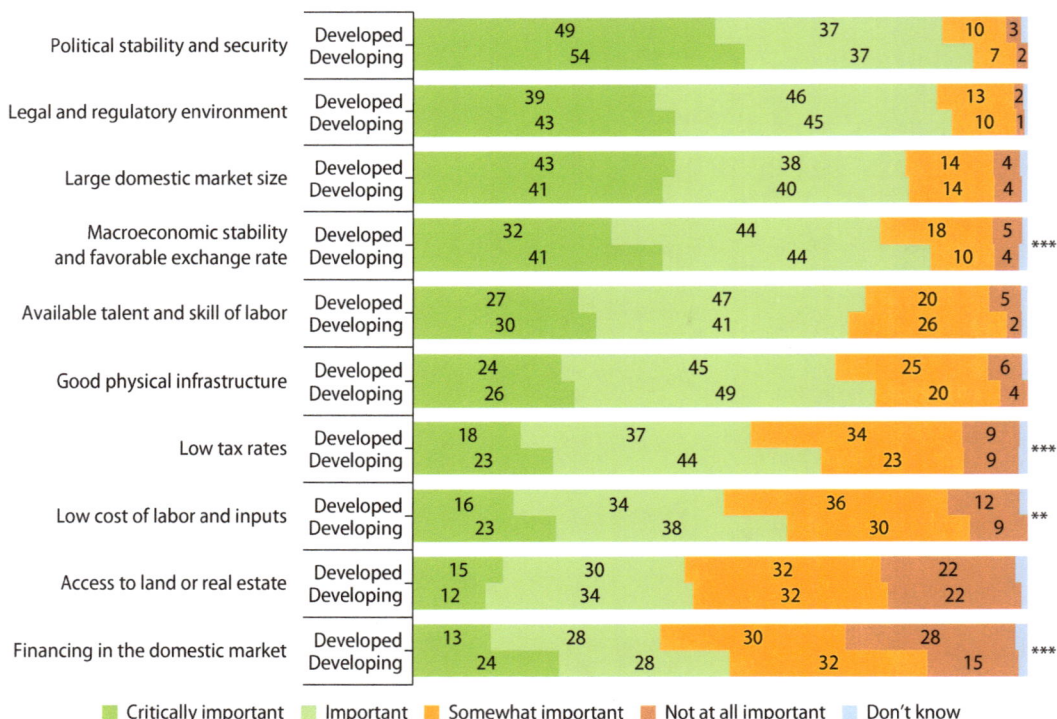

		Critically important	Important	Somewhat important	Not at all important	Don't know
Political stability and security	Developed	49	37	10	3	
	Developing	54	37	7	2	
Legal and regulatory environment	Developed	39	46	13	2	
	Developing	43	45	10	1	
Large domestic market size	Developed	43	38	14	4	
	Developing	41	40	14	4	
Macroeconomic stability and favorable exchange rate	Developed	32	44	18	5	***
	Developing	41	44	10	4	
Available talent and skill of labor	Developed	27	47	20	5	
	Developing	30	41	26	2	
Good physical infrastructure	Developed	24	45	25	6	
	Developing	26	49	20	4	
Low tax rates	Developed	18	37	34	9	***
	Developing	23	44	23	9	
Low cost of labor and inputs	Developed	16	34	36	12	**
	Developing	23	38	30	9	
Access to land or real estate	Developed	15	30	32	22	
	Developing	12	34	32	22	
Financing in the domestic market	Developed	13	28	30	28	***
	Developing	24	28	32	15	

Source: Computation based on the GIC Survey.
Note: The differences between the two groups are significant at ***$p<0.01$, **$p<0.05$ and *$p<0.1$.

FIGURE 1C.3 Importance of Country Characteristics by Parent Company versus Affiliate

Share of respondents (percent)

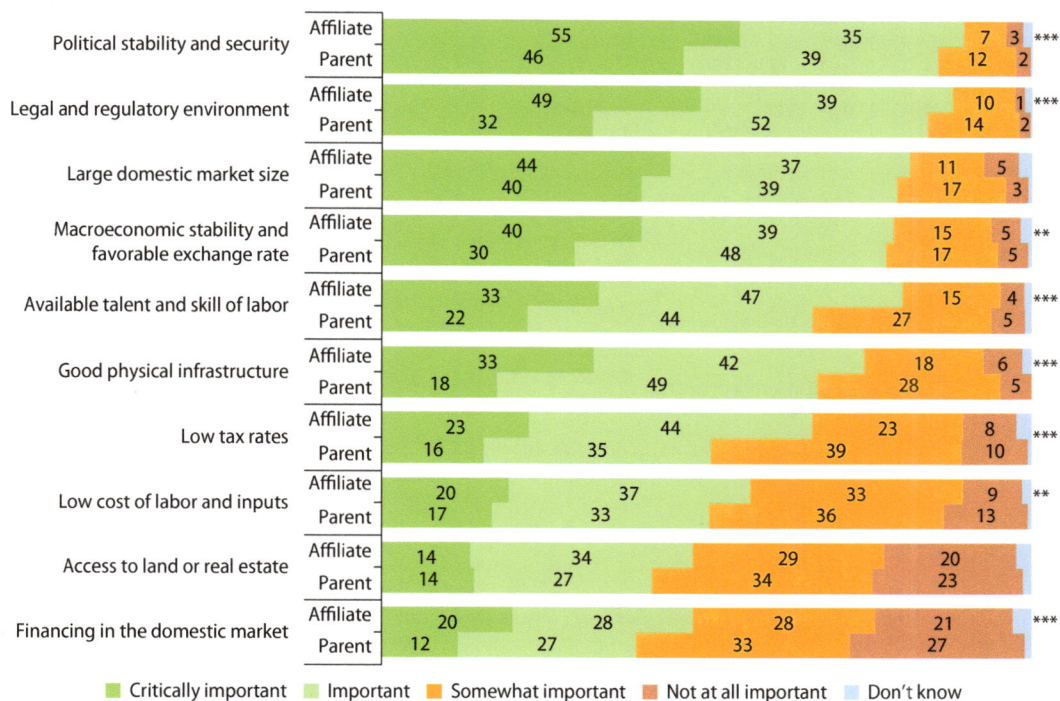

| | | Critically important | Important | Somewhat important | Not at all important | Don't know |

Source: Computation based on the GIC Survey.
Note: The differences between the two groups are significant at ***p<0.01, **p<0.05 and *p<0.1.

FIGURE 1C.4 Importance of Investment Climate Factors by Manufacturing versus Services Firms

Share of respondents (percent)

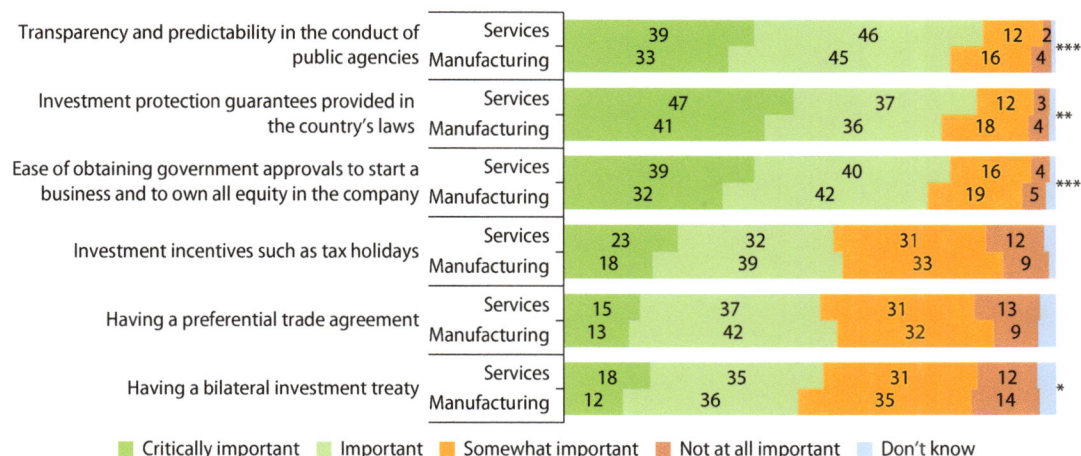

| | | Critically important | Important | Somewhat important | Not at all important | Don't know |

Source: Computation based on the GIC Survey.
Note: The differences between the two groups are significant at ***p<0.01, **p<0.05 and *p<0.1.

FIGURE 1C.5   **Importance of Investment Climate Factors by Developed versus Developing Source Economies**
Share of respondents (percent)

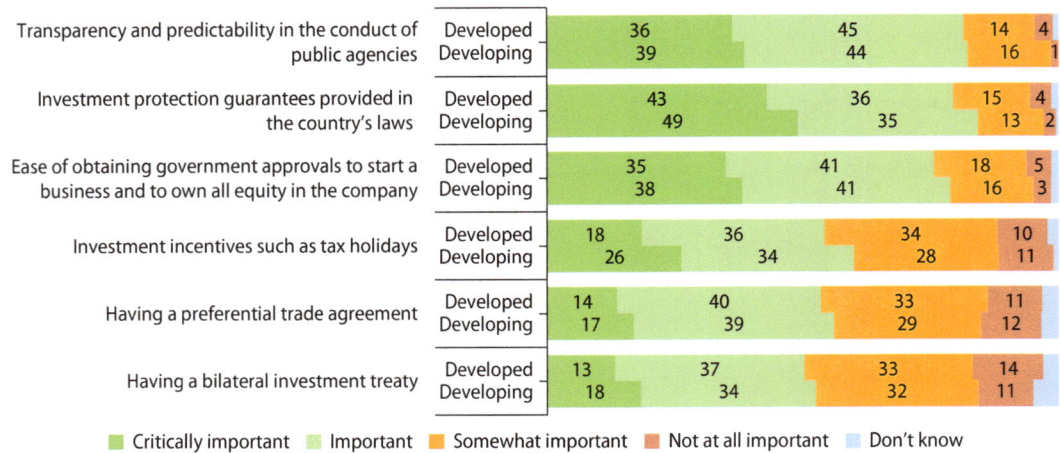

Source: Computation based on the GIC Survey.
Note: None of the differences is statistically significant.

FIGURE 1C.6   **Importance of Investment Climate Factors by Parent Company versus Affiliate**
Share of respondents (percent)

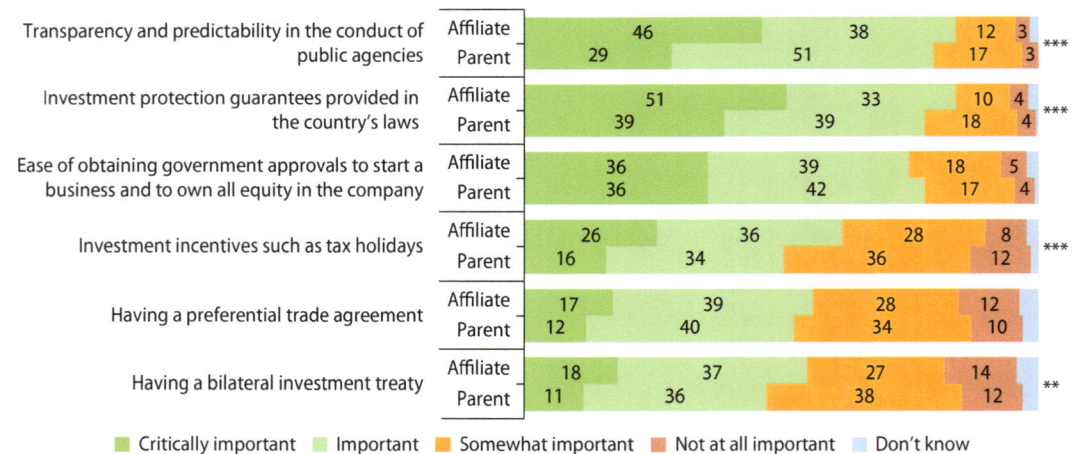

Source: Computation based on the GIC Survey.
Note: The differences between the two groups are significant at ***$p<0.01$, **$p<0.05$ and *$p<0.1$.

climate factors as important compared with respondents based at the companies' global headquarters (figure 1C.6). In particular, these are transparency and predictability in the conduct of public agencies, investment protection guarantees, investment incentives, and having bilateral investment treaties.

Notes

1. This broader definition and use of FDI typology will be further elaborated in a forthcoming World Bank Group publication.
2. In this chapter, "efficiency-seeking" investors are those respondents who said that lowering production costs and establishing a new base for exports was one of their motivations for setting up an affiliate in a developing country.
3. Echandi, Krajcovicova, and Qiang (2015) provide a literature review of local content requirements including studies from UNCTAD (2007), Moran (1998, 2006, 2011), Hufbauer and others (2013).

Bibliography

AON Centre of Innovation and Analytics. 2015. *Global Risk Management Survey*. U.K.: AON Centre of Innovation and Analytics.

A.T. Kearney. 2017. *Foreign Direct Investment Confidence Index: Glass Half Full*. Washington, DC: A.T. Kearney.

Dunning, J.H. 1993. *Multinational Enterprises and the Global Economy*. Addison Wesley.

Dunning, J.H., and S.M. Lundan. 2008. *Multinational Enterprises and the Global Economy*. Cheltenham, U.K.: Edward Elgar Publishing.

Echandi, R., J. Krajcovicova, and C.Z.W. Qiang. 2015. "The Impact of Investment Policy in a Changing Global Economy." Policy Research Working Paper 7437, World Bank, Washington, DC.

Ernst & Young Emerging Markets Center. 2015. *EY's Attractiveness Survey Africa 2015: Making Choices*. London: Ernst & Young Global Limited.

Gómez-Mera, L., T. Kenyon, Y. Margalit, J.G. Reis, and G. Varela. 2015. *New Voices in Investment: A Survey of Investors from Emerging Countries.*

World Bank Studies. Washington, DC: World Bank. doi:10.1596/978-1-4648-0371-0.

Hufbauer, G.C., J.J. Schott, C. Cimino, M. Vieiro, and E. Wada. 2013. "Local Content Requirements: A Global Problem." Policy Analyses 102. Peterson Institute for International Economics, Washington, DC.

MIGA (Multilateral Investment Guarantee Agency). 2013. *World Investment and Political Risk 2013*. Washington, DC: MIGA.

Moran, T. H. 1998. *Foreign Direct Investment and Development: The New Policy Agenda for Developing Countries and Economies in Transition*. Washington, DC: Peterson Institute for International Economics.

———. 2006. *Harnessing Foreign Direct Investment for Development: Policies for Developed and Developing Countries*. Washington, DC: Center for Global Development.

———. 2011. *Foreign Direct Investment and Development: Launching a Second Generation of Policy Research: Avoiding the Mistakes of the First, Re-Evaluating Policies for Developed and Developing Countries*. Washington, DC: Peterson Institute for International Economics.

UNCTAD (United Nations Conference on Trade and Development). 2007. *Elimination of TRIMS: The Experience of Selected Developing Countries*. New York and Geneva: UNCTAD.

———. 2014. *World Investment Prospects Survey: 2013–2015*. New York: UNCTAD.

———. 2016. *World Investment Report 2016: Investor Nationality: Policy Challenges*. Geneva: UNCTAD.

———. 2017. *World Investment Report 2017: Investment and the Digital Economy*. Geneva: UNCTAD.

WEF (World Economic Forum). 2017. *The Global Risks Report 2017, 12th Edition*. Geneva: WEF.

World Bank. 2014. "Conceptual Framework." In *Making Foreign Direct Investment Work for Sub-Saharan Africa: Local Spillovers and Competitiveness in Global Value Chains*, edited by Farole, Thomas, and Deborah Winkler, 23–55. Washington, DC: World Bank.

World Bank Group/MIGA. 2002. *Foreign Direct Investment Survey: A Study Conducted by the Multilateral Investment Guarantee Agency with the Assistance of Deloitte & Touche LLP*. Washington, DC: World Bank Group.

Effects of FDI on High-Growth Firms in Developing Countries | 2

José-Daniel Reyes

Foreign direct investment (FDI) promotes economic growth, job creation, and poverty reduction. Countries more open to trade and investment tend to be more productive and grow faster (Dollar 1992; Harrison 1996; Frankel and Romer 1999). Policy makers seek to attract FDI to create jobs, bring in cutting-edge knowledge and technology, connect to global value chains, and diversify and upgrade their economies' production capabilities.[1] The potential transmission of knowledge between foreign firms and local enterprises is an added benefit of FDI, one that can improve the productivity of domestic enterprises and thus make economic growth more inclusive.

The effects of foreign investment on the host economy are therefore a crucial element in a country's development strategy. These FDI effects—or spillovers—on domestic firms can be positive or negative, depending on whether local firms improve or worsen their performance as a result of FDI. It can have positive effects if it brings foreign technology and frontier knowledge that, if

successfully transmitted to local firms, improves their productivity. At the same time, FDI can exert a negative effect by increasing the competition in local input and output markets, thereby undermining the performance of local firms. The balance between these two forces determine the overall effect of foreign firms on local enterprises. At the sectoral level, greater competition in product and factor markets results in the efficient reallocation of resources from less productive to more productive firms, thereby increasing sectoral productivity over the long run.[2]

FDI can benefit domestic firms through two main channels:[3]

- *Contractual linkages* between foreign firms and local suppliers that promote the formal transmission of foreign firms' knowledge and practices, which may help domestic suppliers upgrade their technical and quality standards.[4]
- The *demonstration effect*, in which domestic firms imitate foreign technologies or

managerial practices either through observation or by hiring workers trained by the foreign company.[5]

This chapter explores the role of these two transmission channels of FDI spillovers on the performance of firms across 50 sectors and 121 economies in the developing world.[6] Employing data from the World Bank's Enterprise Surveys, it constructs sectoral measures of the linkages and demonstration channels and examines their role in the ability of domestic firms in the sector to benefit from FDI. The analysis reveals a large variation of FDI spillovers across local firms. In line with the literature, an average firm in the developing world does not necessarily benefit from these FDI effects (Damijan and others 2013; Fons-Rosen and others 2017). It is primarily the local high-growth firms that are able to internalize FDI spillovers through both linkages and demonstration channels.[7] For the linkages channel, an increase of 1 percentage point in the share of inputs sourced domestically by foreign firms is correlated with a 0.6 unit rise in the measure of output growth of domestic high-growth firms. For the demonstration channel, an increase of 1 percentage point in the share of foreign output in the sector is correlated with a 0.1 unit gain in output growth of high-growth firms.

This chapter therefore focuses on domestic high-growth firms, which the analysis shows benefit from FDI more than other firms. This is likely due to their higher absorptive capacity—their ability to recognize the value of new information, assimilate it, and apply it to improve production processes.[8] High-growth firms account for a sizable share of job creation and productivity gains in developing countries. The distinctive characteristics of these firms have been the subject of study from the perspective of both individual firms interested in sales and revenue growth and policy makers interested in job creation and economic growth.

From a policy perspective, developing countries are interested in spreading the benefits of FDI to the local economy. The evidence presented here shows that linkages programs to connect local suppliers with foreign firms can help achieve this goal. Considering the different absorptive capacities of indigenous firms and the various potential market failures is fundamental for evidence-based policy making. Particularly important is the design of programs that target high-potential suppliers and tackle specific failures, such as information asymmetries, and scale and quality constraints of domestic suppliers. Linkages programs should include a comprehensive set of interventions aimed at the supply side, the demand side, and market exchange. Compulsory local content requirements may cause more harm than good because they may discourage FDI from entering the country, thereby shutting down any channel of positive spillover effects. A comprehensive policy intervention aimed at reducing search costs and tackling constraints of both buyers and sellers is more effective than a piecemeal approach.

High-Growth Firms Are Important for Job Creation, and Are Small and Young

While the private sector is the main engine of countries' economic growth, only a small part of the private sector—the "high-growth" firms—plays a disproportionately large role in job creation (Coad and others 2014; Haltiwanger, Jarmin, and Miranda 2016; Hsieh and Klenow 2014). Identifying them and assessing the constraints that hinder the emergence and performance of these high-growth firms is critical to realize their full potential (box 2.1).

The identification of high-growth firms in this dataset focuses exclusively on domestically owned enterprises to highlight the ability of these firms to benefit from the presence of foreign firms. The analysis uses the rate of firm-level job creation to characterize firm growth.[9,10] In each country, high-growth firms are located in the top fifth percentile of the distribution of firm-level job growth rates

Factors Influencing High-Growth Firms: The Four-Layer Onion Framework

Firm performance, and hence the potential emergence of high-growth firms, is influenced by a variety of factors:

- Individual characteristics of entrepreneurs such as age, education, experience, and motivation.
- Firm-level attributes such as firm age, size, location, sector, and absorptive capacity.

- Personal and professional networks.
- The overall business environment in which firms operate.

The "four-layer onion" provides a representation of these factors (see figure B2.1.1).

FIGURE B2.1.1   The Four-Layer Onion Framework of Growth Factors

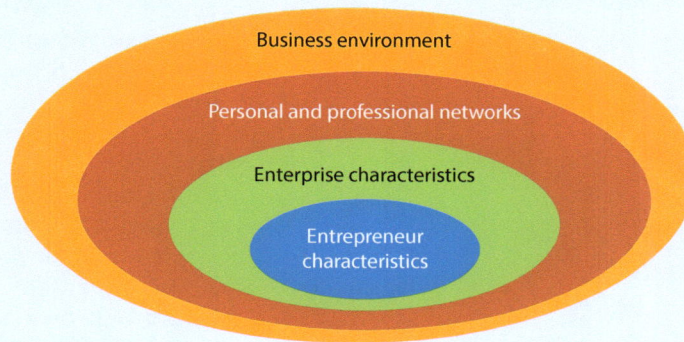

Business environment

Personal and professional networks

Enterprise characteristics

Entrepreneur characteristics

Source: Hampel-Milagrosa, Loewe, and Reeg 2015.

over two years. The key advantage of this method is that it establishes country-specific minimum growth rates required for firms to be classified as high-growth, thereby taking into account characteristics that support or hinder the performance of the private sector in each economy (annex 2A provides the complete list of economies and the years in which each Enterprise Survey was conducted).[11]

The case of Indonesia—where the Enterprise Survey was conducted in 2015—illustrates the identification of high-growth firms. According to the chosen criterion, high-growth firms increased employment by at least 35.3 percent between 2012 and 2014.[12] In figure 2.1, these firms are shown in the shaded right tail of the firm growth distribution.

Applying the criterion to the sample of countries, two common characteristics of

FIGURE 2.1   High-Growth Firms Create the Most Jobs
Distribution of firm-level growth rates in Indonesia, 2012–14

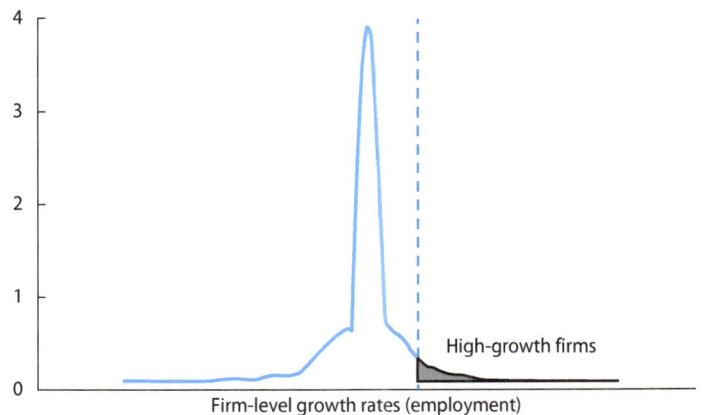

High-growth firms

Firm-level growth rates (employment)

Source: Computation based on data from Enterprise Surveys, the World Bank.
Note: This figure shows the distribution of firm-level mid-point growth rates for Indonesia between 2012 and 2014. The survey was conducted in 2015 and firms were asked about the total number of full-time employees the year before (2014) and three years ago (2012). The dotted line indicates the 95th percentile. The shaded area of the distribution indicates the presence of high-growth firms.

high-growth firms in the developing world emerge: they tend to be small and young. Across countries, they represent 7.9 percent of small firms, relative to 2.3 percent of large firms (figure 2.2). In 89 countries, the median size of these firms is less than 10 employees (annex 2C). High-growth firms are also more common among young enterprises; 6.9 percent of firms younger than 10 years are high-growth while only 2.3 percent older than 50 years are high-growth (figure 2.3). The median age of high-growth firms is lower than the median age of the rest of firms in 105 countries in the sample (annex 2C).[13]

High-growth businesses in the developing world exist in all economic sectors but are more common in services than in manufacturing (table 2.1). Information and communications technology (ICT) and the construction sector show the highest shares of high-growth firms; these firms account for 8.1 percent of all firms in the ICT sector and 6.6 percent of all firms in the construction sector.[14] In terms of output and employment growth, high-growth firms in services outperform those in manufacturing. Overall, high-growth firms in services grew in terms of employment by 133 percent (versus 127 percent in manufacturing) and increased sales by 40 percent over the previous two years (versus 38 percent in manufacturing).

Many variables determine the presence of high-growth firms across sectors in developing economies. As noted above, these elements range from the characteristics of the entrepreneur to the regulatory and institutional framework in which the firm operates. Key determinants also vary across the life cycle of the firm, but the process of internationalization is usually a central element in the firms' success (box 2.2).

In sum, high-growth firms are few in number but critical for job creation. The evidence indicates that they are young, small, present across all economic activities, and diverse in terms of the factors that determine their performance. Their strong performance indicates their superior capabilities relative to other firms in the economy facing the same constraints on operations and growth, which enable them to benefit from the presence of multinational corporations (MNCs).

FIGURE 2.2   High-Growth Firms Tend to Be Small...

Share of high-growth firms, by size bins

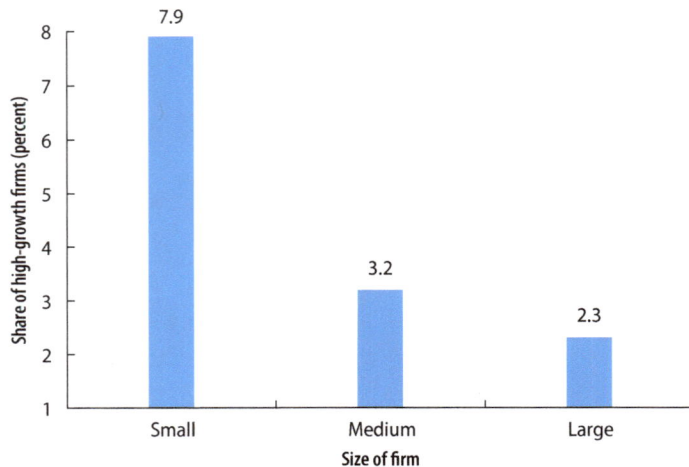

Source: Computation based on data from Enterprise Surveys, the World Bank.
Note: This figure shows the number of high-growth firms as a share of the total number of firms, by size bins. Small firms have fewer than 20 employees, medium firms have 20–100 employees, and large firms have more than 100 employees.

FIGURE 2.3   ... and Young

Share of high-growth firms, by age bins

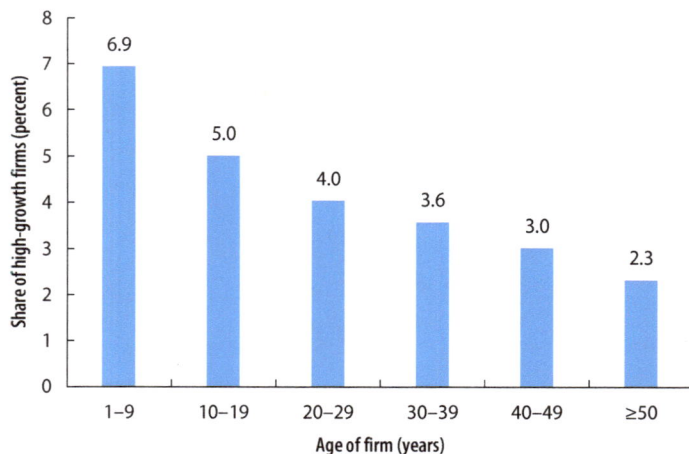

Source: Computation based data from Enterprise Surveys, the World Bank.
Note: This figure shows the number of high-growth firms as a share of the total number of firms, by age bins.

TABLE 2.1   High-Growth Firms Appear in All Economic Sectors

Firm-level employment and output growth across sectors

ISIC codes—sector	High-growth firms [1]	Rest of firms [2]	Share of high-growth firms in the sector [3] = [1]/([1] + [2]), percent	High-growth firms		Rest of firms	
				Employment growth (percent)	Output growth (percent)	Employment growth (percent)	Output growth (percent)
Manufacturing	**1,608**	**27,188**	**5.6**	**127**	**38**	**0**	**14**
17—Textiles	158	2,414	6.1	124	43	0	13
29—Machinery and equipment	123	1,972	5.9	100	33	0	15
18—Apparel and fur	226	3,574	5.9	141	40	0	14
28—Metal products	180	2,938	5.8	150	47	0	17
15—Food products and beverages	393	6,508	5.7	133	35	0	14
36—Furniture	114	1,927	5.6	150	52	0	15
24—Chemicals	150	2,789	5.1	132	35	0	17
26—Nonmetallic mineral products	144	2,684	5.1	130	34	0	11
25—Rubber and plastic	120	2,382	4.8	100	33	0	14
Services	**1,479**	**24,446**	**5.7**	**133**	**40**	**0**	**13**
64 & 72—ICT	116	1,319	8.1	115	53	9	17
45—Construction	173	2,463	6.6	115	53	0	12
50–52—Wholesales and retail trade	929	14,845	5.9	133	39	0	13
60–63—Transport and storage	109	2,251	4.6	150	34	0	11
55—Hotels and restaurants	152	3,568	4.1	130	33	0	9

Source: Computation based on data from Enterprise Surveys, the World Bank.

Note: This table shows the total number of firms by type and their associated employment and output growth across economic sectors. To reduce clutter, sectors with fewer than 100 enterprises have been dropped. Sectors are ranked by the presence of high-growth firms (column [3]). The data use the revision 3.1 of the International Standard Industrial Classification (ISIC). For output and employment, the table presents the median standard growth rate within each cell. ICT = Information and communications technology.

BOX 2.2

AAA Growers: A High-Growth Firm in Kenya

AAA Growers is a company that produces vegetables and flowers in Kenya—and is the largest commercial grower and exporter of chilies in the nation. The company started with 50 employees in 2000 and now owns five farms that employ some 4,000 during peak seasons. The workforce consists of rural workers, 60 percent of whom are women. The main objective of AAA Growers since its inception is to produce vegetables to export, primarily to the U.K. market. Currently, about 98 percent of its production is sold in international markets.

The management team cited three elements as central to the company's success:

- *Family support to set up the business.* Family capital was used to set up and maintain low-scale operations during the company's first three years. This period did not generate positive margins but was central to learning about the dynamics of different crops, the requirements to export, and the need to build professional networks.

box continues next page

AAA Growers: A High-Growth Firm in Kenya (continued)

- *Connection with foreign buyers*. Establishing a commercial presence in international markets was challenging. The owners employed family connections to identify potential buyers in the U.K. market and secured small orders with the goal of building long-term professional relationships. The first three to five years of operations of the company were dedicated mostly to identifying and securing international buyers.
- IFC *funding to set up large-scale operations*. An International Finance Corporation (IFC) loan

allowed AAA Growers to invest in state-of-the-art equipment and installations, which helped not only to expand output but also to comply with stringent production and agricultural standards in the European market.

After growing at a high rate over the last 10 years, the company is now consolidating. The top priority for management is to stabilize the company's operations to ensure sustainable expansion.

High-Growth Firms Benefit from FDI Mainly through the Linkages Channel

This section looks at the two channels through which FDI affects domestic enterprises, with a focus on high-growth firms. The linkages channel is characterized by direct contractual arrangements in which domestic firms become suppliers of foreign firms. The demonstration channel enables domestic firms to replicate foreign technologies or management practices either through observation or by hiring workers trained by foreign firms. Thus, the stronger the presence of FDI in the sector, the more opportunities for the demonstration channel to positively affect local firms.

But while foreign firms bring technology and frontier knowledge that can improve the performance of indigenous firms, they may also increase competitive pressures in the host economy, which could hurt some local businesses (Alfaro and Chen, forthcoming; Fons-Rosen and others 2017). The relative magnitude of these two forces determines the ultimate effect on domestic firms. At the sectoral level, however, more competition promotes the efficient reallocation of factors of production from low-productivity to high-productivity firms, thereby increasing sectoral productivity over the long term.

Because all firms in the same sector face the same degree of competitive pressures posed by the presence of the foreign firm, their ability to ultimately benefit from FDI hinges on whether they can capture positive spillovers through the linkages and demonstration channels.[15] This ability, in turn, depends on their absorptive capacity—the ability to recognize the value of new information, assimilate it, and apply it to improve production processes. By virtue of their fast growth trajectory, which may reflect high absorptive capacity and productivity, high-growth firms may be better able to capture positive spillovers than other local firms.

Using information from the World Bank's Enterprise Surveys, the team constructed indicators of the linkages and demonstration channels across 50 sectors and 121 developing countries. Following the literature, the linkages channel is captured by the average share of inputs of domestic origin that foreign firms acquire in the host country.[16] The demonstration channel is measured as the share of foreign output in total output (see Blalock and Gertler 2009; Farole and Winkler 2015; and annex 2D). These measures represent the importance of the FDI spillover channels within country-sector observations and, therefore, capture the potential for intra-industry spillover effects.[17]

The relevance of the transmission channels of FDI spillovers varies across sectors and countries. On average, linkages are more apparent in manufacturing than in services (table 2.2). In manufacturing, Asia shows the highest prevalence of linkages. In East Asia, for example, foreign manufacturing firms source 70 percent of the inputs locally, relative to the average for the rest of the world of about 60 percent. Demonstration effects are relatively balanced between manufacturing and services; foreign firms account broadly for 20 percent to 30 percent of sectoral output across sectors and regions.

The sole presence of linkages and demonstration channels does not guarantee that domestic enterprises benefit from FDI. Domestic firms can become suppliers of foreign enterprises but may be incapable of using the information acquired to improve their production techniques. Arguably, the transmission of FDI benefits to local firms via the demonstration channel can be even more challenging, given the absence of a direct link between the foreign and domestic enterprises. To examine the relationship between domestic firms' performance and the two channels of FDI spillover, the analysis employs a regression framework to investigate whether firms operating in sectors with high potential for FDI spillover effects—as indicated by the presence and importance of the linkages and demonstration channels—display a higher rate of output growth. The analysis differentiates between high-growth firms and others. The regression controls for other variables relevant to firm growth, specifically, age, export status, and labor productivity (annex 2D).

The results indicate that, on average across firms and countries, FDI benefits are not uniformly transmitted to local firms. While both linkages and demonstration channels are positively correlated with output growth at the firm level, they are not statistically different from zero. In other words, the average firm in the developing world is unable to benefit from the presence of foreign companies. Two self-enforcing mechanisms

explain this: First, the competition that foreign firms bring to the domestic market outweighs the FDI benefits that the average firm internalizes. Second, the low absorptive capacity of the average firm prevents it from capturing more FDI benefits.[18]

Contrary to these aggregate results, the analysis finds that high-growth firms are able to capture the benefit of FDI in their markets through both channels. The results are particularly significant for the linkages channel, where an increase of 1 percentage point in the share of inputs that are sourced domestically by foreign firms is associated with a 0.6 unit gain in the measure of output growth of high-growth firms (figure 2.4).[19] The demonstration effect is also positively related to the performance of high-growth firms, albeit its impact is lower: an increase of 1 percentage point in the share of foreign output in the sector is associated with a 0.1 unit rise in the output growth of high-growth firms.[20] The impact of these channels on the performance of non-high-growth firms is also positive but statistically insignificant.[21]

High-growth firms are better able to internalize foreign technologies and processes to improve their productivity and counterbalance FDI's competitive effect. From a policy perspective, increasing absorptive capacity in domestic enterprises is therefore key to maximizing the benefits of FDI for job creation.

The importance of FDI for the performance of local high-growth firms varies across regions. Employing the same empirical framework, the analysis estimates the role of the linkages and the demonstration channels across six regions of the world (figure 2.5 and annex 2D). The analysis yields three key messages:

- High-growth firms in Sub-Saharan Africa do not internalize FDI spillovers. Since the lion's share of FDI going to Africa is directed to natural resources, this result may indicate that the potential of this type of investment to generate positive spillovers is limited.
- Europe and Central Asia is an outlier because the demonstration channel outweighs the linkages channel. In fact,

TABLE 2.2 **Linkages Are More Important in Manufacturing while Demonstration Effects Are Balanced across Sectors**

Average size of linkages and demonstration channels across sectors and regions

ISIC codes—Sector	East Asia and Pacific		Europe and Central Asia		Latin America and the Caribbean		Middle East and North Africa		South Asia		Sub-Saharan Africa	
	Linkages	Demonstration	Linkages	Demonstration	Linkages	Demonstration	Linkages	Demonstration	Linkages	Demonstration	Linkages	Demonstration
Manufacturing	**0.7**	**0.3**	**0.6**	**0.2**	**0.6**	**0.3**	**0.6**	**0.2**	**0.8**	**0.1**	**0.6**	**0.4**
15—Food products and beverages	0.8	0.3	0.7	0.2	0.7	0.4	0.7	0.2	0.8	0.1	0.7	0.5
17—Textiles	0.8	0.3	0.7	0.2	0.6	0.3	0.7	0.1	0.8	0.1	0.5	0.5
18—Apparel and fur	0.6	0.4	0.5	0.2	0.7	0.2	0.4	0.3	0.6	0.0	0.6	0.2
24—Chemicals	0.7	0.3	0.6	0.4	0.5	0.4	0.5	0.2	0.8	0.1	0.4	0.4
25—Rubber and plastic	0.7	0.1	0.5	0.2	0.4	0.5	0.6	0.1	0.9	0.0	0.4	0.5
26—Nonmetallic mineral products	0.8	0.4	0.7	0.3	0.7	0.2	0.8	0.2	1.0	0.2	0.7	0.4
28—Metal products	0.6	0.2	0.6	0.1	0.5	0.5	0.6	0.2	0.9	0.0	0.5	0.4
29—Machinery and equipment	0.8	0.2	0.6	0.2	0.7	0.5	0.6	0.4	0.9	0.1	0.6	0.3
36—Furniture	0.7	0.3	0.4	0.1	0.8	0.2	0.8	0.1	0.6	0.0	0.6	0.2
Services	**0.3**	**0.2**	**0.0**	**0.1**	**0.3**	**0.3**	**0.7**	**0.2**	**0.0**	**0.0**	**0.4**	**0.4**
45—Construction	—	0.1	0.0	0.1	0.7	0.2	0.7	0.2	—	0.0	0.7	0.4
50–52—Wholesale and retail trade	0.7	0.2	0.0	0.2	0.7	0.3	0.3	0.2	0.0	0.0	0.5	0.3
55—Hotels and restaurants	—	0.2	—	0.2	—	0.3	0.9	0.1	0.0	0.1	0.4	0.5
60–63—Transport and storage	0.7	0.2	0.0	0.1	—	0.3	1.0	0.2	0.0	0.0	0.6	0.3
64 & 72—IT and communications	0.2	0.1	0.0	0.2	—	0.4	0.6	0.2	—	0.1	—	0.3

Source: Computation based on data from Enterprise Surveys, the World Bank.

Note: This table shows the average value of the linkages and the demonstration effects across economic sectors and world regions. For the linkages channel, each figure shows the average share of domestically sourced input for foreign firms within the sector. For the demonstration channel, each figure shows the average share of foreign output as a percentage of total sectoral output.

— = data unavailable.

the role of the demonstration channel is much larger than in other regions.

- The linkages channel is the key engine for FDI spillovers to high-growth firms in Latin America and the Caribbean, East Asia and Pacific, South Asia, and the Middle East and North Africa.

The linkages channel is more important than the demonstration channel for leveraging FDI spillovers in both manufacturing and services for high-growth firms. In services, both linkages and demonstration channels transmit FDI benefits (figure 2.6 and annex 2D). High-growth firms in manufacturing, however, benefit from FDI only through linkages. The findings indicate that a 1 percentage point increase in linkages is associated with a 0.7 unit rise in the measure of sales growth of high-growth firms in manufacturing, and a 0.5 unit gain in service sectors. In services, an increase of 1 percentage point in the demonstration channel is associated with a 0.2 unit increase in the measure of sales growth of domestic high-growth firms. The demonstration channel is not statistically significant for the manufacturing sector's high-growth firms.

FIGURE 2.4 High-Growth Firms Benefit from the Presence of Foreign Firms

Average impact of FDI spillovers on firm growth, by firm type

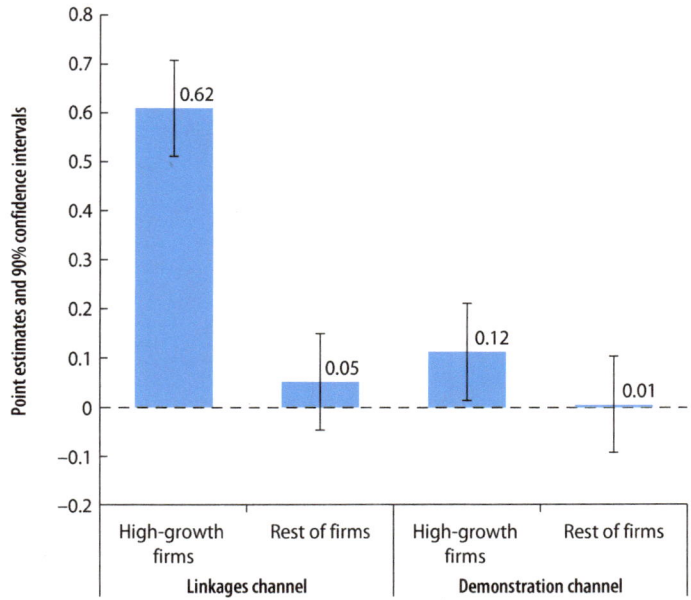

Source: Computation based on data from Enterprise Surveys, the World Bank.
Note: This figure shows the estimated coefficient of the linkages and demonstration channels on high-growth firms and the rest of businesses in a sample of 121 countries. Vertical lines capture 90 percent confidence intervals. The estimates correspond to the estimation shown in column 7 in table 2D.1 in annex 2D. FDI = foreign direct investment.

FIGURE 2.5 The Linkages Channel More Efficiently Transmits FDI Benefits in Nearly All Regions

FDI spillovers to high-growth firms, by region

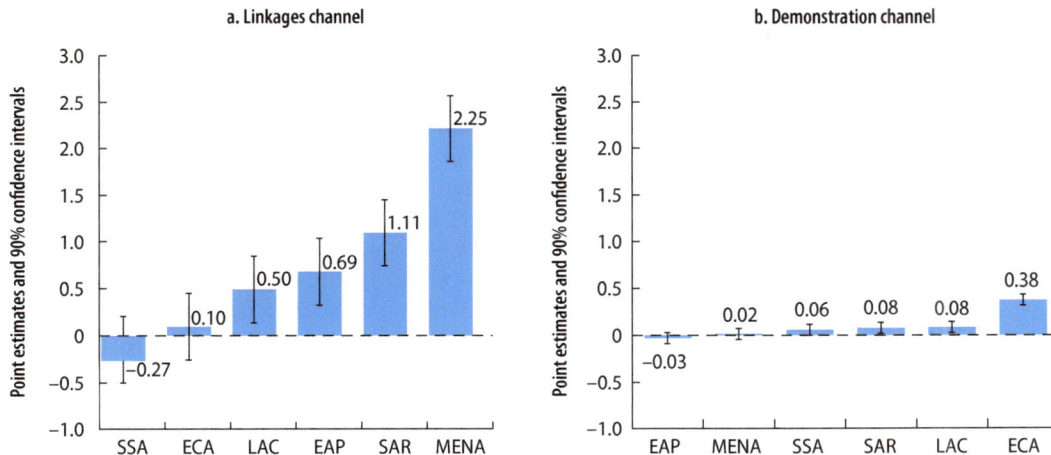

Source: Computation based on data from Enterprise Surveys, the World Bank.
Note: These figures show the estimated coefficient of the role of the channels for foreign direct investment (FDI) spillover effects on high-growth firms, by region. Vertical lines capture 90 percent confidence intervals. Regression results are presented in annex 2D. The regions are EAP = East Asia and Pacific; ECA = Europe and Central Asia; LAC = Latin America and the Caribbean; MENA = Middle East and North Africa; SAR = South Asia; SSA = Sub-Saharan Africa.

FIGURE 2.6 High-Growth Firms Benefit from FDI Mainly through the Linkages Channel, Both in Services and Manufacturing
Average impact of spillover effect on high-growth firms, by sector

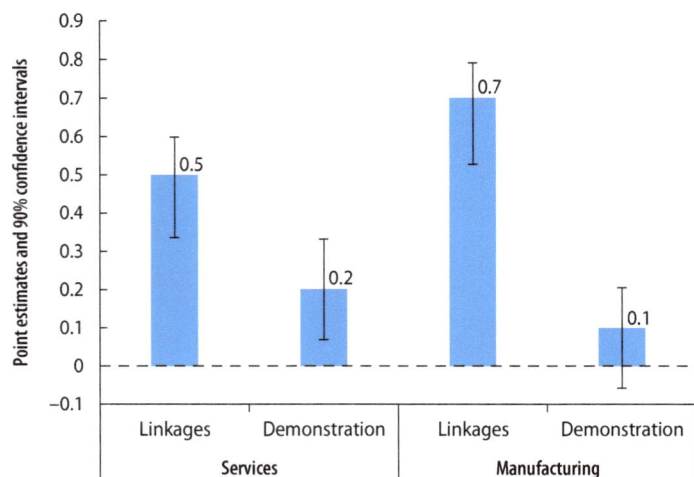

Source: Computation based on data from Enterprise Surveys, the World Bank.
Note: This figure shows the estimated coefficient of the role of foreign direct investment (FDI) spillovers on high-growth firms in manufacturing and services. Vertical lines capture 90 percent confidence intervals. Regression results are presented in annex 2D.

Policies to Maximize the Gains from FDI: Promoting Linkages for Development

While FDI may result in negative distributional effects for particular groups of local firms, countries open to multinational production experience aggregate productivity gains. These benefits can be accrued via positive spillovers for domestic enterprises and the reallocation of factors of production from less productive firms to more productive firms. From a policy perspective, governments are advised to design policies to reduce the adjustment cost of the reallocation process and increase the ability of local enterprises to internalize positive spillovers from the presence of foreign firms. Policies and programs that can increase the absorptive capacities of local enterprises—mainly by promoting domestic linkages—will maximize the potential gains from FDI. While the analysis focuses on connecting domestic firms to MNCs, these policies can be tailored to also support linkages between domestic suppliers and large buyers.

Policy interventions aimed at strengthening linkages programs should tackle specific market failures. The most common failure preventing the development of linkages is asymmetry of information, which increases search costs for both buyers and sellers (Monge-González and Rodríguez-Álvarez 2013). Foreign companies may find it difficult to identify potential local suppliers while domestic enterprises may struggle to identify potential contracting opportunities with foreign enterprises. Another common failure is the small size and scale of domestic suppliers who may find it impossible to respond to large orders from MNCs, yet find it too risky to invest in production expansion. Additionally, domestic enterprises may not have the production standards required to meet minimum quality requirements of foreign enterprises.

Linkages programs should consider a mechanism to identify and support high-potential local firms in becoming suppliers of foreign firms. The evidence presented in this chapter shows that not all domestic firms are equal in terms of their ability to benefit from FDI. High-growth firms have the absorptive capacity allowing them to internalize FDI spillovers that, in turn, improve their productivity and support job creation. There is no empirical basis for setting up linkages programs to support the broad group of small- and medium-sized enterprises (SMEs), yet such programs are rather common in many economies.[22]

Linkages programs should include a comprehensive set of interventions to tackle constraints at the *market level,* the *supply side* (domestic firms), and the *demand side* (foreign company). A comprehensive approach is more effective than a piecemeal one. Interventions at the market level seek to reduce search costs and facilitate matchmaking. For example, they usually tackle information asymmetries by providing information about business opportunities for both buyers and sellers. The most common intervention is the creation of supplier databases that contain contact details and the menu of goods and services offered by potential domestic suppliers. Matchmaking services among buyers and sellers are another common practice for promoting business-to-business transactions. They include organizing trade fairs, supporting supplier audits, and organizing site visits, missions, exhibitions, and seminars.

Supply-level interventions seek to improve the capacity of domestic firms to meet minimum scale and quality standards expected by MNCs. Two common policy instruments are relevant. The first set of policies is aimed at improving firm-level productivity via the creation of supplier development programs that provide targeted training support aligned with buyer requirements. These programs are often based on a partnership between domestic enterprises and foreign firms, and may also include local educational institutions (for example, universities and colleges) and consulting firms in the form of joint research projects, customized training programs, and help in identifying local strategic partners. These

policies may also include more broad-based entrepreneurship development and training programs to support local skills development as well as help in obtaining international quality certifications (box 2.3). The second set of policies leverages and encourages existing business groups (business clusters, for instance) to tackle their capacity constraints. The rationale is that domestic firms acting in a coordinated manner can provide the scale expected by foreign firms, thus allowing the cluster to jointly fulfill large orders from foreign companies.

Demand-level interventions are directed at foreign firms with the goal of encouraging their increased use of domestic inputs. Financial and tax incentives are the most common policy tool. Examples include exempting foreign firms from value added taxes to encourage their use of local rather than imported inputs, treating expenditures incurred in the creation of

---

BOX 2.3

Chile's Supplier Development Program

Chile's Supplier Development Program (SDP) was launched by the Chilean Economic Development Agency (*Corporación de Fomento de la Producción de Chile*; CORFO) in 1998. The program is aimed at improving and stabilizing the commercial linkages already existing between domestic suppliers and their large-firm customers to achieve higher levels of adaptability and guarantee the quality of goods and services at different stages of production. By requiring that a commercial relationship be already established among firms, the program sought to ensure that suppliers were local firms with high potential. The SDP provides partial funding to strengthen the management of local businesses through specialized services, professional advice, training, and technology transfers.

For a large firm to be eligible to participate in the program and receive a subsidy to train the local firms that make up its supply chain, its net annual sales had to be greater than or equal to $42.6 million in August 2010. Each project must include at least 20 domestic firms (in the agriculture and forestry sector), or a minimum of 10 in other economic activity sectors. After the project is approved, the program is implemented in two stages: a diagnostic stage and a development

stage. The diagnostic stage lasts up to six months and identifies areas of intervention that the sponsor (that is, the large firm) wishes to develop with its suppliers. The result is a development plan designed by a consultant or consulting firm. CORFO pays for up to 50 percent of its cost with a ceiling of $16,000. The development stage is the implementation of the development plan and can last up to three years. CORFO pays for up to 50 percent of the cost of this stage with an annual ceiling of $110,000 (or $5,000 per supplier firm). CORFO assesses annually the renewal of the project financing depending on the implementation progress. The implementation of the development plan is the responsibility of the sponsor firm and can be carried out by a consultant or consulting firm or by the sponsor's in-house staff.

A rigorous impact evaluation has shown that the SDP not only increased sales, employment, and the sustainability of suppliers, but also improved the sales of large firms and raised their probability of becoming exporters (Arráiz, Henríquez, and Stucchi 2013). The positive effect on suppliers appeared one year after the firms enrolled in the program while the impact on large firms appeared after two years.

linkages (for example, training or research and development activities) as tax-deductible expenses, incentives for training programs of local suppliers, and co-financing skills development activities (see box 2.3). While compulsory local content requirements are sometimes used, they can discourage the entry of foreign investors and, more important, preclude altogether the entry of foreign technology that could itself be the source of positive spillover effects. In practice, these requirements are also often circumvented by foreign companies, rendering them largely ineffective (Echandi, Krajcovicova, and Qiang 2015; Hufbauer, Schott, and Cimino-Isaacs 2013).

Key elements for creating an enabling policy environment for linkages also include a suitable lead agency, proper coordination mechanisms across institutions, and strong stakeholder engagement. The lead agency should have political clout and a clear mandate to coordinate among the different agencies involved in private sector development. The lead agency, typically associated with the Ministry of Commerce and Industry, should organize the representatives of different agencies involved in supporting linkages programs, which can include the investment promotion agency, the regulators of special economic zones, private sector representatives, the agency to support small and medium enterprises and industry associations. Clear operating rules should govern the coordination mechanism among them to ensure policy coherence along the different parts of the program. A key component of the linkages program is also the constant interaction with the private sector, including feedback mechanisms. Designing and implementing rigorous impact evaluation of the linkages programs are useful for basing policy design and decisions on evidence.

Last, flexible labor markets and better access to finance remain key constraints on the ability of domestic firms to internalize FDI spillovers. A flexible labor market facilitates the movement of managers and skilled workers between foreign and local companies. The shift of experienced workers from foreign firms to domestic enterprises could be the channel through which spillovers are accrued by indigenous firms (the demonstration channel). These workers can also launch successful business ventures on their own.

Lack of access to finance often limits the ability of local firms to strengthen their productivity and, therefore, improve their chances of becoming suppliers of foreign enterprises. Various types of incentives can financially and legally support local firms in obtaining finance to fund further investment in their human capital, technological and managerial capacities; and lower the risks of linkages. Some of these interventions include loans, grants, guarantees, and legal protection against unfair contractual arrangements.

Conclusion

Foreign investors bring a wide range of knowledge and know-how with the potential to bring positive spillovers for the host economy. These benefits, however, are not guaranteed. Indeed, foreign firms may also generate competitive pressures in the local economy to the detriment of some local firms. The balance between these potentially positive and negative impacts determines the overall effect of foreign firms on local enterprises.

Over the long run, competitive pressures encourage the efficient reallocation of factors within sectors, thereby increasing sectoral productivity. Foreign knowledge and technology can be transferred to domestic firms through two main channels. The first is *linkages* between foreign firms and domestic suppliers. The second is the *demonstration* channel through which domestic firms imitate and replicate foreign technologies and management practices in their own production processes.

Employing a firm-level dataset for 121 developing economies, this chapter evaluates the role of these channels in supporting the performance of local firms across the developing world. It finds that high-growth firms internalize positive spillover effects mainly through the linkages channel. This points to their superior absorptive capacities, which make them ideal targets for policy interventions aimed at maximizing the benefits of FDI in the local economy.

Governments can implement an array of policies to maximize the potential for FDI spillover. Government interventions should seek to offset specific market failures, which usually take the form of information asymmetries or the small scale and low quality of domestic firms. Linkages programs should consider a mechanism to identify domestic suppliers with potential to connect with foreign firms. Supplier databases and matchmaking services are the most common tools to promote linkages. Supplier development programs and support for cluster development are interventions that seek to improve the capacity of domestic firms to connect to foreign firms. Financial and tax incentives are also used to encourage the use of domestic inputs by foreign enterprises. A flexible labor market can go a long way to support workers' movement from foreign firms into the domestic economy.

More policy-oriented research is needed to better understand the role of FDI on the performance of domestic high-growth firms. One aspect is the long-term consequences of FDI spillovers, particularly on productivity, innovation, and the ability of high-growth firms to create better jobs. Another aspect that merits further study is the different potential of FDI spillovers that different types of FDI bring to developing countries. Reyes (forthcoming) finds that FDI embedded in global value chains may have higher potential to generate FDI spillovers than FDI that seeks to serve mostly the domestic market.

But regardless of the distributional impact of foreign firms on domestic businesses, countries open to multinational production tend to experience aggregate productivity gains. These benefits are accrued through spillover effects on domestic firms and the reallocation of factors of production from less productive firms to more productive firms.

Annex 2A. Economies Included in the Analysis

East Asia and Pacific	Cambodia (2016), China (2012), Fiji (2009), Indonesia (2015), Lao PDR (2016), Malaysia (2015), Micronesia, Fed. Sts. (2009), Mongolia (2013), Myanmar (2014), Papua New Guinea (2015), Philippines (2015), Samoa (2009), Solomon Islands (2015), Thailand (2016), Timor-Leste (2015), Tonga (2009), Vanuatu (2009), Vietnam (2015)
Europe and Central Asia	Albania (2013), Armenia (2013), Azerbaijan (2013), Belarus (2013), Bosnia and Herzegovina (2013), Bulgaria (2013), Macedonia, FYR (2013), Georgia (2013), Hungary (2013), Kazakhstan (2013), Kosovo (2013), Kyrgyz Republic (2013), Moldova (2013), Montenegro (2013), Romania (2013), Serbia (2013), Tajikistan (2013), Turkey (2013), Ukraine (2013), Uzbekistan (2013)
Latin America and the Caribbean	Argentina (2010), Belize (2010), Bolivia (2010), Brazil (2009), Colombia (2010), Costa Rica (2010), Dominica (2010), Dominican Republic (2010), Ecuador (2010), El Salvador (2010), Grenada (2010), Guatemala (2010), Guyana (2010), Honduras (2010), Jamaica (2010), Mexico (2010), Nicaragua (2010), Panama (2010), Paraguay (2010), Peru (2010), St. Lucia (2010), St. Vincent and the Grenadines (2010), Suriname (2010), Venezuela, RB (2010)
Middle East and North Africa	Djibouti (2013), Egypt, Arab Rep. (2013), Iraq (2011), Jordan (2013), Lebanon (2013), Morocco (2013), Tunisia (2013), West Bank and Gaza (2013), Yemen, Rep. (2013)
South Asia	Afghanistan (2014), Bangladesh (2013), Bhutan (2015), India (2014), Nepal (2013), Pakistan (2013), Sri Lanka (2011)
Sub-Saharan Africa	Angola (2010), Benin (2009), Botswana (2010), Burkina Faso (2009), Burundi (2014), Cameroon (2009), Cabo Verde (2009), Central African Republic (2011), Chad (2009), Congo, Dem. Rep. (2013), Congo, Rep. (2009), Côte d'Ivoire (2009), Eritrea (2009), Ethiopia (2015), Gabon (2009), Gambia, The (2006), Ghana (2013), Guinea (2006), Guinea-Bissau (2006), Kenya (2013), Lesotho (2009), Liberia (2009), Madagascar (2013), Malawi (2014), Mali (2010), Mauritania (2014), Mauritius (2009), Mozambique (2007), Namibia (2014), Niger (2009), Nigeria (2014), Rwanda (2011), Senegal (2014), Sierra Leone (2009), South Africa (2007), South Sudan (2014), Sudan (2014), Swaziland (2006), Tanzania (2013), Togo (2009), Uganda (2013), Zambia (2013), Zimbabwe (2011)

Source: World Bank Enterprise Survey.
Note: This table presents the economies included in the analysis using the World Bank Enterprise Survey data. The year in which the survey was implemented in each country is in parentheses. The information was accessed on September 8, 2016.

Annex 2B. Measuring Firm Growth

When characterizing firm performance, there are at least three issues that need to be considered: the indicator of growth, the measure of growth, and the study period.

The indicator of growth refers to the variable over which growth is observed. The most commonly used indicators in the high-growth firm literature are sales and number of employees (Daunfeldt, Elert, and Johansson 2014). Because we are interested in the role of high-growth businesses in job creation, we use the number of permanent, full-time employees of the firm as our growth indicator.

The number of possible indicators for measuring firm-level employment growth is ample. The two most basic approaches are the absolute and relative changes in the indicator of growth. The first one examines the simple difference in employment between two points in time while the second presents this difference relative to the initial size of the firm. These two measures can lead to different results. Almus (2002) and Daunfeldt, Elert, and Johansson (2014) show that measures of absolute growth are biased toward larger firms, while measures of relative growth favor small firms. To reduce these biases, we employ

the midpoint growth rate, a measure proposed by Davis, Haltiwanger, and Schuh (1998) that uses absolute changes relative to the *average* size of the firm across the period of time considered in the study. This measure is formally defined as follows:

$$g_{i,t} = \frac{emp_{i,t} - emp_{i,t-2}}{\frac{1}{2}\left(emp_{i,t-2} + emp_{i,t}\right)},$$

where $emp_{i,t}$ refers to total number of permanent, full-time employees that firm i reports in year t. By construction, this growth rate is symmetric around zero and bounded between −2 and 2. It is also monotonically related to the conventional growth rate measure ($G_{i,t}$), and it approximates the latter for small growth rates. Both growth measures are linked by the following identity: $G_{i,t} \approx \frac{2g_{i,t}}{(2 - g_{i,t})}$

The underlying statistical properties of this growth rate are discussed in detail in Törnqvist, Vartia, and Vartia (1985).

The time period of study of our analysis is two years. The surveys ask firms about total employment during the last fiscal year and in the three previous fiscal years. Three- or four-year periods are used in most studies examining high-growth firms, although some studies have used shorter periods (Coad and others 2014; Reyes, Roberts, and Xu 2017).

Annex 2C. Median Size and Age of High-Growth Firms and Rest of Businesses

	High-growth firms		Rest of firms			High-growth firms		Rest of firms	
	Employment	Age	Employment	Age		Employment	Age	Employment	Age
Afghanistan	6	7	12	9	Liberia	3	8	6.5	7
Albania	3	10	9	12	Macedonia, FYR	5.5	8	9	16.5
Angola	9	9	15	10	Madagascar	7.5	11	12	12
Argentina	10	15	36	28	Malawi	6	14.5	15	16
Armenia	6.5	8	18	13	Malaysia	13.5	18	32	17
Azerbaijan	10	15	16	12	Mali	4	12	10	10
Bangladesh	20	17	26	18	Mauritania	7	16	19.5	14
Belarus	8	8	17	15	Mauritius	5	5	15	16
Belize	9.5	20	16	15	Mexico	6.5	12	44	20

table continues next page

	High-growth firms		Rest of firms			High-growth firms		Rest of firms	
	Employment	Age	Employment	Age		Employment	Age	Employment	Age
Benin	3	6	7	14	Micronesia, Fed. Sts.	2.5	3.5	10	16
Bhutan	5.5	7	13	15	Moldova	8	13	15	13
Bolivia	8	15	35	23	Mongolia	10	10.5	15	12
Bosnia and Herzegovina	12.5	13	15	16	Montenegro	7	12	10	15
Botswana	6	7	20	14	Morocco	7.5	15	30	18
Brazil	5	16	25	18	Mozambique	3.5	7	10	12
Bulgaria	5	11	15	17	Myanmar	10	10	11	14
Burkina Faso	8	6	10.5	12	Namibia	3	6	12	9
Burundi	10	4.5	16	12	Nepal	3.5	10.5	12	15
Cabo Verde	4.5	6.5	19.5	13	Nicaragua	6	18	24	19
Cambodia	3.5	14	15	13	Niger	4	6	14	11
Cameroon	10	12	20	16	Nigeria	4	14	9	14
Central African Republic	3	12	10	10	Pakistan	10	15	20	20
Chad	4	11	12	14	Panama	20	18	28.5	17
China	20	10	56	11	Papua New Guinea	79.5	41.5	44	25
Colombia	9	15	30	20	Paraguay	4	7	25	18
Congo, Dem. Rep.	4	6	9	9	Peru	9	11	30	16
Congo, Rep.	2.5	7.5	14	11	Philippines	20	14.5	35	19
Costa Rica	20	12	26.5	21	Romania	5	9	15	17
Côte d'Ivoire	3	6	7.5	9	Rwanda	6	5	16	9
Djibouti	5	10	12	14	Samoa	4	9	12	16
Dominica	3	9	13.5	10	Senegal	3.5	10	10	14
Dominican Republic	5	11	35	17	Serbia	8	11	18	17
Ecuador	12	11	30	22	Sierra Leone	2.5	14.5	10	14
Egypt, Arab Rep.	11	13	28	18	Solomon Islands	8.5	5.5	19	18.5
El Salvador	15	12	35	20	South Africa	6	9	25	15
Eritrea	15	8	16	13	South Sudan	3	5	7	6
Ethiopia	5.5	9	16	12	Sri Lanka	5	13	18	19
Fiji	9	13	15	23	St. Lucia	4.5	9	18	13
Gabon	5	7	10	12	St. Vincent and the Grenadines	3	11.5	9	18
Gambia, The	8	6	9	9	Sudan	10	11	15	11
Georgia	3	4.5	11	10	Suriname	34	17.5	20	18.5
Ghana	2	8	10	13	Swaziland	2	8	10	10
Grenada	2	24	13.5	20	Tajikistan	6.5	9.5	17	10
Guatemala	7	13	32	21	Tanzania	2	15	10	13
Guinea	2	6.5	6	8	Thailand	15	16	27	19
Guinea-Bissau	2.5	10.5	7	10	Timor-Leste	6	9	10	11
Guyana	12.5	17.5	30	19	Togo	3	6	13	11
Honduras	4	17.5	20	20	Tonga	3	4	7	10
Hungary	6.5	11	13	16	Tunisia	10	10.5	35	20

table continues next page

	High-growth firms		Rest of firms			High-growth firms		Rest of firms	
	Employment	Age	Employment	Age		Employment	Age	Employment	Age
India	15	13	30	16	Turkey	9	10	22	16
Indonesia	20	15	30	19	Uganda	6	10	10	13
Iraq	3	12	9	10	Ukraine	20	12	20	14
Jamaica	10	10	24	20	Uzbekistan	6	7	25	14
Jordan	7.5	9	22	15	Vanuatu	7	6	12	19
Kazakhstan	10	8	17	12	Venezuela, RB	6	11.5	16	13
Kenya	9.5	13.5	20	18	Vietnam	10	8	28	11
Kosovo	5	7	15	13	West Bank and Gaza	3	11	10	16
Kyrgyz Republic	20	10	22.5	15	Yemen, Rep.	9	16	14	20
Lao PDR	5	12.5	13	16	Zambia	7	8	12	12
Lebanon	7	7	19	22	Zimbabwe	13	19	40	31
Lesotho	4	11	15	10					

Source: Computation based on data from Enterprise Surveys, the World Bank.
Note: This table reports the median employment and age of firms at the beginning of the period under consideration (that is, two years before the implementation of the survey).

Annex 2D. Identifying the Role of FDI Spillover in High-Growth Firms[23]

To capture the role of FDI spillovers on the performance of domestic enterprises, we regress measures of linkages and demonstration effects on the growth rate of domestic firms' output as follows:

$$g_{ijc} = \beta_1 linkages_{jc} + \beta_2 demonstration_{jc} + BX_{ijc} + \gamma_c + \gamma_j + \varepsilon_{ijc} \quad (1)$$

where the subscript i stands for firm, j for sector, and c for country. γ_c represents country fixed effects and γ_j sector fixed effects, introduced to the specification in order to account for unobserved heterogeneity within each one of these dimensions. Sector fixed effects are defined at the two-digit International Standard Industrial Classification (ISIC) level. g_{ijc} is the sales midpoint growth rate of firm i over the last two years in which the survey was implemented in each country (see annex 2B).

The *linkages* channel (*linkages_{jc}*) is defined by the average share of inputs of domestic origin that foreign firms in sector j (two-digit ISIC codes) acquire in each country. In line with the literature, foreign firms are identified

as firms with at least 10 percent foreign ownership. Specifically, this variable is constructed as

$$linkages_{jc} = \frac{1}{n} \sum_{i=1}^{n} \frac{input_{ijc}^{dom}}{input_{ijc}^{tot}} \quad (2)$$

where $input_{ijc}^{dom}$ represents the value of inputs of domestic origin used by the foreign firm, and $input_{ijc}^{tot}$ corresponds to total value inputs, regardless of their origin. The total number of foreign firms in the sector is n.

The *demonstration* channel (*demonstration_{jc}*) is defined by the share of foreign output as a percentage of total output at the sectoral level. This measure is standard in the literature to measure intra-industry spillover effects. See Farole and Winkler (2015) and references therein.

$$demonstration_{jc} = \frac{\sum_i output_{ijc}^{fgn}}{\sum_i output_{ijc}^{all}} \quad (3)$$

where $output_{ijc}^{fgn}$ represents the sales of foreign firms exclusively, while $output_{ijc}^{all}$ accounts for the sales of all firms in each sector, country, and year.

The model controls for firm-specific attributes contained in the matrix X_{ijc}, including a log transformation of the firm age (defined as the years between the beginning of operations of the firm and the application of the survey), a log transformation of the labor productivity (US$ sales per worker), and a dummy variable to capture exporter status, taking a value of one if direct exports accounted for more than 5 percent of the local firm's total sales. We retained country-sector cells with presence of foreign firms. The final sample of the regressions included about 33,000 domestic firms in 121 economies.

The coefficients β_1 and β_2 provide the *average* impact of linkages and demonstration effects on domestic firms' sales growth across countries and sectors. To test the different impact that these effects have on high-growth firms, we modify equation [1] to include a dummy variable indicating if the firm is a high-growth business and interact this term with the FDI spillover channels. A high-growth firm is defined as an enterprise located in the top fifth percentile of the distribution of employment growth in each country. The results of these estimations are presented in table 2D.1.

To examine how FDI spillovers vary across countries, we run the specification separately for six regions of the world, following the World Bank Group country classification. We also separate the sample between manufacturing and services sectors. The results are presented in tables 2D.1 and 2D.2.

TABLE 2D.1 **Role of FDI Spillovers on Firm Performance**

Variables	(1)	(2)	(3)	(4)	(5)	(6)	(7)
Linkages channel		0.023		0.028	0.053		0.053
		(0.051)		(0.052)	(0.050)		(0.051)
Demonstration channel			0.010	0.011		0.002	0.006
			(0.015)	(0.019)		(0.019)	(0.019)
High-growth firm					0.207***	0.207***	0.190***
					(0.019)	(0.021)	(0.021)
X Linkages channel					0.678***		0.568***
					(0.190)		(0.201)
X Demonstration channel						0.171***	0.109*
						(0.061)	(0.063)
Log age	−0.068***	−0.068***	−0.068***	−0.068***	−0.061***	−0.061***	−0.061***
	(0.005)	(0.005)	(0.005)	(0.005)	(0.005)	(0.005)	(0.005)
Exporter	−0.001	−0.001	−0.001	−0.001	−0.003	−0.003	−0.003
	(0.010)	(0.010)	(0.009)	(0.010)	(0.010)	(0.010)	(0.010)
Log labor productivity	0.082***	0.082***	0.082***	0.082***	0.083***	0.083***	0.083***
	(0.005)	(0.005)	(0.002)	(0.005)	(0.005)	(0.005)	(0.005)
Constant	−0.783***	−0.784***	−0.785	−0.786***	−0.813***	−0.816***	−0.816***
	(0.059)	(0.059)	(0.551)	(0.059)	(0.060)	(0.059)	(0.059)
Country fixed effects	Yes	Yes	Yes	Yes	Yes	Yes	Yes
Sector fixed effects	Yes	Yes	Yes	Yes	Yes	Yes	Yes
Observations	33,305	33,305	33,305	33,305	33,305	33,305	33,305
R-squared	0.165	0.165	0.165	0.165	0.174	0.174	0.174

Source: Computation based on data from Enterprise Surveys, the World Bank.
Note: Standard errors (in parentheses) are clustered at the country-sector level. FDI = foreign direct investment.
***$p<0.01$; **$p<0.05$; *$p<0.1$.

TABLE 2D.2   Role of FDI Spillovers on Firm Performance, by Regions and Sectors

Variables	World Bank regions						Economic sectors	
	East Asia and Pacific	Europe and Central Asia	Latin America and the Caribbean	Middle East and North Africa	South Asia	Sub-Saharan Africa	Manufacturing	Services
Linkages channel	−0.123	0.299	0.009	−0.092	0.349	−0.059	0.092	−0.111*
	(0.103)	(0.265)	(0.108)	(0.164)	(0.647)	(0.098)	(0.108)	(0.064)
Demonstration channel	0.047	−0.051	0.042	−0.003	−0.086	−0.001	−0.003	−0.009
	(0.050)	(0.047)	(0.036)	(0.043)	(0.101)	(0.034)	(0.023)	(0.037)
High-growth firm	0.238***	0.171***	0.212***	0.241***	0.127***	0.294***	0.181***	0.235***
	(0.067)	(0.065)	(0.056)	(0.066)	(0.025)	(0.071)	(0.021)	(0.061)
X Linkages channel	0.814***	−0.202	0.491	2.342***	0.764***	−0.207	0.570*	0.581**
	(0.309)	(0.892)	(0.320)	(0.700)	(0.240)	(0.439)	(0.307)	(0.284)
X Demonstration	−0.076	0.427**	0.042	0.019	0.163	0.059	0.078	0.211**
	(0.118)	(0.192)	(0.127)	(0.208)	(0.201)	(0.147)	(0.077)	(0.115)
Log age	−0.056***	−0.086***	−0.059***	−0.059***	−0.045***	−0.088***	−0.059***	−0.069***
	(0.015)	(0.016)	(0.011)	(0.012)	(0.006)	(0.017)	(0.006)	(0.012)
Exporter	−0.000	0.017	−0.065***	0.015	−0.009	0.064	−0.013	0.083*
	(0.023)	(0.029)	(0.019)	(0.021)	(0.014)	(0.045)	(0.010)	(0.043)
Log labor productivity	0.062***	0.086***	0.107***	0.099***	0.038***	0.122***	0.075***	0.108***
	(0.009)	(0.011)	(0.007)	(0.009)	(0.006)	(0.011)	(0.005)	(0.012)
Constant	−0.579***	−0.718***	−0.679***	−0.983***	0.062	−0.641***	−0.444***	−0.734***
	(0.100)	(0.171)	(0.089)	(0.128)	(0.104)	(0.131)	(0.078)	(0.119)
Country fixed effects	Yes	Yes	Yes	Yes	Yes	Yes	Yes	Yes
Sector fixed effects	Yes	Yes	Yes	Yes	Yes	Yes	Yes	Yes
Observations	5,876	2,749	5,557	4,086	9,155	5,882	26,398	6,893
R-squared	0.103	0.171	0.116	0.306	0.050	0.184	0.175	0.190

Source: Computation based on data from Enterprise Surveys, the World Bank.
Note: Standard errors (in parentheses) are clustered at the country-sector level. FDI = foreign direct investment.
***$p<0.01$; **$p<0.05$; *$p<0.1$.

Notes

1. Moran (2011, 2015) provides a comprehensive overview of the challenges countries face when using FDI to reach these policy goals.
2. Alfaro and Chen (forthcoming) provide empirical evidence on the positive impact of FDI spillovers and the reallocation of factors on aggregate productivity using a rich cross-country database.
3. See Alfaro and others (2006), Alfaro and Chen (forthcoming), Lipsey (2004), Barba Navaretti and Venables (2004), and Alfaro and Rodriguez-Claire (2004) for an overview of the empirical literature about the channels of FDI spillovers.
4. Linkages can increase the productivity of domestic firms in at least three other ways: First, greater demand for intermediates produced by domestic suppliers can increase potential for scale economies. Second, domestic suppliers may face incentives to improve product quality and increase efficiency, owing to more stringent requirements from the foreign firms. Third, competition for other local firms for foreign consumers may also spur productivity upgrading. The analysis in this chapter focuses on the knowledge diffusion impact of linkages.
5. Some studies such as Morrissey, López, and Sharma (2015), separate the learning process from observation from the labor turnover effect. Given data limitations, this chapter compounds these two channels into the demonstration effect.
6. The dataset covers a broad range of business environment topics including access to finance, corruption, infrastructure, crime,

competition, and firm-level performance measures. The raw data include information for various waves of surveys for 139 countries. This analysis retains the latest survey conducted in each country and economies classified as low- and middle-income countries by the World Bank Group. In total, information for about 63,000 firms in 121 developing economies is analyzed.

7. These findings are in line with Damijan and others (2013), which employs 10 transition economies to find positive effects of horizontal spillovers only on large and high-productivity domestic enterprises.

8. A growing body of literature aims to understand the conditions under which the benefits of FDI materialize at the firm level. Some firm characteristics have been linked to their absorptive capacity, including elements such as the size of their technology gap (Wang and Blomström 1992), their share of skilled labor (Blalock and Gertler 2009), and their size (Meyer and Sinani 2004).

9. Although the Enterprise Surveys allow the systematic study of firm performance across a broad range of developing countries, some important caveats are in order. First, firm performance outcomes are available for just two points in time, separated by only two years. Second, the surveys are representative only of the broad manufacturing and services sectors, not at the detailed two-digit ISIC codes. Third, the data include only firms that survived between the two points of time, not those that exited. Fourth, there may be some differences across countries in the minimum size of firms included in the surveys.

10. Because standard growth rates are relative to the initial size of the firm and, therefore, biased toward smaller firms, the analysis uses midpoint growth rates representing the change in employment relative to the average size of the firm between the fiscal year before the survey was administered and three fiscal years prior. Annex 2B discusses the characterization of firm growth adopted in this study.

11. While this methodology is based on previous literature, there is no general agreement on the definition of high-growth firms. Growth rate thresholds have been employed by Schreyer (2000) and Davidsson and Henrekson (2002), among others. Henrekson and Johansson (2010) provide a meta-analysis of the empirical literature

of identifying high-growth businesses. The Organisation for Economic Co-operation and Development (OECD) defines them as firms with 10 or more employees that have an average annualized growth higher than 20 percent for three consecutive years (Ahmad 2008; OECD 2008, 2010). But this definition is overly restrictive for developing countries where 95 percent of businesses have nine or fewer workers (McKenzie 2017).

12. This threshold changes in every country. On average, across countries in the database, firms need to double the number of employees in two years to be considered high-growth firms (Reyes, forthcoming).

13. The fact that high-growth firms are an important source of job creation and tend to be young is a well-established empirical fact in the literature (Coad and others 2014). When firm growth is computed in relative terms—as in this analysis—small firms are also overrepresented among high-growth firms (Delmar, Davidsson, and Gartner 2003).

14. This finding is in line with Henrekson and Johansson (2010), who find that high-growth businesses exist in all industries but tend to be overrepresented in services.

15. Jiménez-Barrionuevo, García-Morales, and Molina (2011) propose a scale of 18 items to measure the absorptive capacity of firms. They are grouped under four categories: They are grouped under four categories: *acquisition* (interaction, trust, friendship, and reciprocity); *assimilation* (common language, complementarity, similarity, and organization culture and management style); *transformation* (communications, meetings, documents, transmission, time, and flows); and *exploitation* (responsibility and application).

16. This approach on backward linkages, which focuses on the demand for inputs from foreign companies, is also used in Sánchez-Martín, De Piniés, and Antoine (2015) and complements that in Javorcik (2004) and Blalock and Gertler (2008), who adopt the perspective of the local supplying sector and look for foreign presence downstream in the supply chain. Forward linkages, which focus on the relationship with upstream sectors, can also be important, particularly in the services sector. Hoekman and Shepherd (2017) find strong impacts of services efficiency and the productivity of downstream manufacturing firms.

17. Owing to limitations with the level of sectoral disaggregation of the World Bank's Enterprise Surveys data, the channels for FDI spillovers are defined at a broader sectoral classification (two-digit ISIC codes). Consequently, in addition to horizontal spillovers, the measures are likely to capture some vertical spillovers. For example, manufacture of leather and related products (classified under ISIC 15) includes both final footwear and the tanning and dressing of leather—an input for footwear. Thus, FDI in this sector could affect domestic final producers of footwear as well as domestic suppliers of footwear production.

18. The finding that intra-industry spillover effects are rarely accrued by domestic firms is standard in the literature. Meyer and Sinani (2009) and Görg and Strobl (2001) provide two meta-analyses reviewing this literature.

19. This effect is statistically significant at the 1 percent level.

20. This effect is statistically significant at the 10 percent level.

21. These findings are robust to 80 percent and 90 percent thresholds to identify high-growth firms. See Reyes (forthcoming).

22. The argument that medium-sized and large indigenous firms are usually better candidates to qualify as suppliers of MNCs is also made by Freund and Moran (2017).

23. For a discussion of the identification strategy see Reyes (forthcoming).

Bibliography

Ahmad, N. 2008. "A Proposed Framework for Business Demography Statistics." In *Measuring Entrepreneurship*, edited by Emilio Congregado, 113–74. Boston, MA: Springer.

Alfaro, L., A. Chanda, S. Kalemli-Ozcan, and S. Sayek. 2006. "How Does Foreign Direct Investment Promote Economic Growth? Exploring the Effects of Financial Markets on Linkages." NBER Working Paper 12522, National Bureau of Economic Research, Cambridge, MA.

Alfaro, L., and A. Rodriguez-Clare. 2004. "Multinationals and Linkages: Evidence from Latin America." *Economia* 4: 113–70.

Alfaro, L., and M. X. Chen. Forthcoming. "Selection and Market Reallocation: Productivity Gains from Multinational Production." *American Economic Journal: Economic Policy*.

Almus, M. 2002. "What Characterizes a Fast-Growing Firm?" *Applied Economics* 34 (12): 1497–1508.

Arráiz, I., F. Henríquez, and R. Stucchi. 2013. "Supplier Development Programs and Firm Performance: Evidence from Chile." *Small Business Economics* 41 (1): 277–93.

Barba Navaretti, G., and A. Venables. 2004. *Multinational Firms in the World Economy*. Princeton, NJ: Princeton University Press.

Blalock, G., and P. J. Gertler. 2008. "Welfare Gains from Foreign Direct Investment through Technology Transfer to Local Suppliers." *Journal of International Economics* 74 (2): 402–21.

———. 2009. "How Firm Capabilities Affect Who Benefits from Foreign Technology." *Journal of Development Economics* 90 (2): 192–99.

Coad, A., S. Daunfeldt, W. Hölzl, D. Johansson, and P. Nightingale. 2014. "High-Growth Firms: Introduction to the Special Section." *Industrial and Corporate Change* 23 (1): 91–112.

Damijan, J. P., M. Rojec, B. Majcen, and M. Knell. 2013. "Impact of Firm Heterogeneity on Direct and Spillover Effects of FDI: Micro-Evidence from Ten Transition Countries." *Journal of Comparative Economics* 41 (3): 895–922.

Daunfeldt, S., N. Elert, and D. Johansson. 2014. "The Economic Contribution of High-Growth Firms: Do Policy Implications Depend on the Choice of Growth Indicator?" *Journal of Industry, Competition and Trade* 14 (3): 337–65.

Davis, S. J., J. C. Haltiwanger, and S. Schuh. 1998. *Job Creation and Destruction*. MIT Press Books.

Davidsson, P., and M. Henrekson. 2002. "Determinants of the Prevalence of Start-Ups and High-Growth Firms." *Small Business Economics* 19 (2): 81–104.

Delmar, F., P. Davidsson, and W. B. Gartner. 2003. "Arriving at the High-Growth Firm." *Journal of Business Venturing* 18 (2): 189–216.

Dollar, D. 1992. "Outward-Oriented Developing Economies Really Do Grow More Rapidly: Evidence from 95 LDCs, 1976–1985." *Economic Development and Cultural Change* 40 (3): 523–44.

Echandi, R., J. Krajcovicova, and C. Z. W. Qiang. 2015. "The Impact of Investment Policy in a Changing Global Economy: A Review of the Literature." Policy Research Working Paper 7437, World Bank, Washington, DC.

Farole, T., and D. Winkler. 2015. "The Role of Foreign Firm Characteristics, Absorptive Capacity and the Institutional Framework for FDI Spillovers." *Journal of Banking and Financial Economics* 1 (3): 77–112.

Fons-Rosen C., S. Kalemli-Ozcan, B. T. Sorensen, C. Villegas-Sanchez, and V. Volosovych. 2017. "Foreign Investment and Domestic Productivity: Identifying Knowledge Spillovers and Competition Effects." NBER Working Paper 22643, National Bureau of Economic Research, Cambridge, MA, August.

Frankel, J. A., and D. Romer. 1999. "Does Trade Cause Growth?" *American Economic Review* 89 (3): 379–99.

Freund, C., and T. Moran. 2017. "Multinational Investors as Export Superstars: How Emerging-Market Governments Can Reshape Comparative Advantage." Working Paper 17-1, Peterson Institute for International Economics, Washington, DC.

Görg, H., and E. Strobl. 2001. "Multinational Companies and Productivity Spillovers: A Meta Analysis." *The Economic Journal* 111 (475): 723–39.

Haltiwanger, J., R. S. Jarmin, and J. Miranda. 2013. "Who Creates Jobs? Small versus Large versus Young." *Review of Economics and Statistics* 95 (2): 347–61.

Hampel-Milagrosa, A., M. Loewe, and C. Reeg. 2015. "The Entrepreneur Makes a Difference: Evidence on MSE Upgrading Factors from Egypt, India, and the Philippines." *World Development* 66: 118–30.

Harrison, A. 1996. "Openness and Growth: A Time-Series, Cross-Country Analysis for Developing Countries." *Journal of Development Economics* 48 (2): 419–47.

Henrekson, M., and D. Johansson. 2010. "Gazelles as Job Creators: A Survey and Interpretation of the Evidence." *Small Business Economics* 35 (2): 227–44.

Hsieh, C., and P. J. Klenow. 2014. "The Life Cycle of Plants in India and Mexico." *The Quarterly Journal of Economics* 129 (3): 1035–84.

Hoekman, B., and B. Shepherd. 2017. "Services Productivity, Trade Policy and Manufacturing Exports." *The World Economy* 40 (3): 499–516.

Hufbauer, G. C., J. Schott, and C. Cimino-Isaacs. 2013. *Local Content Requirements: A Global Problem*. Columbia University Press.

Javorcik, B. 2004. "Does Foreign Direct Investment Increase the Productivity of Domestic Firms? In Search of Spillovers through Backward Linkages." *The American Economic Review* 94 (3): 605–27.

Jiménez-Barrionuevo, M. M., V. J. García-Morales, and L. M. Molina. 2011. "Validation of an Instrument to Measure Absorptive Capacity." *Technovation* 31 (5): 190–202.

Lipsey, R. E. 2004. "Home- and Host-Country Effects of Foreign Direct Investment." In *Challenges to Globalization: Analyzing the Economics*, edited by Robert E. Baldwin and L. Alan Winters, 333–82. University of Chicago Press.

McKenzie, D. 2017. "Identifying and Spurring High-Growth Entrepreneurship: Experimental Evidence from a Business Plan Competition." *American Economic Review* 107 (8): 2278–2307

Meyer, K. E., and E. Sinani. 2004. "Spillovers of Technology Transfer from FDI: The Case of Estonia." *Journal of Comparative Economics* 32 (3): 445–66.

———. 2009. "When and Where Does Foreign Direct Investment Generate Positive Spillovers? A Meta-Analysis." *Journal of International Business Studies* 40 (7): 1075–94.

Monge-González, R., and J. A. Rodríguez-Álvarez. 2013. "Impact Evaluation of Innovation and Linkage Development Programs in Costa Rica: The Cases of PROPYME and CR Provee." IDB Working Paper Series IDB-WP-461, Inter-American Development Bank, Washington, DC.

Moran, T. 2011. *Foreign Direct Investment and Development: Launching a Second Generation of Policy Research: Avoiding the Mistakes of the First, Reevaluating Policies for Developed and Developing Countries*. Columbia University Press.

Moran, T. H. 2015. "The Role of Industrial Policy as a Development Tool: New Evidence from the Globalization of Trade-and-Investment." Policy Paper 071, Center for Global Development, Washington, DC.

Morrissey, O., R. López, and K. Sharma, eds. 2015. *Handbook on Trade and Development*. Cheltenham, U.K.: Edward Elgar Publishing.

OECD (Organisation for Economic Co-Operation and Development). 2008. *OECD Framework for the Evaluation of SME and Entrepreneurship Policies and Programmes*. Paris: OECD Publishing.

———. 2010. *What Governments Can Do to Make a Difference*. OECD Studies on SMEs and Entrepreneurship High-Growth Enterprises. Paris: OECD Publishing.

Reyes, J-D. Forthcoming. "FDI Spillovers and High-Growth Firms in Developing Countries." Mimeo, World Bank, Washington, DC.

Reyes, J-D., M. Roberts, and L. C. Xu. 2017. "The Heterogeneous Growth Effects of the Business Environment: Firm-Level Evidence for a Global Sample of Cities." Policy Research Working Paper 8114, World Bank, Washington, DC.

Sánchez-Martín, M. E., J. De Piniés, and K. Antoine. 2015 "Measuring the Determinants of Backward Linkages from FDI in Developing Economies: Is It a Matter of Size?" Policy Research Working Paper 7185, World Bank, Washington, DC.

Schreyer, P. 2000. "High-Growth Firms and Employment." OECD Science, Technology and Industry Working Paper 2000/3, Organisation for Economic Co-operation and Development, Paris.

Törnqvist, Leo, Pentti Vartia, and Yrjö O. Vartia. 1985. "How Should Relative Changes Be Measured?" *The American Statistician* 39 (1): 43–46.

Wang, J., and M. Blomström. 1992. "Foreign Investment and Technology Transfer. A Simple Model." *European Economic Review* 36 (1): 137–55.

Corporate Tax Incentives and FDI in Developing Countries | 3

Maria R. Andersen, Benjamin R. Kett, and Erik von Uexkull

Policy makers in developing countries often find themselves in a dilemma over the use of tax incentives to attract foreign direct investment (FDI). They would likely prefer that no country offer tax incentives and that all firms contribute equitably to public coffers. But given that most other countries—including high-income ones—offer incentives, investment promotion practitioners often feel obliged to match, or even surpass, the competition to attract FDI.[1] Binding international coordination could resolve this dilemma, but such a solution does not appear to be on the horizon. Although efforts to increase international coordination are under way at both the regional and global levels,[2] and countries are well advised to continue these, the process is slow and often leaves gaps.[3] In the meantime, developing countries continue to make heavy and increasing use of tax incentives.

While general principles for incentives reform are well documented, this chapter contributes practical evidence to help developing country policy makers design and implement reforms to make their incentives regimes more effective for FDI attraction. It provides sector- and firm-level evidence to show how to target incentives more efficiently, based on a new dataset on tax incentives in developing countries compiled by the World Bank Group. The analysis considers whether and how developing countries use tax incentives by sector and over time, links the effectiveness of incentives to a simple framework of investor motivation, and presents new evidence on the relevance of tax incentives for investors. The chapter also reviews priorities for design, transparency, and administration reforms of incentives regimes.

Tax incentives are more effective in attracting efficiency-seeking FDI motivated by lowering production costs than for other types of investment. Yet many developing countries offer incentives to all investors, including those motivated by access to natural resources or the domestic market, who are less likely to respond to incentives. While some developing countries target their incentives at efficiency-seeking FDI, many also offer incentives to market- and natural resource–seeking FDI. In most cases, this is not because incentives are deliberately targeting these investors but rather because they are offered indiscriminately. At the same time, efficiency-seeking FDI also requires that host countries have a more favorable overall investment climate than natural resource– or market-seeking FDI. Incentives do not compensate for such shortcomings and are likely to succeed only if they are part of a broader strategy to address investment climate constraints.

Tax incentive regimes in developing countries often suffer from weak design, lack of transparency, and cumbersome administration. Tax holidays and preferential tax rates remain by far the most widely used incentive instruments in developing countries, despite their well-documented shortcomings. Lack of transparency and high administrative costs also diminish the attractiveness of incentives and raise their indirect costs in terms of economic distortions and potential for corruption.

Even in the short run, developing countries can undertake unilateral reforms to make tax incentives better targeted and more cost-efficient. By focusing incentives on those types of investors most likely to respond, developing countries can reduce the unnecessary loss of tax revenue resulting from incentives granted to firms that would have invested anyway. At the same time, reforms to improve the design, transparency, and administration of incentives can help reduce unintended effects and costs, such as economic distortions, red tape, and corruption. Although these policy reforms do not obviate the need for regional and global solutions, they can substantially improve the cost–benefit ratio of incentives.

Developing Countries Make Wide Use of Tax Incentives

A "Developing Country Tax Incentives Database"[4] compiled for this report provides data on the use of tax incentives in the developing world. Information on tax incentives is often freely available to the public, in particular through the tax summaries published by global accounting firms. In many cases, information is also available from a country's investment promotion agency (IPA), but this information is typically provided in qualitative form and does not lend itself to quantitative research. The new tax incentives database compiled for this report quantifies information from publicly available sources on a number of frequently used incentive instruments (box 3.1).

BOX 3.1

The Developing Country Tax Incentives Database

The Developing Country Tax Incentives Database provides information on 107 countries for the period 2009–15 (table 3A.1). Data are broken down by 22 economic sectors to the extent that incentives explicitly target a specific sector. The following information is covered:

- The standard corporate income tax (CIT) rate.
- The availability and maximum duration of tax holidays.
- The availability and level of preferential rates below the standard CIT rate for a specific sector or type of investment.
- The availability of investment tax allowances or credits that grant investors the right to deduct

investment expenses from taxable income or credit them against payable taxes. Information on the magnitude of these instruments was not collected owing to methodological challenges.

The database also contains information on three conditions for receiving incentives, tracked by type of incentive and by sector:

- Investment location, including requirements for establishment in a certain region of the country or a special economic zone (SEZ).
- Company exporting status, including requirements to sell a certain share of output to other exporting companies.

box continues next page

BOX 3.1

The Developing Country Tax Incentives Database (continued)

- Other conditions, such as requirements to undertake research and development (R&D) or incentives specific to income from intellectual property.

The data were collected through desk research of public sources for country-level tax information in July and August of 2016. As a default, Ernst and Young's "Global Tax Guides" and PricewaterhouseCoopers' "Worldwide Tax Summaries" for the years 2009–15 were consulted and compared. In cases of missing information or discrepancies, other publicly available data sources were consulted, such as the website of a country's investment promotion agency (IPA) or relevant country reports.

A few caveats bear mention: While the World Bank Group made significant efforts to ensure accuracy, it did not corroborate the tax and incentives information reported by the sources mentioned above. In addition, many countries provide tax incentives at the subnational level and these are not covered by the data sources used. Moreover, some countries negotiate ad hoc tax incentives and other discretionary deals with potential investors, and these are also not captured by the database. Finally, the database focuses on corporate tax incentives, excluding information on incentives through indirect taxes such as customs duties and VAT exemptions, or other types of incentives such as subsidies or regulatory advantages. Many countries make incentives available to both domestic and foreign investors. The database registers all such incentives, unless foreign investors are explicitly excluded.

While tax incentives are common in developing countries, they vary at the sector, regional, and income levels. Across sectors, 49–72 percent of all developing countries offer tax holidays, preferential or very low general tax rates, or tax allowances. Tax incentives are most common for construction, information technology (IT) and electronics, machinery and equipment, and other manufacturing sectors. The share of countries offering incentives in services sectors is lower but the majority do offer incentives for most services sectors.

Some developing countries deliberately target incentives to manufacturing sectors and construction to attract investors, but most apply incentives across the board. While about 30 percent of developing countries have incentives that specifically target certain manufacturing sectors (figure 3.1, blue bar), targeting is less common for services and natural resource sectors. Forty percent of developing countries have incentive systems that grant either incentives or low general corporate income tax (CIT) rates across all or most sectors.

Countries deliver tax incentives through a number of different instruments. Among developing countries, tax holidays are the most widely used instrument (table 3A.2). More than half of the developing countries in the database offer tax holidays in at least one sector. Across regions, the highest incidence of tax holidays is in construction and manufacturing sectors, where up to 46 percent of developing countries use them. Their application is less common in services and natural resource sectors, with retail showing the lowest use (23 percent). The median duration of tax holidays across regions and sectors is 10 years.

Most developing countries that grant tax holidays condition them on location requirements within the country (77 percent), which mostly consist of either special economic zone (SEZ) locations or requirements to establish in a designated region of the country. Thirty percent of developing countries also condition tax holidays on a requirement to export or sell to exporting firms, which raises concerns about compliance with World Trade Organization (WTO) rules.[5] Forty percent of developing countries have additional requirements in place, such as spending on research and development (R&D).

FIGURE 3.1 **Tax Incentives Are Widespread in Developing Countries, Especially in Construction and Manufacturing**

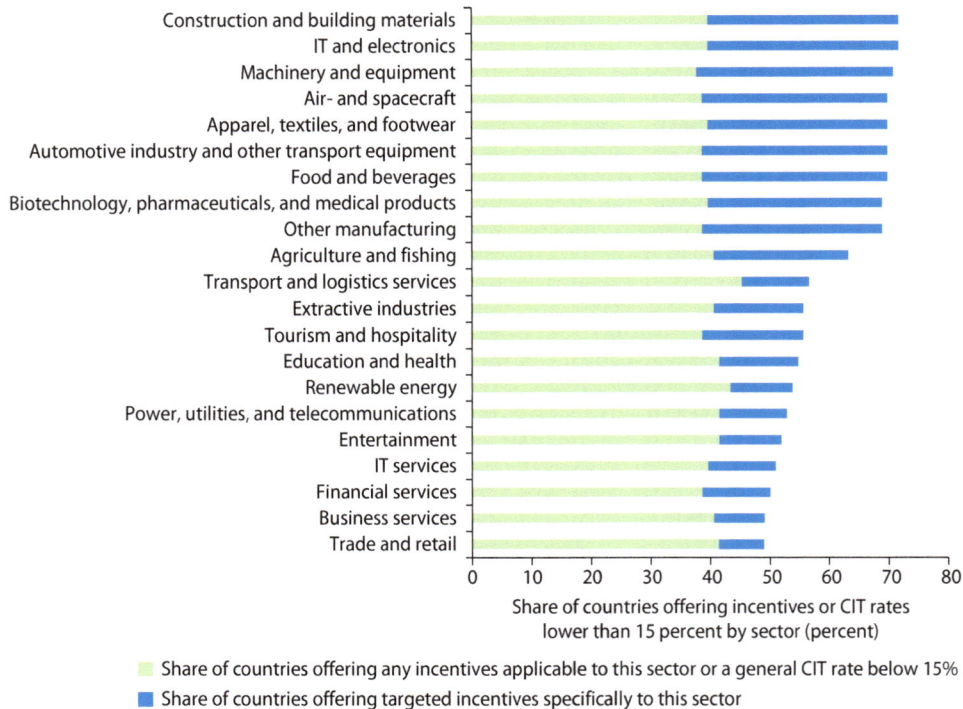

Source: Developing Country Tax Incentives Database.
Note: Incentives specifically targeted to a sector, shown by the dark blue bar, are those applicable to less than 15 out of 22 sectors. This is to account for a small share of incentives generally available across the board, but excluding a limited number of sectors. Some countries also exclude specific sectors from overall low CIT rates. Such exclusions explain the slight variation in the green graph, showing the share of countries offering general incentives applicable to this sector or a general CIT rate below 15 percent. CIT = corporate income tax; IT = information technology.

Preferential tax rates below the standard CIT rate for specific sectors or investors are also common, with 40 percent of countries in the database offering them for at least one sector (table 3A.3). The median preferential margin[6] is 13 percentage points. Conditions on location (45 percent), exporting (32 percent), and other investment project characteristics (46 percent) are also common albeit with significant regional variation. As with tax holidays, preferential rates are most widely used in the manufacturing sector (led by food and beverages) and IT and electronics, where 31 percent of developing countries offer preferential tax rates.

Tax allowances and credits that grant investors the right to deduct investment expenses from taxable income or credit them

against payable taxes are much less common in developing countries; just 16 percent of countries offer them in at least one sector (table 3A.4). Tax allowances and credits also mainly target the manufacturing sector. Almost all tax allowances and credits come with conditions, which is consistent with the performance-based character of this instrument. Receiving the allowance or credit is typically linked to making specific investments, such as R&D or the purchase and installation of new machinery or technology.

Profit-based incentives, such as tax holidays and preferential rates, have serious limitations. They lower the tax rate for any amount of profit earned by the firm, including setting the tax rate to zero for a limited period during a tax holiday. The value of the incentive for such an instrument is thus a direct function of the company's profits. As a result, the incentive heavily favors firms with high profits, which least need government support. This can lead to high redundancy of expenditure on incentives since an investor anticipating high profits would likely have proceeded anyway. Also, host governments face the risk of losing substantial revenue when a firm earns extraordinary profits in a given year. The risk of tax evasion through profit shifting is high for profit-based incentives as firms can artificially allocate profits within the firm to a plant or subsidiary enjoying preferential tax treatment (UNCTAD 2015). The widespread use of these incentive instruments in developing countries is a significant shortcoming in the design of tax incentives.

Cost-based instruments, such as tax allowances and credits, offer superior design features. Unlike profit-based incentives, cost-based ones lower the cost of a specific input or production factor. In the case of investment allowances or credits, the government may grant a firm the right to deduct a certain share of the investment value from its taxable income. The magnitude of the benefit to the company is independent of its profit level and instead depends on the size of the investment that

is undertaken. Such instruments have various advantages: They do not suffer from the bias of profit-based incentives in favor of highly profitable firms and are thus less likely to be biased toward firms that would have invested anyway. They are also less prone to abuse through profit shifting, and their magnitude is directly linked to the policy outcome on which they are conditioned. Still, only a few developing countries currently use these more advanced instruments in granting corporate tax incentives. Part of the reason may be insufficient tax administration capacity. Table 3.1 provides a more detailed overview of the respective strengths and weaknesses of these instruments.

Policy makers have continued to reduce CIT rates across developing countries. In the Middle East and North Africa, East Asia and Pacific, Latin America and the Caribbean, Sub-Saharan Africa, and South Asia, average CIT rates fell between 2009 and 2015; in contrast, Europe and Central Asia showed a small increase in average CIT rates (figure 3.2). Variation in average tax rates across regions is substantial, ranging from 38 percent in South Asia to 15 percent in Europe and Central Asia.

At the same time, developing countries also continued to implement new tax incentives and to make existing ones more generous. More specifically, 46 percent of countries

TABLE 3.1 Pros and Cons of Various Tax Incentives Instruments

Profit-based instruments	
• Tax holidays: Time-bound exemption of new firms or investments from taxes (typically CIT)	
• Concessionary/preferential tax rates: Reduced tax rates that act as a partial exemption of the standard CIT rate	

Pros	Cons
• Strong signaling effect to investors, easy to communicate and advertise.	• Disproportionately favors investments with high profit margins that would have likely occurred anyway and investment with short time horizons (in the case of time-bound holidays and concessions). • Typically granted against up-front assurances from the investor rather than actual performance in terms of expected outcomes such as investment or jobs generated. • Prone to abuse through profit shifting within firms. • High fiscal risk owing to little predictability of actual fiscal cost.
• Tax holidays only: Investors may appreciate complete liberation from interaction with tax authorities for the duration of the holiday.	• Tax holidays only: Liberating investors from tax filing requirements makes it impossible to monitor costs of incentives in terms of forgone revenue.

table continues next page

TABLE 3.1   Pros and Cons of Various Tax Incentives Instruments (continued)

Cost-based instruments

- Tax allowance: Deduction of a share of the cost of investment from taxable income.
- Tax credit: Deduction of a share of the cost of investment from taxes owed.
- Accelerated depreciation: Depreciation of fixed assets for tax purposes at a faster schedule than what is normally applied.

Pros	Cons
• Amount of benefit to investor is directly linked to amount invested. • Tax revenue loss is more predictable than under profit-based instruments. • Less prone to abuse through profit shifting than profit-based instruments. • Does not liberate firms from filing taxes, which makes the process more transparent and allows tracking of costs in terms of foregone revenue. • Accelerated depreciation only: Nominal tax burden is not actually reduced, but payment is merely deferred to a later stage of the investment.	• More challenging to administer. • May bias production technology toward more capital-intensive investment.

introduced new tax incentives or increased the generosity of existing ones in at least one sector during the period covered by the dataset (2009–15). At the median, developing countries that made incentives more generous or introduced new ones expanded tax holidays by seven years or dropped concessionary tax rates by five percentage points. In contrast, only 24 percent of developing countries abolished tax incentives or made them less generous in at least one sector over the same period (figure 3.3 and table 3A.5).

In the Middle East and North Africa, the shares of countries introducing new tax incentives and of countries abolishing existing ones during this period are high—at 50 percent each—reflecting reforms undertaken in both directions. The strongest growth in incentives was in Sub-Saharan Africa, where 65 percent of countries introduced new or more generous incentives, while only 21 percent removed existing incentives or made them less generous. South Asia is the only region in which more countries reduced the use of tax incentives relative to countries that increased them.

These trends in CIT rates and changes in incentives are consistent with a global pattern of lower taxation of geographically mobile capital, as governments around the world strive to attract investment and jobs (Klemm and Van Parys 2012; OECD 1998). This underscores the risk of tax competition when a country that introduces lower taxes or new incentives triggers a similar action by a competing country. Such retaliation diminishes the intended effect of incentives to attract more FDI and also reduces both

FIGURE 3.2   Policy Makers Continue Cutting Corporate Income Tax (CIT) Rates in Most Regions

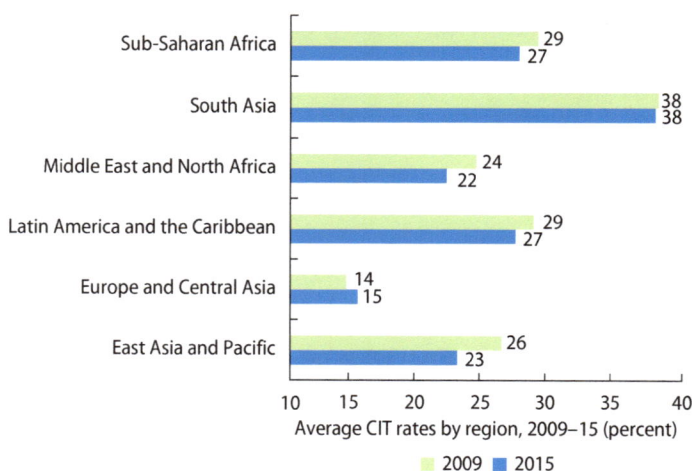

Sub-Saharan Africa: 29 (2009), 27 (2015)
South Asia: 38 (2009), 38 (2015)
Middle East and North Africa: 24 (2009), 22 (2015)
Latin America and the Caribbean: 29 (2009), 27 (2015)
Europe and Central Asia: 14 (2009), 15 (2015)
East Asia and Pacific: 26 (2009), 23 (2015)

Average CIT rates by region, 2009–15 (percent)

■ 2009   ■ 2015

Source: Developing Country Tax Incentives Database.

FIGURE 3.3 **Nearly Half of Developing Countries Have Introduced New Tax Incentives or Increased the Generosity of Existing Ones**

Share of countries with changes in use of tax incentives, 2009–15 (percent)

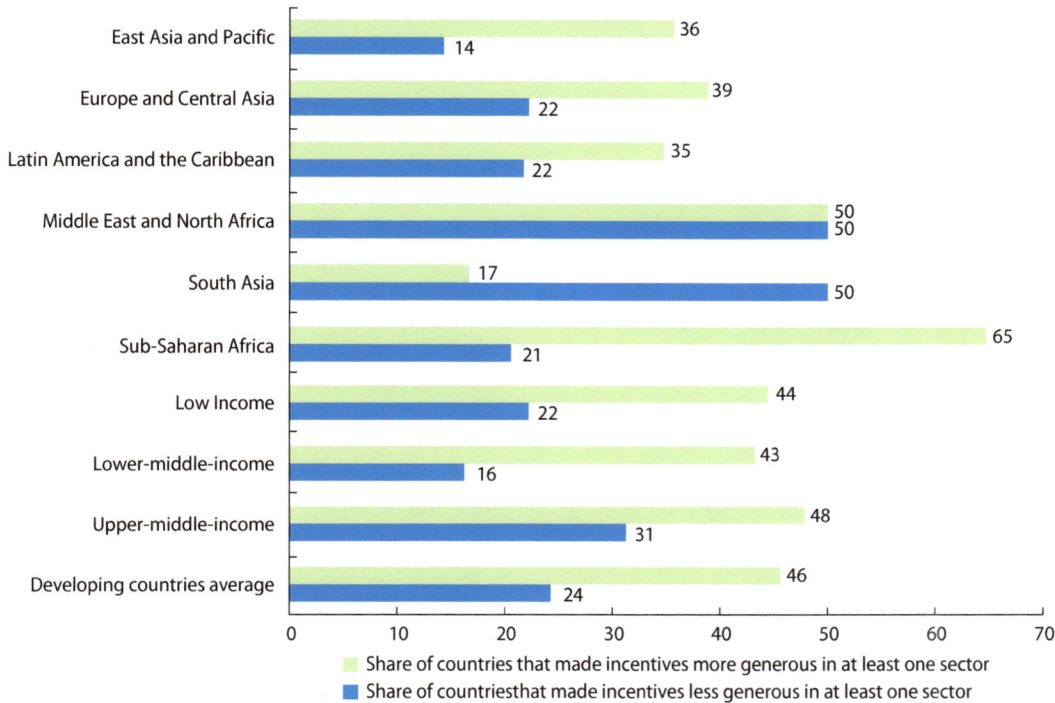

Source: Developing Country Tax Incentives Database.
Note: Making a tax incentive more generous refers to either extending the maximum duration of a tax holiday or reducing the preferential tax rate offered.

countries' fiscal revenues. Global and regional approaches to reducing harmful tax competition are thus warranted to reach a sustainable equilibrium of corporate taxation.

Tax Incentives Are Generally Not Cost-Effective

Tax incentives impose significant costs on the countries using them, though these costs are not always easily visible:

- *Fiscal losses* resulting from the non-collection of taxes that would otherwise be due, also referred to as tax expenditure. Such expenditure can be very significant, especially in developing countries. While data limitations are often severe, recent World Bank technical assistance has estimated tax expenditures from incentives

to be as high as 5.9 (Cambodia), 5.2 (Ghana), and 3.9 (Dominican Republic) percent of GDP. Such expenditure through forgone revenue often does not undergo the same scrutiny and public control as regular government spending, and in many developing countries tax expenditure is not even systematically measured or published.

- *Rent-seeking* by firms engaging in nonproductive behavior to obtain an incentive, or outright corruption where decision makers are bribed to grant incentives (James 2009). Such costs are often amplified by a lack of transparency in the design and administration of incentives.

- *Tax planning and evasion* by the private sector, for example, through shifting of profits from nonexempted to exempted affiliates in the same firm by manipulating internal transfer prices (Heckemeyer and Overesch 2013; UNCTAD 2015).

- *Administrative costs* for both firms and the government due to cumbersome procedures for granting and monitoring incentives.
- *Economic distortions* resulting from reallocating resources to activities benefitting from incentives, including a "status quo bias," in that already-established firms or sectors tend to be more successful than newcomers in lobbying to extend incentives (Zolt 2013).
- *Retaliation* against new or more generous incentives by competing investment locations (Klemm and Van Parys 2012; OECD 1998).

Evidence on the benefits of incentives for FDI attraction is mixed and that for developing countries is particularly limited. While high corporate tax rates clearly have a negative effect on FDI entry (Bénassy-Quéré, Fontagne, and Lahreche-Revil 2005; Bellak, Leibrecht, and Damijan 2009; Desai, Fritz Foley, and Hines 2006; Djankoff and others 2010; Egger and others 2008; Hebous, Ruf, and Weichenrieder 2010; Overesch and Wamser 2008), evidence on the impact of tax incentives is much more mixed. Several studies (Allen and others 2001; James 2009; James and van Parys 2010; Klemm and van Parys 2012; van Parys 2012) find them to be of limited effectiveness at the aggregate level. But the research base for a targeted approach to incentives in developing countries remains small as most existing studies focus on OECD countries and often do not allow sector- or investor-type-specific conclusions on the effectiveness of incentives.

Incentives are rarely among the top characteristics that multinational corporations (MNCs) initially consider in their location decisions, but they can play an important role in the final decision among shortlisted locations. The Global Investment Competitiveness (GIC) survey results in the first chapter confirm that such variables as political stability, regulatory quality, and market size are generally considered more important by investors than tax rates and

incentives, which is consistent with previous survey results on the subject (UNIDO 2011). Nonetheless, incentives often play a role in the final stage of negotiations between investors and governments of the shortlisted investment locations (Freund and Moran 2017). One reason countries offer incentives is precisely because they can make a difference among similar countries on the investor's shortlist. Incentives, by themselves, will not get a country on the list. But when several countries are on the shortlist, with similar conditions, incentives can be decisive. In other words, the effectiveness of incentives is likely conditional upon other factors that determine whether a country "makes the shortlist" in the first place.

This underscores the importance of taking a closer look at investor motivation and firm and country characteristics to understand the effectiveness of tax incentives for FDI promotion. Even where incentives are able to influence an investor's location decision, the benefits do not always justify the costs. Rather than judging the success of an incentive by the absolute amount of FDI it has attracted, countries should weigh the benefits of this FDI in terms of its contribution to such development outcomes as job creation, technology transfer, or other positive externalities, against the above described costs.

The Effectiveness of Incentives Varies by FDI Motivation

Not all FDI is the same; it differs, among other things, in terms of the motivation of the investor (see box 1.2 in chapter 1). Investor motivation is difficult to observe in available global FDI data, and a one-to-one categorization of sectors by FDI motivation is not possible. In fact, FDI in the same sector can be driven by different motives across countries or even within the same country.[7] But for illustrative purposes, a basic distinction between predominantly market-seeking relative to efficiency-seeking FDI sectors can be made on the basis of the share of revenue that is derived from exports versus domestic sales. The third type of motivation—natural resource–seeking

FDI—can be broadly identified with the extractive and agricultural sectors.

Table 3.2 shows the underlying data and approach for this approximate classification for the purposes of this chapter. For well-informed decision making on the targeting of incentives, this analysis must be conducted more thoroughly according to firm-level data on the activities of foreign affiliates in a specific host country. FDI that

TABLE 3.2 **Efficiency-Seeking FDI Is Clustered in Few Locations While Natural Resource– and Market-Seeking FDI Is Geographically Dispersed**

FDI in developing countries by sector and likely primary FDI motivation

Sector	Export share (percentage of total sales) of U.S. foreign affiliates[a]	Within firm sales (percentage of total sales to affiliated parties) of U.S. foreign affiliates[b]	Number of FDI projects in developing countries in fDi Markets database	Herfindahl-Hirschman Index of geographic concentration of FDI projects[c]	
				All developing countries	Excl. China and India
Mainly natural resource–seeking					
Agriculture and fishing	36	47	555	0.05	0.03
Extractive industries	58	31	1,112	0.03	0.03
Renewable energy	n.a.	n.a.	45	0.05	0.05
Total mainly natural resource–seeking	**47**	**39**	**1,712**	**0.04**	**0.04**
Mainly market-seeking					
Business services	n.a.	19	3,690	0.07	0.04
Construction and building materials	11	8	1,840	0.07	0.03
Education and health	n.a.	n.a.	546	0.11	0.03
Entertainment	n.a.	n.a.	179	0.07	0.04
Financial services	1	0	4,082	0.04	0.02
Food and beverages	28	27	1,150	0.06	0.04
Power, utilities, and telecommunications	n.a.	n.a.	1,878	0.04	0.03
Tourism and hospitality	n.a.	n.a.	872	0.08	0.03
Trade and retail	13	5	3,902	0.07	0.05
Total mainly market-seeking	**13**	**12**	**18,139**	**0.07**	**0.04**
Mainly efficiency-seeking					
Air- and spacecraft	n.a.	n.a.	371	0.12	0.13
Apparel, textiles, and footwear	52	24	544	0.07	0.07
Automotive industry and other transport	50	46	2,867	0.12	0.10
Biotechnology, pharmaceuticals, and medical products	43	48	640	0.11	0.04
IT and electronics	60	45	2,167	0.13	0.06
IT services	n.a.	33	3,275	0.10	0.07
Machinery and equipment	51	36	2,657	0.13	0.07
Other manufacturing	46	25	2,164	0.09	0.06
Transport and logistics services	59	11	2,909	0.07	0.04
Total mainly efficiency-seeking	**51**	**34**	**17,594**	**0.10**	**0.07**
Total all sectors			**37,445**	**0.08**	**0.05**

Source: Computation based on data from Bureau of Economic Analysis (BEA) Statistics on activities of US foreign affiliates (Table II.E 11. Goods Supplied by Affiliates, Industry of Affiliate by Destination, 2014), and fDi Markets database (2009–15), the Financial Times.

Note: FDI = foreign direct investment; IT = information technology; n.a. = not applicable.

a. The export share by sector is calculated as non-host country sales divided by total sales based on the BEA data. Sectors are classified as natural resource–seeking if the sector description clearly indicates a direct link with natural resources. Remaining sectors are classified as efficiency-seeking if the share of exported sales exceeds 40 percent, and as market-seeking otherwise. Sectors with no BEA data availability are classified based on authors' intuition.

b. Because of data limitations in more recent years, this indicator is based on the 2008 BEA data on US foreign affiliates.

c. The Herfindahl-Hirschman Index (HHI) of geographic concentration is defined as the sum of the squares of all developing countries' shares in the total number of FDI projects for a given sector. It would hence take the value of 1 in a hypothetical case where all FDI projects in a given sector went to one country and approach zero the more dispersed FDI projects are across countries. China and India are excluded in the last column as a robustness check owing to their high share in the overall number of investment projects.

is primarily in natural resource– or efficiency-seeking sectors is associated with a large share of exports, while market-seeking investment, by definition, leads mainly to domestic sales. On the basis of this categorization, FDI in mainly market-seeking sectors accounts for 48 percent of projects in developing countries, followed by projects that are efficiency-seeking (47 percent) and natural resource–seeking (5 percent). FDI projects in natural resources, however, tend to be large in terms of the size of capital investment, and thus account for a higher share of overall FDI value than their share in the number of projects.

Natural resource– and efficiency-seeking FDI tends to exhibit much higher shares of intrafirm sales than market-seeking FDI (table 3.2). In the case of efficiency-seeking FDI, this finding reflects firms' attempts to organize and control their global value chains (GVCs) across different production locations. Being able to attract efficiency-seeking FDI is therefore often a prerequisite for countries to integrate with GVCs and to export to the markets they serve.

Efficiency-seeking FDI tends to cluster in relatively few successful host countries while market- and natural resource–seeking FDI are more geographically dispersed (table 3.2). Such a pattern of clustering is consistent with efficiency-seeking FDI being highly mobile and driven by firms strategically organizing their value chains by locating in cost-competitive host countries. Depending on the industry, this means that countries must compete for efficiency-seeking FDI and that not all of them win. On the other hand, market- and natural resource–seeking FDI, by definition, must go where the market or natural resource is located, and are thus more geographically dispersed.

In sectors where FDI is predominantly efficiency-seeking, competition for FDI is high and incentives are commonly offered by developing countries. For FDI in such efficiency-seeking sectors as IT and electronics, machinery and equipment, automotive, air- and spacecraft, and biotechnology and pharmaceuticals, most FDI projects are clustered in a limited number of host countries; at the same time,

these sectors show the highest prevalence of incentives (figure 3.4, upper right quadrant). The IT services sector is somewhat of an outlier in that, while it is highly geographically concentrated and mainly efficiency-seeking, fewer developing countries offer incentives for this sector than for other mainly efficiency-seeking sectors.

This suggests that some developing countries use incentives strategically in sectors with high shares of efficiency-seeking FDI where competition is particularly intense. It also shows that, while incentives may be an important part of the value proposition to investors, they are not a sufficient condition for FDI in these sectors as FDI is concentrated in relatively few locations despite the widespread availability of incentives for these sectors.

On the other hand, FDI in mainly market- and natural resource–seeking sectors also flows to less competitive locations; and, while incentives remain common, they may not be necessary. FDI projects in extractives, power and utilities, and financial services, for example, are among the most dispersed geographically. Incentives are less common in these sectors yet are still offered by about 50 percent of developing countries (figure 3.4, lower left quadrant). As competition for FDI is more limited in these sectors, and location decisions are likely dominated by questions of market demand and availability of natural resources, such incentives are good candidates for further study and possible elimination as they may well be redundant.

In the GIC survey results, the share of respondents rating incentives such as tax holidays as important or critically important for their investment decision is considerably lower for market- and natural resource–seeking investors (47 percent) than for efficiency-seeking investors (64 percent). The GIC survey also finds that developing country–based efficiency-seeking investors care more about incentives, relative to efficiency-seeking companies of developed countries. But country-specific analysis of FDI motivation and costs and benefits of incentives is an important step in confirming these broad trends before reforming a country's incentives regime (box 3.2).

FIGURE 3.4 **Incentives Are Used Most in Sectors with Heavy Competition for Efficiency-Seeking Investment**
Prevalence of incentives and FDI concentration

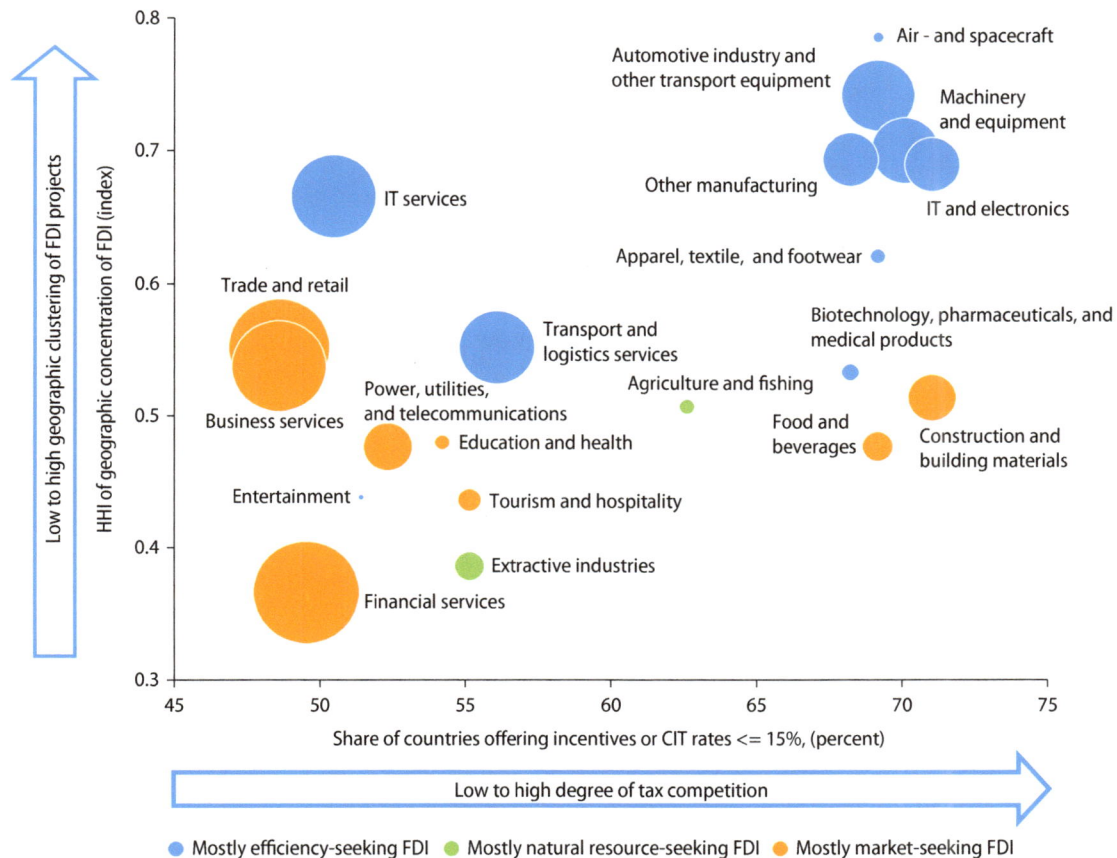

Source: Computation based on Developing Country Tax Incentives Database and FDI data from fDi Markets database, the Financial Times.
Note: The size of each bubble represents the number of FDI projects within the sector in developing countries. This was constructed based on information from the fDi Markets database. CIT = corporate income tax; FDI = foreign direct investment; IT = information technology.

BOX 3.2

Methodologies and Results from Country-Level Cost-Benefit Analysis of Incentives

This box summarizes recent work on cost–benefit analysis (CBA) of tax incentives for FDI attraction in developing countries where data availability is often limited. Even in low data environments, basic analytical steps can help promote a more informed policy dialogue on tax incentives.

To analyze the costs of incentives, a minimum requirement is to collect a list of firms, by sector, benefitting from incentives. While not explicitly covering costs, such information can be a useful starting point to see which sectors enjoy the most incentives. It can also highlight distortions to competition if

box continues next page

BOX 3.2

Methodologies and Results from Country-Level Cost-Benefit Analysis of Incentives (continued)

incentives benefit only a few firms within a sector. A sector-level analysis to motivate further data collection and research can be done by merging data on the prevalence of incentives with outcome variables (for example, employment and investment) from secondary sources such as an Enterprise Census or Labor Force Survey. While falling short of a proper CBA, this basic approach can help a country identify sectors with an obvious disproportion between the granting of incentives and the benefits of doing so. For example, a recent study on Côte d'Ivoire (World Bank 2016b) found that while almost 15 percent of companies receiving incentives were in the construction sector, this sector accounted for only about 5 percent of total investment and 2 percent of employment in the country.

A much better starting point for understanding the costs of incentives is a tax expenditure analysis. This entails assessing the corporate and indirect taxes that would have been due from a given company in the absence of incentives. Such information can be produced by the tax authorities using individual companies' tax returns. Collecting and publishing this data on a regular basis increases the transparency of incentives and enables policy makers and other stakeholders to better assess their cost. Countries such as Colombia,[a] Morocco,[b] and South Africa[c] follow this practice; but many others neither track nor publish tax expenditure.

Confidentiality concerns often limit the ability of the tax administration to share firm-level tax expenditure data for analytical purposes. In such a case, aggregate results at the sector level can nevertheless provide useful policy guidance by identifying disproportions between tax expenditure and benefits generated by a sector. Research in Sri Lanka (World Bank 2016a), for example, shows that, although the communication sector absorbed 27 percent of total tax expenditure, it accounted for only 1 percent of total employment.

A more rigorous assessment of costs and benefits is possible when firm-level data are available. One possibility is to analyze a firm's return on investment

with and without the incentive. While this approach involves judgment in defining a credible minimum return for an investment to proceed, it can lead to intuitive yet highly policy-relevant insights. For example, the above-mentioned analysis of Sri Lanka also revealed that firms in the communication sector averaged high returns on investment, and that these returns would have remained above the country average even without the incentives they received. Such a finding suggests that incentives granted to this sector were likely redundant and that the investment would have been undertaken in any case.

A formal quantitative assessment of the tax incentive's costs and benefits is offered by the user cost of capital (UCC) methodology. This approach is more data intensive as it requires firm-level data from balance sheets and/or tax returns over a period of several years. It can produce an econometrically solid estimate of the tax-investment relationship in a country by isolating the marginal investment effect of a given tax concession. The UCC can be regarded as the pretax minimum rate of return required for an investment to be considered profitable. By construction, the investment elasticities to UCC will vary across time and firm (or group of firms); thus, comparing these trends with what the UCC would have been without tax incentives permits an estimation of the change in fixed assets that is due to existing tax incentives. Recent analytical work based on this methodology has produced rigorous measures of the net fiscal costs per job created, or unit of investment, for different sectors and incentive instruments in the Dominican Republic, Malaysia, and South Africa. But its heavy data needs make this approach difficult to replicate in many lower-middle-income countries.

A more easily replicable approach to shed light on the question of attribution of benefits to tax incentives is an investor motivation survey. Such surveys ask firms a series of questions about the role of incentives and other characteristics in their location decisions. Firms are classified as marginal investors if attracted by an incentive versus nonmarginal investors that would have come anyway based on their responses.

box continues next page

Methodologies and Results from Country-Level Cost-Benefit Analysis of Incentives (continued)

While this classification by survey responses requires some nontrivial judgment, the approach has been used widely across developing countries.

At the aggregate level, the share of investors who would have invested without an incentive (redundancy rate) is often high, ranging from 32 percent in El Salvador to 92 percent in Guinea and 98 percent in Rwanda, based on a recent series of investor motivation surveys (James 2013). However, because of significant variation by sector and investor motivation, aggregate results are insufficient to derive credible cost–benefit results. Thus, the survey sample size must be large enough to disaggregate the resulting redundancy rates by sector and motivation of the investor, which is costly. If such a detailed breakdown were available, sector-specific redundancy ratios could be

combined with information on tax expenditure and benefits in terms of jobs, investment, and other variables to calculate cost–benefit ratios.

a. "Article 87 of Act 788 (2002) established the Colombian government's obligation to present a detailed report in which the fiscal impact of benefits must be evaluated and made explicit. The Oficina de Estudios Económicos de la Dirección de Impuestos y Aduanas Nacionales (DIAN) (National Customs and Tax Directorate's Economic Research Office) has systematically published Colombia's tax expenditure estimates since 2003 and presents the principal categories of preferential treatments for the last 10 years, making the distinction between those treatments to individuals and companies." Villela, Lemgruber, and Jorratt (2010).
b. Morocco publishes a detailed account of tax expenditure as part of its annual budget. Expenditure is presented by tax instrument, by type of beneficiary, and by industrial sector. The detailed report also contains information on the types of incentives granted, their legal basis, the intended objectives, and the eligible beneficiaries. The full document for 2015 is available at http://www.finances.gov .ma/Docs/2014/DB/dep_fisc_fr.pdf.
c. South Africa publishes supplementary information to the National Budget that provides some detail on tax expenditure.

Firm- and Country-Level Variables Influence the Impact of Incentives

The effectiveness of tax incentives in attracting FDI also depends on several firm- and country-level variables. Previous research has differentiated between greenfield investment versus mergers and acquisitions (Hebous, Ruf, and Weichenrieder 2010), export- versus domestic-oriented FDI (James 2009), and horizontal versus vertical FDI (Overesch and Wamser 2008). It has found a stronger effect of tax incentives on greenfield FDI (Hebous, Ruf, and Weichenrieder 2010), export-oriented FDI (James 2009), and vertical FDI (Overesch and Wamser 2008). As all these firm characteristics are consistent with efficiency-seeking FDI, the findings generally confirm that efficiency-seeking FDI is more responsive to tax incentives. Investment incentives have

also been shown to be more effective in countries with better infrastructure (Bellak and others 2009) and investment climates (James 2009).

Linking the Developing Country Tax Incentives Database to data from the World Bank's Enterprise Surveys sheds light on the role of incentives, and firm and country characteristics in developing countries. The Enterprise Surveys systematically collect firms' perceptions concerning a number of obstacles they face in their operations, including the tax burden. While there is some evidence linking this indicator to actual FDI inflows (Kinda 2010), the observed effect of incentives on investors' perceptions of the tax system is more reasonably interpreted as a necessary, but not sufficient, condition for the incentive to lead to more FDI. Companies may be facing other obstacles and thus still not invest, even if their perception of the tax system improves owing to an incentive. But if companies do not even see an incentive as an improvement in the tax system they face, it is logical to conclude that this incentive is not effective. Merging the Developing Country Tax Incentives Database with information on perceptions of foreign firms from the Enterprise Surveys yields useful insights (table 3A.6):

Not surprisingly, the CIT rate is positively associated with the likelihood that firms will rank taxes as an obstacle. A 10-percentage-point drop in the CIT rate is associated with a 3.6 to 4 percentage point fall in the probability of foreign firms perceiving the tax rate as an obstacle.

A tax holiday offered in the firm's sector of operation is associated with a 3.3 to 6.9 percentage point drop in the likelihood of ranking the tax rate as an obstacle. This average finding masks significant variation of the effect depending on firm and country characteristics. For example, the link between tax holidays and a firm's perception of the tax rate is much stronger for exporting firms. Among exporters, the probability of ranking tax rates as an obstacle declines by 12 percentage points if a country offers tax holidays in their sector of operation. The corresponding figure for nonexporters is 3.8 percentage points.

This finding is in line with results recorded by the GIC survey, suggesting that incentives matter more for efficiency-seeking investors: 29 percent of efficiency-seeking firms reported that tax holidays were critical when deciding to invest or expand in developing countries. The Enterprise Surveys include only manufacturing and services firms and no natural resource–seeking firms, so export-oriented firms can be equated with efficiency-seeking investors in this dataset, confirming the previous finding that incentives matter more for this type of FDI.[8]

Similarly, the link between the existence of tax holidays and firms' perceptions of taxes as a barrier appears to be stronger for large firms (9.8 percentage points) than for small ones (3.3 percentage points). This may reflect the widespread use of minimum investment requirements

for incentives. It could also suggest a problem with high up-front costs of obtaining incentives—such as determining the requirements to qualify for them and going through cumbersome application processes—that make incentives worthwhile only for larger firms. This raises serious efficiency and equity concerns. Transparency-enhancing reforms (box 3.3) can mitigate up-front costs of incentives and also help avoid indirect costs attributable to corruption and economic distortions.

The link between tax holidays and the perceptions of old versus new firms does not seem to differ. This should be reason for concern because tax holidays are typically intended to promote new investments rather than sustain existing ones. In practice, existing investors often use rent-seeking behavior, including lobbying and strategic reinvestments, to extend tax holidays beyond their intended duration, which may explain this finding in the data. These types of targeting problems seriously limit the effectiveness of tax incentives for FDI promotion. A predetermined sunset clause for incentives can help better shield policy decision making from such pressures.

The positive link between tax holidays and firms' perceptions of the tax rate does not hold in countries with poor transport or investment climates. This is consistent with literature showing that incentives are ineffective in promoting FDI in such environments (Bellak, Leibrecht, and Damijan 2009; James 2009). Tax holidays thus apparently cannot compensate for shortcomings in these areas and may be benefiting mainly firms that would have invested anyway. Efficiency-seeking FDI, the most likely to respond to incentives, is particularly sensitive to the quality of the investment climate and transport costs, and prone to clustering in the most competitive locations. This finding may thus result from efficiency-seeking investors avoiding countries with weak investment climates regardless of incentives, while market- and natural resource–seeking investors are less responsive and operate in these countries regardless of the investment climate.

BOX 3.3

Examples of Transparency-Enhancing Reforms of Tax Incentives

Incentives Inventories

Publishing up-to-date information on the types of incentives offered, their legal basis, granted amounts, eligibility criteria, administration process, and other relevant information is an important first step toward increasing transparency. Often, this information is not available in developing countries in a comprehensive manner and needs to be compiled by reviewing laws and regulations that may include incentives—a process that also yields important insights into incentives design. For investors, the inventory can be used to publicize relevant information and create a more level playing field. A good example of an incentives inventory in a developing country is Jordan. The Jordan Investment Commission publishes on its website, in a user-friendly format, a list of incentives available to investors across all laws, as well as administrative procedures for applying for incentives. This inventory is underpinned by an internal IT system and is updated annually by a dedicated team. Another recent example is Pakistan, where the Federal Board of Investment publishes on its website all tax and customs duty incentives available to investors through federal-level legislation.

Consolidating All Incentive Provisions in the Tax Law

Keeping incentives in the tax law avoids scattering them through a country's legislation (often including the investment code, mining code, agricultural code, or special economic zone law). It also ensures that the legislature reviews the incentives as part of the annual budget process. Furthermore, it supports the ability of the tax administration to keep track of, and monitor, incentives effectively. At the same time, granting incentives based only on tax law avoids the discretionary practice of concluding individual agreements with investors and thus limits the scope for rent-seeking and corruption. In Tunisia, the new Investment Code approved in 2016, instead of providing for incentives, refers to a Fiscal Incentives Decree connected to the Tax Code. In Sri Lanka, the new Inland Revenue Act being considered would move all existing tax incentives into the tax code, no longer allowing the Sri Lanka Bureau of Investment to grant incentives under its own authority.

Minimizing Discretion and Establishing Clear, Objective Eligibility Criteria for Granting Incentives

Reducing the discretion of agencies administering or awarding incentives enhances predictability for investors and reduces opportunities for rent-seeking and corruption. For tax incentives, a good practice is awarding incentives to qualified investors based on the criteria set out in the law, rather than through a separate approval process. Costa Rica, for example, has established clear eligibility criteria for incentives through its Free Trade Zone Law, which identifies the thresholds and practices for granting incentives.

Conclusion

While efforts to reduce harmful tax competition remain a priority on the multilateral agenda, developing country governments can take unilateral steps to use tax incentives in a more targeted and cost-efficient manner. They can do this by implementing tailored reform strategies based on two pillars:

- Targeting incentives at those investors whose decision to invest is most likely swayed by incentives. This requires a thorough understanding of the type of and motivation for FDI in the country and the costs and benefits of existing incentives.
- Improving the design, transparency, and administration of incentives to reduce indirect costs and avoid unintended consequences.

An important starting point for any incentives system is to achieve clarity and consensus among stakeholders as to the specific and measurable policy goals to be pursued through the incentives. Leaving objectives undefined, or trying to accomplish too many or vaguely defined goals, makes it impossible to assess the success of incentives and is bound to lead to failure. A robust monitoring and evaluation framework to track progress toward such objectives is indispensable to justify the public cost of tax incentives, and detect and adjust redundant or inefficient expenses.

Tax incentives should be targeted at efficiency-seeking investors, but fundamentals of the investment climate must be addressed first. Getting a "piece of the cake" of globally mobile efficiency-seeking FDI requires more effort in terms of proactive government involvement. Tax competition for efficiency-seeking FDI is intense; for some sectors with the highest shares of efficiency-seeking FDI, almost all developing countries offer some sort of corporate tax incentives. But efficiency-seeking FDI is also considerably more demanding than other forms of FDI in that it requires a higher-quality investment climate, basic infrastructure, reasonable transport costs, and a policy framework favoring investment. If these elements are lacking, investors are unlikely to respond to even the most generous incentives. Thus, for developing countries with poor performance along these dimensions, the most promising strategy is to avoid the use of incentives and instead protect their revenue base to support investment in infrastructure and improvement of the investment climate while formulating a medium-term strategy to become more competitive for efficiency-seeking FDI. On the other hand, countries that already have the attributes to attract efficiency-seeking FDI may in some cases find targeted incentives for this type of FDI useful to bolster their locational competitiveness.

Tax incentives for natural resource– and market-seeking investors are often redundant and should be primary targets for further evaluation and potential removal. Countries across geographic regions and income groups continue to offer investment incentives to market- and natural resource–seeking FDI. In most cases, these investors are not explicitly targeted by incentives but benefit from incentives offered to all or most investors in a country. For these investors, incentives have a higher likelihood of being redundant in that the investments they support may have proceeded anyway.

Country-specific cost–benefit analysis of incentives, including an assessment of redundancy by analyzing the return on investment with or without an incentive, is important in further tailoring this recommendation to country-specific circumstances.

Developing countries can improve the design of incentives by moving away from profit-based to cost-based instruments linked to clear policy goals. Most developing countries continue to rely heavily on tax holidays and preferential tax rates. The shortcomings of such profit-based instruments have been well established in that they are more attractive for firms with already high profits and short time horizons, as opposed to cost-based instruments, such as tax allowances and credits, that directly lower the cost of investment. Profit-based incentives are also more prone to abuse through tax planning and profit shifting.

As cost-based incentives can be tailored more closely to policy goals, host countries should identify a realistic set of policy goals and design instruments accordingly. Monitoring and evaluation systems should be put in place to track progress against the intended results. Finally, throughout this experiential process, policy makers should be taking steps to learn and adapt accordingly.[9]

By enhancing transparency and administration practices, developing countries can reduce the indirect costs of incentives resulting from rent-seeking and corruption, and avoid excessive administrative costs. This includes avoiding the use of discretionary or ad hoc incentives by mandating that all incentives be clearly laid out in the relevant law. Consolidating the legal basis for incentives in the tax law can also help enhance transparency and facilitate control by the tax administration. On the administration side, reducing discretion in awarding incentives and, ideally, awarding them automatically to any investors qualified under the law can reduce up-front costs that can render incentives unattractive, especially for smaller investors. Finally, to avoid capture and perpetual renewal of incentives by established firms that in practice often make tax incentives ineffective in terms of generating new investment, incentives should always be temporary in nature, including through a pre-announced sunset clause.

The evidence on the use of tax incentives in developing countries clearly needs to be developed further. The current version of the Developing Country Tax Incentives Database covers only CIT incentives; an extension, in particular to customs and value added tax incentives, would be desirable, as would be the inclusion of subnational data.[10] Given the limitations of existing data and methodologies to systematically explore causal effects between incentives and FDI, a key priority is to collect longer-term time series data on incentives and FDI, by sector, for developing countries.

Another avenue of research could focus on globally comparable firm-level data and look at the micro effects of incentives (for example, returns on investment and firm expansion). Such micro-based research could also move beyond the focus on FDI entry and consider the role of incentives for FDI retention, linkages between foreign and domestic firms, employment, or other behavioral characteristics of firms receiving incentives.

Annex 3A

TABLE 3A.1   **Countries in Developing Country Tax Incentives Database**

Low-income countries		Lower-middle-income countries		Upper-middle-income countries	
Haiti	LAC	Cambodia	EAP	China	EAP
Afghanistan	SAR	Indonesia	EAP	Fiji	EAP
Nepal	SAR	Lao PDR	EAP	Malaysia	EAP
Burundi	SSA	Mongolia	EAP	Thailand	EAP
Chad	SSA	Myanmar	EAP	Albania	ECA
Congo, Dem. Rep.	SSA	Papua New Guinea	EAP	Azerbaijan	ECA
Ethiopia	SSA	Philippines	EAP	Belarus	ECA
Gambia, The	SSA	Samoa	EAP	Bosnia and Herzegovina	ECA
Guinea	SSA	Sri Lanka	EAP	Bulgaria	ECA
Liberia	SSA	Timor-Leste	EAP	Georgia	ECA
Madagascar	SSA	Vietnam	EAP	Kazakhstan	ECA
Malawi	SSA	Armenia	ECA	Macedonia, FYR	ECA
Mozambique	SSA	Moldova	ECA	Montenegro	ECA
Rwanda	SSA	Tajikistan	ECA	Romania	ECA
Senegal	SSA	Ukraine	ECA	Serbia	ECA
Sierra Leone	SSA	Uzbekistan	ECA	Turkey	ECA
South Sudan	SSA	Bolivia	LAC	Turkmenistan	ECA
Tanzania	SSA	Guatemala	LAC	Argentina	LAC
Uganda	SSA	Honduras	LAC	Belize	LAC
Zimbabwe	SSA	Nicaragua	LAC	Brazil	LAC
		Egypt, Arab Rep.	MENA	Colombia	LAC
		Morocco	MENA	Costa Rica	LAC
		Tunisia	MENA	Dominica	LAC
		Bangladesh	SAR	Dominican Republic	LAC
		India	SAR	Ecuador	LAC
		Pakistan	SAR	Grenada	LAC
		Cameroon	SSA	Guyana	LAC
		Cabo Verde	SSA	Jamaica	LAC
		Congo, Rep.	SSA	Mexico	LAC
		Côte d'Ivoire	SSA	Panama	LAC
		Ghana	SSA	Paraguay	LAC
		Kenya	SSA	Peru	LAC
		Lesotho	SSA	Saint Lucia	LAC
		Mauritania	SSA	Suriname	LAC
		Nigeria	SSA	Venezuela, RB	LAC
		São Tomé and Príncipe	SSA	Algeria	MENA
		Sudan	SSA	Iraq	MENA
		Swaziland	SSA	Jordan	MENA
		Zambia	SSA	Lebanon	MENA
				Libya	MENA
				Maldives	SAR
				Angola	SSA
				Botswana	SSA
				Equatorial Guinea	SSA
				Gabon	SSA
				Mauritius	SSA
				Namibia	SSA
				South Africa	SSA

Source: Developing Country Tax Incentives Database.
Note: EAP = East Asia and Pacific: ECA = Europe and Central Asia; LAC = Latin America and Caribbean; MENA = Middle East and North Africa; SAR = South Asia; SSA = Sub-Saharan Africa.

TABLE 3A.2   **Global Use of Tax Holidays, 2015**

	East Asia and Pacific	Europe and Central Asia	Latin America and the Caribbean	Middle East and North Africa	South Asia	Sub-Saharan Africa	Low-income	Lower-middle-income	Upper-middle-income	Total
Number of countries covered in database	15	18	23	8	6	37	20	39	48	107

Prevalence of tax holidays by sector and region (share of countries offering tax holidays in a given sector, percent)

	East Asia and Pacific	Europe and Central Asia	Latin America and the Caribbean	Middle East and North Africa	South Asia	Sub-Saharan Africa	Low-income	Lower-middle-income	Upper-middle-income	Total
Construction and building materials	71	56	48	50	50	32	35	47	52	47
Machinery and equipment	71	56	48	50	50	30	30	47	52	46
Air- and spacecraft	64	56	48	50	50	30	30	47	50	45
Automotive industry and other transport	64	56	48	50	50	30	30	47	50	45
IT and electronics	71	56	48	50	33	30	30	45	52	45
Apparel, textiles, and footwear	64	56	48	50	33	30	30	45	50	44
Food and beverages	64	56	48	50	33	30	30	45	50	44
Other manufacturing	64	56	48	50	33	30	30	45	50	44
Biotechnology, pharmaceuticals, and medical products	57	56	48	50	33	30	30	42	50	43
Agriculture and fishing	64	39	30	13	33	32	30	42	33	36
Tourism and hospitality	50	33	35	38	33	24	25	37	33	33
Extractive industries	29	39	26	25	33	24	20	32	29	28
Transport and logistics services	43	33	22	13	33	24	20	29	29	27
Education and health	50	28	22	13	50	19	15	32	27	26
IT services	50	39	22	13	17	19	15	26	31	26
Financial services	29	39	26	13	17	19	15	21	31	25
Power, utilities, and telecommunications	36	28	22	13	50	19	15	29	25	25
Renewable energy	29	33	26	13	33	19	15	26	27	25
Business services	43	28	26	13	17	16	15	24	27	24
Entertainment	43	28	22	13	17	19	15	24	27	24
Recycling	29	28	22	13	17	22	15	24	25	23
Trade and retail	29	33	22	13	17	19	15	21	27	23
Total (countries with tax holidays in at least one sector)	71	61	48	50	50	41	40	55	52	51

Median duration of tax holidays by sector and region, years

	East Asia and Pacific	Europe and Central Asia	Latin America and the Caribbean	Middle East and North Africa	South Asia	Sub-Saharan Africa	Low-income	Lower-middle-income	Upper-middle-income	Total
Air- and spacecraft	10.0	6.0	15.0	10.0	5.0	10.0	8.5	9.5	10.0	10.0
Apparel, textiles, and footwear	9.0	6.0	15.0	10.0	7.5	10.0	8.5	9.0	10.0	10.0
Automotive industry and other transport	9.0	6.0	15.0	10.0	5.0	10.0	8.5	8.5	10.0	10.0
Biotechnology, pharmaceuticals, and medical products	9.0	6.0	15.0	10.0	7.5	10.0	8.5	9.0	10.0	10.0
Business services	9.0	5.0	12.0	10.0	10.0	10.0	10.0	10.0	9.0	10.0
Construction and building materials	8.5	6.0	15.0	10.0	10.0	10.0	7.0	10.0	10.0	10.0
Financial services	9.0	5.0	12.0	10.0	10.0	10.0	10.0	10.0	9.0	10.0
Food and beverages	9.0	6.0	15.0	10.0	7.5	10.0	8.5	9.0	10.0	10.0
IT and electronics	8.5	6.0	15.0	10.0	7.5	10.0	8.5	9.0	10.0	10.0
Machinery and equipment	8.5	6.0	15.0	10.0	5.0	10.0	8.5	8.5	10.0	10.0
Other manufacturing	9.0	6.0	15.0	10.0	7.5	10.0	8.5	9.0	10.0	10.0
Power, utilities, and telecommunications	10.0	5.0	9.0	10.0	10.0	10.0	10.0	10.0	8.5	10.0
Tourism and hospitality	8.0	6.5	10.0	10.0	6.5	10.0	5.0	7.5	10.0	10.0

table continues next page

TABLE 3A.2   Global Use of Tax Holidays, 2015 (continued)

	East Asia and Pacific	Europe and Central Asia	Latin America and the Caribbean	Middle East and North Africa	South Asia	Sub-Saharan Africa	Low-income	Lower-middle-income	Upper-middle-income	Total
Trade and retail	9.0	6.5	9.0	10.0	10.0	10.0	10.0	10.0	9.0	10.0
Transport and logistics services	9.5	6.5	9.0	10.0	7.5	10.0	7.5	10.0	9.5	10.0
Extractive industries	10.0	5.0	12.0	10.0	8.5	10.0	7.5	10.0	8.5	9.5
Recycling	9.0	5.0	9.0	10.0	10.0	10.0	10.0	10.0	8.5	9.5
Renewable energy	9.0	5.0	12.0	10.0	7.5	10.0	10.0	7.5	9.0	9.5
Entertainment	8.5	5.0	9.0	10.0	10.0	10.0	10.0	10.0	8.0	9.0
Agriculture and fishing	9.0	5.0	15.0	10.0	7.5	8.5	6.0	9.5	8.5	8.5
Education and health	8.0	5.0	9.0	10.0	5.0	10.0	10.0	7.0	8.0	8.5
IT services	8.0	5.0	9.0	10.0	10.0	10.0	10.0	9.0	8.0	8.5
Total	9.0	5.0	15.0	10.0	10.0	10.0	10.0	10.0	10.0	10.0
Prevalence of conditions for getting the tax holiday by type, percent										
Conditional on location (province or SEZ)	92	68	69	100	91	72	57	83	78	77
Conditional on exporting or selling to exporters	40	16	25	81	30	24	38	49	33	30
Subject to other conditions (for example, R&D, use of advanced machinery)	65	24	32	48	34	38	24	40	23	40

Source: Developing Country Tax Incentives Database.
Note: IT = information technology; R&D = research and development; SEZ = special economic zone.

TABLE 3A.3   Global Use of Preferential Tax Rates, 2015

	East Asia and Pacific	Europe and Central Asia	Latin America and the Caribbean	Middle East and North Africa	South Asia	Sub-Saharan Africa	Low-income	Lower-middle-income	Upper-middle-income	Total
Number of countries covered in database	15	18	23	8	6	37	20	39	48	107
Prevalence of preferential rates by sector and region (share of countries offering concessions in a given sector, percent)										
Food and beverages	40	33	22	25	67	27	25	46	21	31
IT and electronics	33	39	22	25	67	27	25	46	21	31
Air- and spacecraft	33	33	22	25	67	27	25	44	21	30
Automotive industry and other transport	33	33	22	25	67	27	25	44	21	30
Biotechnology, pharmaceuticals, and medical products	33	33	22	25	67	27	25	44	21	30
Machinery and equipment	33	33	22	25	67	27	25	44	21	30
Construction and building materials	40	33	22	13	50	27	25	38	23	29
Other manufacturing	33	33	22	25	50	27	25	41	21	29
Apparel, textiles, and footwear	27	33	22	25	50	27	25	38	21	28
Agriculture and fishing	33	33	13	0	67	14	20	31	15	21
Power, utilities, and telecommunications	27	28	17	0	50	19	20	28	17	21
Tourism and hospitality	27	28	17	13	50	16	20	28	17	21
Education and health	20	28	17	13	50	16	20	23	19	21

table continues next page

TABLE 3A.3 **Global Use of Preferential Tax Rates, 2015 (continued)**

	East Asia and Pacific	Europe and Central Asia	Latin America and the Caribbean	Middle East and North Africa	South Asia	Sub-Saharan Africa	Low-income	Lower-middle-income	Upper-middle-income	Total
Financial services	27	28	17	0	33	19	20	26	17	21
IT services	33	28	17	0	50	14	15	26	19	21
Transport and logistics services	20	28	17	13	50	16	20	23	19	21
Entertainment	27	28	17	0	50	14	15	23	19	20
Extractive industries	13	22	13	13	50	22	30	23	13	20
Recycling	20	28	17	0	50	16	20	23	17	20
Renewable energy	20	28	17	0	50	16	20	23	17	20
Business services	20	28	17	0	50	14	15	23	17	19
Trade and retail	13	28	17	0	50	14	15	21	17	18
Total	60	39	26	38	67	38	40	56	27	40

Median preferential margin (standard CIT rate—preferential rate by sector and region, percent)

	East Asia and Pacific	Europe and Central Asia	Latin America and the Caribbean	Middle East and North Africa	South Asia	Sub-Saharan Africa	Low-income	Lower-middle-income	Upper-middle-income	Total
Air- and spacecraft	16.0	10.0	25.0	18.0	16.0	13.5	11.0	15.0	15.0	15.0
Apparel, textiles, and footwear	14.5	10.0	25.0	18.0	13.0	13.5	11.0	15.0	15.0	15.0
Automotive industry and other transport	16.0	10.0	25.0	18.0	16.0	13.5	11.0	15.0	15.0	15.0
Biotechnology, pharmaceuticals, and medical products	16.0	10.0	25.0	18.0	16.0	13.5	11.0	15.0	15.0	15.0
Machinery and equipment	15.5	10.0	24.5	0.0	15.0	12.0	11.5	15.5	12.5	15.0
Construction and building materials	14.5	10.0	25.0	18.0	16.0	13.5	11.0	15.0	15.0	15.0
Other manufacturing	16.0	10.0	25.0	18.0	16.0	13.5	11.0	15.0	15.0	15.0
Apparel, textiles, and footwear	16.0	10.0	25.0	18.0	16.0	13.5	11.0	15.0	15.0	15.0
Agriculture and fishing	16.0	10.0	25.0	18.0	15.0	13.5	12.0	15.0	15.0	15.0
Power, utilities, and telecommunications	16.5	10.0	24.5	0.0	10.0	15.0	11.5	25.0	12.5	15.0
Construction and building materials	12.0	10.0	25.0	15.0	13.0	13.5	11.0	15.0	15.0	13.0
Entertainment	15.5	10.0	24.5	0.0	13.0	12.0	12.0	13.0	15.0	13.0
Transport and logistics services	16.0	10.0	24.5	15.0	13.0	13.5	11.5	13.0	15.0	13.0
Business services	16.0	10.0	24.5	0.0	13.0	12.0	12.0	13.0	12.5	12.5
IT services	16.0	10.0	24.5	0.0	13.0	12.0	11.5	18.0	10.0	12.5
Agriculture and fishing	13.0	9.5	26.0	0.0	13.0	11.0	12.0	13.0	10.0	12.0
Education and health	12.0	10.0	24.5	12.0	13.0	12.0	12.0	13.0	12.0	12.0
Extractive industries	22.5	9.5	26.0	12.0	13.0	11.0	11.0	15.0	15.0	12.0
Recycling	16.0	10.0	24.5	0.0	13.0	12.0	12.0	13.0	12.5	12.0
Renewable energy	16.0	10.0	24.5	0.0	13.0	12.0	12.0	13.0	12.5	12.0
Tourism and hospitality	14.5	10.0	24.5	12.0	13.0	12.0	12.0	13.0	16.0	12.0
Trade and retail	17.0	10.0	24.5	0.0	13.0	12.0	12.0	13.0	12.5	12.0
Total	16.0	10.0	25.0	15.0	13.0	12.0	12.0	15.0	15.0	13.0

Prevalence of conditions for getting the tax allowance by type, percent

	East Asia and Pacific	Europe and Central Asia	Latin America and the Caribbean	Middle East and North Africa	South Asia	Sub-Saharan Africa	Low-income	Lower-middle-income	Upper-middle-income	Total
Conditional on location (province or SEZ)	53	31	54	95	43	41	54	34	57	45
Conditional on exporting or selling to exporters	34	18	9	95	56	35	44	47	5	32
Subject to other conditions (for example, R&D, use of advanced machinery)	46	10	23	14	67	81	67	47	35	46

Source: Developing Country Tax Incentives Database.
Note: CIT = corporate income tax; IT = information technology; R&D = research and development; SEZ = special economic zone.

TABLE 3A.4   Global Use of Tax Allowances and Credits, 2015

	East Asia and Pacific	Europe and Central Asia	Latin America and the Caribbean	Middle East and North Africa	South Asia	Sub-Saharan Africa	Low-income	Lower-middle-income	Upper-middle-income	Total
Number of countries covered in database	15	18	23	8	6	37	20	39	48	107
Prevalence of tax allowances by sector and region (share of countries offering tax allowance in a given sector, percent)										
Machinery and equipment	20	11	4	13	17	14	20	10	10	12
Apparel, textiles, and footwear	20	11	4	13	0	14	20	10	8	11
Automotive industry and other transport	13	11	4	13	0	14	20	8	8	10
Biotechnology, pharmaceuticals, and medical products	20	11	4	13	0	11	20	10	6	10
Construction and building materials	20	11	4	13	0	11	20	8	8	10
Food and beverages	20	11	4	13	0	11	20	10	6	10
IT and electronics	13	11	4	13	0	14	20	8	8	10
Air- and spacecraft	13	11	4	13	0	11	20	8	6	9
Other manufacturing	13	11	4	13	0	11	20	8	6	9
Tourism and hospitality	13	11	0	13	0	14	20	8	6	9
Renewable energy	13	11	4	13	0	8	15	5	8	8
Education and health	13	11	0	13	0	8	10	5	8	7
Entertainment	13	11	0	13	0	8	5	8	8	7
Power, utilities, and telecommunications	13	11	4	13	0	5	10	5	8	7
Agriculture and fishing	13	11	0	13	0	5	10	5	6	7
IT services	20	11	0	13	0	3	5	5	8	7
Recycling	13	11	0	13	0	5	10	5	6	7
Trade and retail	20	11	0	13	0	3	5	8	6	7
Transport and logistics services	13	11	0	13	0	5	10	5	6	7
Business services	13	11	0	13	0	3	5	5	6	6
Financial services	13	11	0	13	0	3	5	5	6	6
Extractive industries	13	11	0	0	0	3	5	3	6	5
Total	33	11	9	13	17	16	25	13	15	16
Prevalence of conditions for getting the tax allowance by type, percent										
Conditional on location (province or SEZ)	20	0	18	100	100	76	58	61	19	44
Conditional on exporting or selling to exporters	14	0	100	100	100	60	58	7	16	41
Subject to other conditions (for example, R&D, use of advanced machinery)	96	100	100	0	100	84	100	95	99	83

Source: Developing Country Tax Incentives Database.
Note: IT = information technology; R&D = research and development; SEZ = special economic zone.

TABLE 3A.5   **Changes in Tax Incentives, 2009–15**

	East Asia and Pacific	Europe and Central Asia	Latin America and the Caribbean	Middle East and North Africa	South Asia	Sub-Saharan Africa	Low-income	Lower-middle-income	Upper-middle-income	Total
Number of countries covered in database	14	18	23	8	6	34	18	37	48	103
Share of countries introducing new tax incentives between 2009 and 2015 or making existing incentives more generous, percent										
Agriculture and fishing	36	33	22	25	17	44	28	32	35	33
Air- and spacecraft	36	39	22	25	17	35	22	30	35	31
Apparel, textiles, and footwear	36	39	22	25	17	32	17	30	35	30
Automotive industry and other transport	36	39	22	25	17	32	17	30	35	30
Biotechnology, pharmaceuticals, and medical products	36	39	22	25	17	32	17	30	35	30
Business services	36	33	30	50	17	35	22	30	42	34
Construction and building materials	36	39	22	25	17	32	17	30	35	30
Education and health	36	33	26	50	17	41	22	32	42	35
Entertainment	36	33	30	50	17	44	22	35	44	37
Extractive industries	36	33	22	13	17	32	28	32	25	28
Financial services	36	33	26	38	17	35	22	24	42	32
Food and beverages	36	39	22	25	17	32	17	30	35	30
IT services	36	39	26	50	0	38	22	30	42	34
IT and electronics	36	39	22	25	17	32	17	30	35	30
Machinery and equipment	36	39	22	25	17	32	17	30	35	30
Other manufacturing	36	39	22	25	17	32	17	30	35	30
Power, utilities, and telecommunications	36	33	26	38	0	38	17	30	40	32
Recycling	36	33	26	50	17	41	22	35	40	35
Renewable energy	36	33	26	50	17	38	22	32	40	34
Tourism and hospitality	36	39	26	50	17	41	22	35	42	36
Trade and retail	36	33	26	50	17	35	22	32	38	33
Transport and logistics services	36	33	26	50	17	38	17	32	42	34
Total (countries with more generous incentives in at least one sector)	36	39	35	50	17	65	44	43	48	46
Share of countries removing tax incentives between 2009 and 2015 or making them less generous, percent										
Air- and spacecraft	7	22	17	38	33	12	17	14	21	17
Apparel, textiles, and footwear	0	17	17	38	33	12	17	11	19	16
Automotive industry and other transport	7	17	17	38	33	15	17	14	21	17
Biotechnology, pharmaceuticals, and medical products	0	17	17	38	33	12	17	11	19	16
Business services	0	17	17	38	33	12	17	11	19	16
Construction and building materials	7	17	9	13	33	12	17	11	13	13
Financial services	0	17	17	25	33	12	17	8	19	15
Food and beverages	7	17	9	13	33	12	17	11	13	13
IT and electronics	0	17	9	13	33	12	17	8	13	12
Machinery and equipment	0	17	17	38	33	15	22	8	21	17
Other manufacturing	0	17	9	13	17	12	17	8	10	11

table continues next page

TABLE 3A.5   **Changes in Tax Incentives, 2009–15 (continued)**

	East Asia and Pacific	Europe and Central Asia	Latin America and the Caribbean	Middle East and North Africa	South Asia	Sub-Saharan Africa	Low-income	Lower-middle-income	Upper-middle-income	Total
Power, utilities, and telecommunications	0	17	17	38	33	12	17	11	19	16
Tourism and hospitality	7	17	9	13	33	15	17	11	15	14
Trade and retail	0	17	17	38	33	12	17	11	19	16
Transport and logistics services	0	17	17	38	33	12	17	11	19	16
Extractive industries	0	17	17	38	33	12	17	11	19	16
Recycling	0	17	9	13	50	15	17	11	15	14
Renewable energy	0	17	9	13	33	12	17	8	13	12
Entertainment	0	17	4	13	33	12	17	8	10	11
Agriculture and fishing	7	17	13	13	33	12	17	8	17	14
Education and health	0	17	9	13	33	15	17	8	15	13
IT services	7	17	9	13	33	12	17	11	13	13
Total (countries with less generous incentives in at least one sector)	14	22	22	50	50	21	22	16	31	24

Source: Developing Country Tax Incentives Database.
Note: IT = information technology.

TABLE 3A.6   **Regression Results on Tax Incentives and Foreign Firms' Perceptions of Tax Rates as a Business Obstacle**

Variables		(1) Margins	(2) Margins	(3) Margins	(4) Margins	(5) Margins	(6) Margins	(7) Margins
CIT	Corporate income tax rate	**0.0037*****	**0.0036*****	**0.0037*****	**0.0037*****	**0.0036*****	**0.0040*****	**0.0036*****
		(0.0008)	(0.0009)	(0.0009)	(0.0009)	(0.0009)	(0.0010)	(0.0009)
HOLIDAY	1 = Availability of tax holiday in country and sector of operation	**−0.0686*****	**−0.0600*****	**−0.0384***	**−0.0327****	**−0.0608*****	0.0099	−0.0262
		(0.0163)	(0.0172)	(0.0220)	(0.0163)	(0.0167)	(0.0195)	(0.0175)
EXPORTER	1 = Exporting firm (>50% of sales)		**−0.0633*****	−0.0268	**−0.0642*****	**−0.0634*****	**−0.0631*****	**−0.0646*****
			(0.0169)	(0.0201)	(0.0169)	(0.0169)	(0.0186)	(0.0173)
LARGE	1 = Large firm (>50% of sales)		0.0081	0.0069	**0.0332****	0.0081	0.0096	0.0111
			(0.0153)	(0.0151)	(0.0162)	(0.0153)	(0.0160)	(0.0148)
NEW	1 = New firm (10 years or younger)		−0.0175	−0.0169	−0.0175	−0.0184	−0.0157	−0.0172
			(0.0160)	(0.0160)	(0.0161)	(0.0175)	(0.0165)	(0.0159)
LPI	1 = Above median Logistics Performance Index Score		0.0055	0.0038	0.0090	0.0055	**0.0586*****	0.0119
			(0.0181)	(0.0165)	(0.0181)	(0.0181)	(0.0158)	(0.0172)
DB	1 = Above median Doing Business DTF (excl. "paying taxes")		**−0.0322*****	**−0.0291*****	**−0.0295****	**−0.0322*****	**−0.0231***	−0.0104
			(0.0122)	(0.0110)	(0.0123)	(0.0121)	(0.0138)	(0.01435)
	Interaction HOLIDAY*EXPORTER			**−0.0819*****				
				(0.0310)				
	Interaction HOLIDAY*LARGE				**−0.0655*****			
					(0.0204)			

table continues next page

TABLE 3A.6 **Regression Results on Tax Incentives and Foreign Firms' Perceptions of Tax Rates as a Business Obstacle (continued)**

Variables		(1) Margins	(2) Margins	(3) Margins	(4) Margins	(5) Margins	(6) Margins	(7) Margins
	Interaction HOLIDAY*NEW					0.0024 (0.0173)		
	Interaction HOLIDAY*LPI						**−0.1330*** (0.0320)	
	Interaction HOLIDAY*DB							**−0.0700** (0.0333)
Other controls		GDP, GDP per capita						
Fixed effects		Sector, year						
Observations		5,396	5,191	5,191	5,191	5,191	5,191	5,191

Source: Computation based on data from World Bank Developing Country Tax Incentives Database and Enterprise Surveys, the World Bank. The Doing Business variable excludes the tax component of this indicator to avoid collinearity with the tax variables.

Note: The table shows marginal effects from a logit regression linking foreign-owned firms' responses to the World Bank Enterprise Surveys question on how severe a business obstacle tax rates represent for them to the CIT rate, availability of a tax holiday in their sector of operation in the year the survey was taken, and a number of firm- and country-specific control variables. Coefficients can be interpreted as the estimated change in probability of thinking tax rates present a "major" or "very severe" business obstacle given a change in the value of the relevant explanatory variables and holding all other explanatory variables at their mean value. The Doing Business variable, *DB*, measures the "Distance to the Frontier" (DTF) of highest-performing countries, with tax-related components removed to avoid endogeneity issues. The sample contains 5,396 manufacturing and services firms with a foreign ownership share of at least 10 percent, distributed across 81 developing countries with Enterprise Surveys available between 2009 and 2015. The results have a potential selection bias, meaning that the extension to marginal investors warrants caution. Specifically, the set of survey respondents are either firms that have opted to invest despite whatever weakness in the investment environment or, conversely, firms that have invested because of the availability of special tax incentives. Similar selection effects may also be reflected in firm size and export status. Similar results to those for tax holidays can be obtained for the availability of preferential tax rates. Tax allowances and credits are not used widely enough in developing countries to replicate results. The results for tax holidays are also robust to including controls for preferential taxes rate and tax allowances/credits. Standard errors in parentheses, clustered at sector level.

***p<0.01; **p<0.05; *p<0.1. Results at 10 percent or greater significance are shown in bold.

Notes

1. Following James (2009), investment incentives can be defined as "measurable economic advantages that governments provide to specific enterprises or groups of enterprises, with the goal of steering investment into favored sectors or regions, or of influencing the character of such investments. These benefits can be fiscal (as with tax concessions) or non-fiscal (as with grants, loans, or rebates to support business development or enhance competitiveness)." This definition raises two important distinctions: locational incentives (intended to influence the location decision of investors) versus behavioral incentives (intended to influence the character of the investment) and fiscal (through tax concession) versus nonfiscal. This chapter focuses on locational fiscal incentives.

2. Examples include the base erosion and profit sharing (BEPS) process under the umbrella of the OECD and EU rules on state aid. Developing countries have also made some progress in this regard, including regional organizations such as the West African Economic and Monetary Union (WAEMU) and the East African Community (EAC), which adopted a code of conduct for member countries' use of tax incentives.

3. For example, the WAEMU Treaty seeks to reduce distortions to intracommunity trade and mobilize domestic tax revenue. To this end, member countries have agreed on an advanced mechanism for tax coordination that has led to some convergence in members' corporate tax rates. But regional coordination rules allow exemptions for incentives granted under member countries' investment codes, creating what Mansour and Rota-Graziosi (2013) characterize as the "Achilles heel" of the agreement. The same authors present evidence of the proliferation of investment incentives under various legal bases in member countries that have, in fact, undermined the purpose of the tax harmonization mechanism.

4. The database is available on request for research purposes. Interested researchers can contact the author of this chapter, Erik von Uexkull, at jvonuexkull@worldbank.org.

5. The WTO Subsidies and Countervailing Measures Agreement (SCM) prohibits export subsidies for most products and defines measures against such subsidies (for example, requiring companies to export a certain share of production to be eligible for an incentive, as well as requirements to buy local over imported inputs). Certain exceptions apply for low-income countries.

6. The preferential margin refers to the difference between the standard CIT rate and the preferential rate granted as an incentive.

7. For example, one car manufacturer may set up a plant in a country to serve the domestic market while another may do so as part of a global offshoring strategy to export.

8. Incentives conditional on firms' exporting status were removed from these estimations in order to isolate how different types of firms react to the same type of incentives. This would not be a valid conclusion if incentives available only to exporters were left in the database.

9. Andrews, Pritchett, and Woolcock (2017): The Problem Driven Iterative Adaptation approach emphasizes the importance of experimenting, learning, iterating, and adapting in order to address a problem.

10. As the current database includes only information on locational incentives, the evidence for behavioral incentives in investor decisions for developing countries is not explored in this chapter.

Bibliography

Allen, N. J., J. Morisset, N. Pirnia, and L. T. Wells, Jr. 2001. "Using Tax Incentives to Compete for Foreign Investment: Are They Worth the Costs?" Foreign Investment Advisory Service Occasional Paper 15, World Bank, Washington, DC.

Andrews, M., L. Pritchett, and M. Woolcock. 2017. *Building State Capability: Evidence, Analysis, Action.* Oxford, U.K.: Oxford University Press.

Bellak, C., M. Leibrecht, and J. P. Damijan. 2009. "Infrastructure Endowment and Corporate Income Taxes as Determinants of Foreign Direct Investment in Central and Eastern European Countries." *The World Economy* 32 (2): 267–90.

Bénassy-Quéré, A., L. Fontagne, and A. Lahreche-Revil. 2005. "How Does FDI React to Corporate Taxation?" *International Tax and Public Finance* 12 (5): 583–603.

Desai, M. H., C. Fritz Foley, and J. R. Hines, Jr. 2006. "Taxation and Multinational Activity: New Evidence, New Interpretations." *Survey of Current Business* 86 (2): 16–22.

Djankoff, S., T. Ganser, C. McLiesh, R. Ramalho, and A. Schleifer. 2010. "The Effect of Corporate Taxes on Investment and Entrepreneurship." *American Economic Journal: Macroeconomics* 2 (3): 31–64.

Dunning, J. H. 1980. "Toward an Eclectic Theory of International Production: Some Empirical Tests." *Journal of International Business Studies* 11 (1): 9–31.

Dunning, J. H. 1993. *Multinational Enterprises and the Global Economy.* Addison Wesley.

Egger, P. H., S. Loretz, M. Pfaffermayr, and H. Winner. 2008. "Bilateral Effective Tax Rates and Foreign Direct Investment." Oxford University Centre for Business Taxation Working Papers 0802. Oxford, UK.

Freund, C., and T. H. Moran. 2017. "Multinational Investors as Export Superstars: How Emerging-Market Governments Can Reshape Comparative Advantage." Working Paper 17-1, Peterson Institute for International Economics, Washington, DC.

Hebous, S., M. Ruf, and A. Weichenrieder. 2010. "The Effects of Taxation on the Location Decision of Multinational Firms: M&A vs. Greenfield Investments." CESifo Working Paper 3076. Munich, Germany.

Heckemeyer, J., and M. Overesch. 2013. "Multinationals' Profit Response to Tax Differentials: Effect Size and Shifting Channels." ZEW Discussion Paper 13-045, Zentrum für Europäische Wirtschaftsforschung, Mannheim.

Hunady, J., and M. Orviska. 2014. "Determinants of Foreign Direct Investment in EU Countries— Do Corporate Taxes Really Matter?" *Procedia Economics and Finance* 12: 243–50.

IMF (International Monetary Fund), OECD (Organisation for Economic Co-operation and Development), UN (United Nations), and World Bank. 2015. "Options for Low Income Countries' Effective and Efficient Use of Tax Incentives for Investment." In *International Monetary Fund Report to the G-20 Development Working Group.*

James, S. 2009. "Tax and Non-Tax Incentives and Investments: Evidence and Policy Implications." Foreign Investment Advisory Service, World Bank, Washington, DC.

———. 2013. "Tax and Non-Tax Incentives and Investments: Evidence and Policy Implications." Investment Climate Advisory Services, World Bank, Washington, DC.

James, S., and S. Van Parys. 2010. "The Effectiveness of Tax Incentives in Attracting Investment: Panel Data Evidence from the CFA Franc Zone." *International Tax and Public Finance* 17 (4): 400–29.

Kinda, T. 2010. "Investment Climate and FDI in Developing Countries: Firm-Level Evidence." *World Development* 38 (4): 498–513.

Klemm, A., and S. Van Parys. 2012. "Empirical Evidence on the Effects of Tax Incentives." *International Tax and Public Finance* 19 (3): 393–423.

Mansour, M., and G. Rota-Graziosi. 2013. "Tax Coordination, Tax Competition, and Revenue Mobilization in the West African Economic and Monetary Union." IMF Working Paper 13/163, International Monetary Fund, Washington, DC.

OECD (Organisation for Economic Co-operation and Development). 1998. "Harmful Tax Competition: An Emerging Global Issue." OECD, Paris.

Overesch, M., and G. Wamser. 2008. "Who Cares about Corporate Taxation? Asymmetric Tax Effects on Outbound FDI." IFO Working Papers 59, IFO Institute for Economic Research, University of Munich.

UNCTAD (United Nations Conference on Trade and Development). 2015. *World Investment Report: Reforming International Investment Governance.* Geneva: UNCTAD.

UNIDO (United Nations Industrial Development Organization). 2011. *Africa Investor Report: Towards Evidence-Based Investment Promotion Strategies.* Geneva: UNIDO.

Van Parys, S. 2012. "The Effectiveness of Tax Incentives in Attracting Investment: Evidence from Developing Countries." *Reflets et perspectives de la vie économique* 2012/3: 129–41.

Villela, L., A. Lemgruber, and M. Jorratt. 2010. "Tax Expenditure Budgets: Concepts and Challenges for Implementation." IDB Working Paper 131, Inter-American Development Bank, Washington, DC.

World Bank. 2016a. "Sri Lanka: Moving toward a New Investment Incentives Framework." Mimeo, World Bank, Washington, DC.

———. 2016b. "Examen du régime d'incitations à l'investissement en République de Côte d'Ivoire." Mimeo, World Bank, Washington, DC.

Zolt, E. M. 2013. "Tax Incentives and Tax Base Protection Issues." Papers on Selected Topics in Protecting the Tax Base of Developing Countries Draft Paper 3, United Nations, New York, NY.

Outward FDI from Developing Countries | 4

Jose Ramon Perea and Matthew Stephenson

Outward foreign direct investment (OFDI) by firms from developing countries[1] has grown dramatically in recent years, accounting for nearly one-fifth of global foreign direct investment (FDI) flows in 2015, up from just 4 percent in 1995. While larger developing countries, especially the BRICS (Brazil, the Russian Federation, India, China, and South Africa), are driving this phenomenon, many developing countries are now engaged in OFDI, regardless of their size or level of development. The increasing importance of such OFDI calls for a better understanding of it and its implications. OFDI has economic effects not only in recipient economies, as research shows, but also in source economies ("home effects"). Growing OFDI may thus require that developing country governments adopt new investment policy reforms and investment promotion efforts to maximize the benefits for both the home economy and its firms.

This chapter describes the rise of OFDI by developing country firms, its development impact, and policy implications. It draws on several global data sources to assess changes over time in the investment decisions of developing country multinational corporations (MNCs). The chapter also looks at findings from a gravity model on FDI flows and qualitative evidence on developing country MNC investments across several industries—including pharmaceuticals, wind turbines, household appliances, and automobiles.

The analysis answers three questions, whose answers have important implications for policy makers, firms, and development practitioners:

1. What are the salient features of developing country OFDI, especially with respect to trends, destinations, sectors, and entry modes?
2. Does OFDI benefit the source economy, and if it does, what are the facilitating or mediating factors?
3. What role does OFDI-related policy play and what further research is needed to better understand and shape it?

Several key findings emerge:

OFDI from developing countries has boomed in recent years, leading to a greater relative share of total OFDI, across both flows and stocks. In absolute terms, BRICS investors are the key drivers of developing country OFDI, accounting for 62 percent of total developing country OFDI stock in 2015—with China alone accounting for 36 percent.

Developing country governments have moved gradually from restricting to supporting OFDI, although some form of restriction remains in half of all developing countries— especially lower-income countries. In some cases, developing country governments have even begun to provide incentives to target strategic sectors. One reason is the increasing evidence that OFDI can boost innovation and exports in the home economy. However, limited absorptive capacity in developing economies, vis-à-vis developed economies, is a key constraint on positive home effects from outward investment.

These findings suggest several policy considerations. Investment promotion agencies (IPAs) may wish to target not only traditional sources of FDI but also new sources such as developing country OFDI. At the same time, policy makers may wish to review their countries' OFDI regulatory frameworks, given that restrictions may be undermining the positive effects on the home economy. Policy makers may also wish to consider measures that expand firm-level and economy-level absorptive capacity to realize the full positive effects of OFDI in home economies. More policy-oriented research is clearly needed to help developing country officials better tailor and target future policy interventions.

The Rise of Developing Country OFDI

The rise of developing country OFDI has occurred in three "waves" (Gammeltoft 2008). The first, during the 1960s and 1970s, saw import-substitution industrialization

restrict the entry of FDI and the potential emergence of OFDI, as developing countries aimed to nurture domestic industries and keep capital at home (Cuervo-Cazurra 2008; Gammeltoft, Barnard, and Madhok 2010). Protectionist measures reduced incentives for domestic firms to become internationally competitive, limiting their ability to expand outside their home markets. The small amount of developing country OFDI that did take place generally went to other developing countries in the same region and was mostly a combination of natural resource–seeking[2] (as developing countries sought primary inputs they lacked) and market-seeking (as a few developing countries sought to expand sales in culturally and geographically close neighbors) (Dunning, Kim, and Park 2008; Ramamurti 2009; Wells 2009).

The second wave, during the 1980s and 1990s, saw investment patterns shift significantly. Structural reforms and export-oriented industrialization opened developing countries to FDI, with countries seeking to attract the foreign capital, knowledge, and skills needed to make their exports competitive. With trade and investment liberalization progressing rapidly, developing country OFDI also began to grow. About two-thirds of OFDI flows went to developed economies, while the remaining third went to developing countries, mostly neighbors (Aykut and Ratha 2004). It became increasingly efficiency-seeking, as developing countries began to plug into global value chains (GVCs) by locating some manufacturing activities in lower-cost locations and integrating into international production networks (UNCTAD 2013).

The third wave, from the early 2000s to the present, is witnessing a fresh rise in developing country OFDI, across both flows and stocks. While OFDI from both developed and developing economies has been dynamic, the relative share of developing country OFDI flows in total FDI (figure 4.1) surged from 4 percent in 1995 to 27 percent in 2014, equivalent to $315 billion. Developing country OFDI stocks (figure 4.2) have also increased as a share of total FDI stocks, although at a slower pace. Between 1995 and

FIGURE 4.1 **Developing Country OFDI Flows**

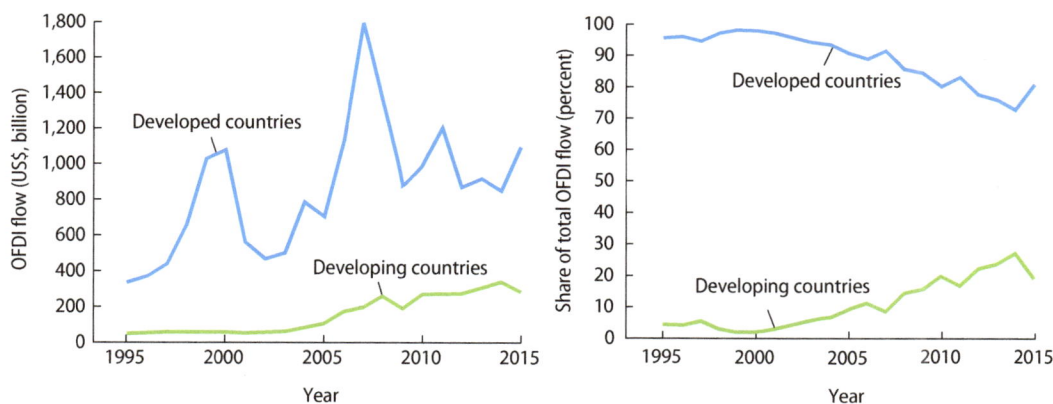

Source: Computation based on United Nations Conference on Trade and Development (UNCTAD).
Note: OFDI = outward foreign direct investment.

FIGURE 4.2 **Developing Country OFDI Stocks**

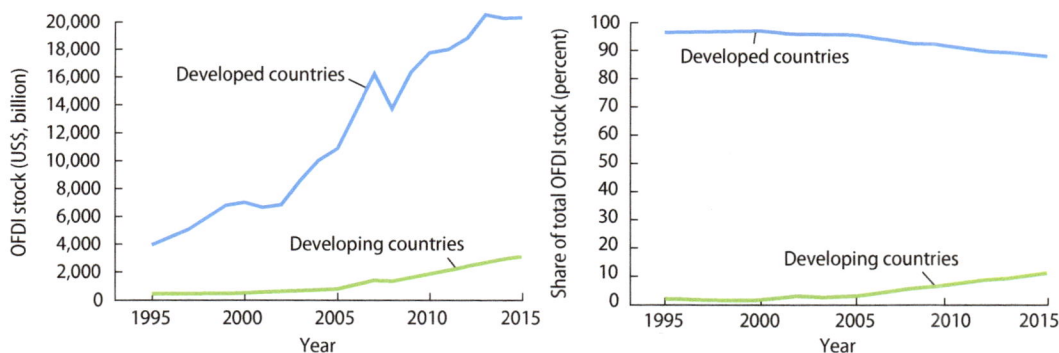

Source: Computation based on UNCTAD.
Note: OFDI = outward foreign direct investment.

2015, developing countries tripled their share in global FDI stocks, increasing from 4 percent to 12 percent, equal to $2.8 trillion.

Both domestic policy choices in developing countries and global economic conditions helped shape these changes in the investment landscape. In terms of domestic policy, liberalization and deregulation reforms embraced in the second wave (the 1980s–90s) raised competitive pressures in many developing countries, eventually "pushing" firms out of their home markets (Sauvant 2008). At the same time, firms in Singapore and other high-growth economies embraced OFDI in the late 1990s as a development strategy to "achieve efficiency in

resource allocation and diversify risks from economic shocks in any one region" (Lee, Lee, and Yeo 2016). Firms in other developing countries soon followed, with OFDI increasingly seen as a means to access markets, capital, technology, and knowledge in international markets—and thus boost national competitiveness (Luo, Xu, and Han 2010). Supportive policy measures, in the form of generous financing and incentives, helped.

Global economic conditions also "pulled" developing market firms into OFDI. First, rapid and sustained growth in much of the developing world during this decade facilitated firms to grow and prosper and, consequently, internationalize. Second, the boom in commodity prices during the same decade gave commodity exporters in the developing world large windfalls, creating substantial liquidity that they used in part to finance OFDI.

Zooming In: Who, Where, What, and How

This section looks at trends in OFDI by developing country firms as revealed by various global datasets (UNCTAD, fDi Markets, and Thomson Reuters) and identifies the main geographic origins and destinations of these flows, principal modes of entry (greenfield versus mergers and acquisitions [M&A]), and sectoral distribution, among other patterns.

Who? Sources of Developing Country OFDI

East Asia and Pacific has gradually become the major source of OFDI among developing regions (figure 4.3). It generated 22 percent of total OFDI from developing country firms during 2000–04, surging to 49 percent in 2010–15.[3] In contrast, Europe and Central Asia, and Latin America and the Caribbean have reduced their relative shares over time. Latin America and the Caribbean held a share of 37 percent of developing country OFDI during the second half of the 1990s, falling to 15 percent during 2010–15.[4] And Europe and Central Asia's share fell to 25 percent in 2010–15 from a peak of 36 percent in 2000–04.[5] Finally, outward flows from Sub-Saharan Africa, the Middle East and North Africa, and South Asia maintained more marginal shares across all periods.

As noted earlier, the BRICS are a key source of developing country OFDI (figure 4.4). These five countries generated 62 percent of such OFDI in 1995, a share that remained essentially unchanged in 2015. These numbers, however, largely align with other aspects of these countries' participation in the global economy.[6] Aside from the BRICS, other large or relatively higher-income developing countries (for example, Chile, Malaysia, and Mexico) are also top investors among developing countries. In fact, when classified across income thresholds (annex 4A), developing country OFDI is driven largely by higher-income developing countries. During 1995–99, 78.8 percent of FDI flows from the developing world originated in upper-middle-income countries, with 13.8 percent from developing high-income countries, 7.1 percent from lower-middle-income, and only 0.3 percent from low-income countries. Such relative shares did not change much during 2010–15 when

FIGURE 4.3   **East Asia and Pacific Leads in Developing Country OFDI**

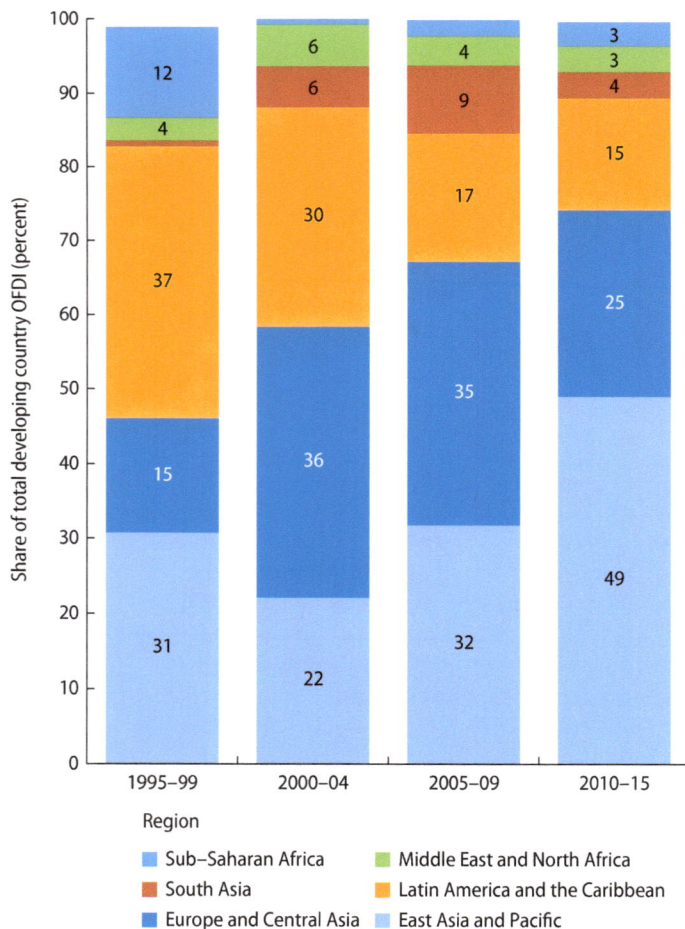

Source: Calculation based on UNCTAD.
Note: OFDI = outward foreign direct investment.

upper-middle-income countries accounted for 79.9 percent of total developing country OFDI stocks, high-income countries for 11 percent, lower-middle-income for 8.7 percent, and low-income countries for 0.3 percent. In this way, upper-middle-income and high-income countries have consistently accounted for the vast majority of developing country OFDI.

China in particular has become the main driver of developing country OFDI, accounting for 36 percent of the total (figure 4.4). When measured across flows, Chinese OFDI sustained a steady upward trend since 2004—moving from 10 percent of total developing country OFDI flows to 49 percent in 2015. China is also the main reason for the rise of East Asia and Pacific as the leading

FIGURE 4.4   Top Developing Country Outward Investors

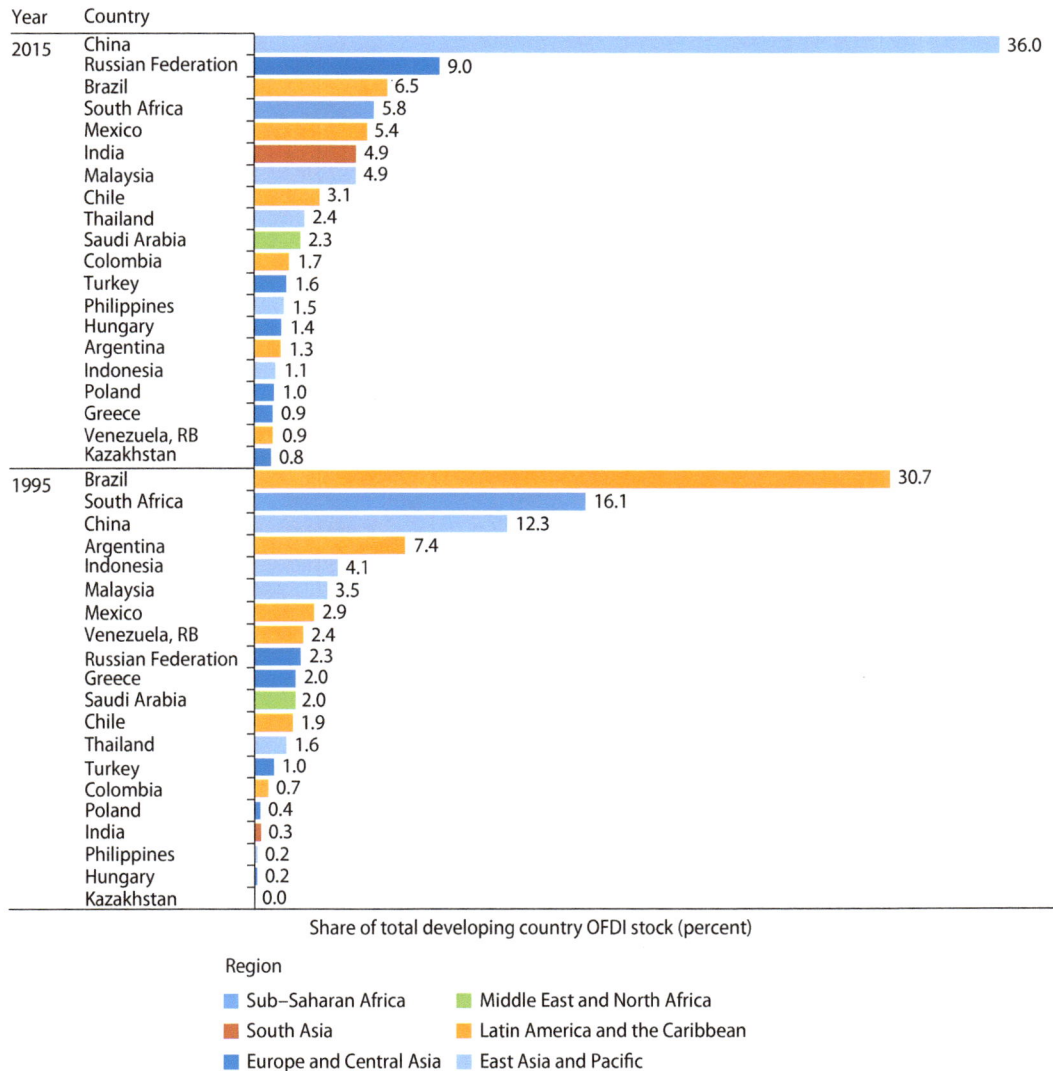

Share of total developing country OFDI stock (percent)

Region

- Sub–Saharan Africa
- Middle East and North Africa
- South Asia
- Latin America and the Caribbean
- Europe and Central Asia
- East Asia and Pacific

Source: Computation based on UNCTAD.
Note: OFDI = outward foreign direct investment.

developing region generating OFDI (figure 4.3). The country has gone from accounting for 40 percent of East Asia and Pacific OFDI flows during 1995–99 to 75 percent in 2010–15. The dynamism of Chinese OFDI reflects a unique institutional and regulatory framework that supports firm internationalization (box 4.1).

A different set of countries emerges if OFDI activity is assessed relative to the size of the national economy. The ratio of OFDI stock to gross domestic product (GDP)[7] (map 4.1) reveals the extent to which

countries are internationalized through OFDI. This ratio shows that developing country OFDI is a relatively recent phenomenon: in 1995, 87 out of 135 developing countries had a positive OFDI stock. Yet virtually all developing countries had very low ratios of OFDI to GDP with only three economies (Botswana, Nigeria, and South Africa, all in Sub-Saharan Africa) having stocks above 10 percent of GDP. A more diverse picture emerges in 2015, with 109 developing countries having positive OFDI stocks and,

BOX 4.1

The Evolving Role of OFDI in China's Economy

OFDI from China accounts for more than a third of all developing country OFDI stock, and the country has been at the vanguard of OFDI policy reform. Trends in Chinese OFDI are remarkable. From 2000 to 2015, its OFDI flows on average more than doubled each year (UNCTADstat) so that, by 2016, it had attained two milestones: OFDI overtook inward FDI for the first time, and Chinese OFDI flows were the second highest in the world after the United States. This meant that China generated the sixth-largest OFDI stock (UNCTAD 2017). Nevertheless, in terms of the ratio of OFDI to GDP, China's OFDI exposure is still below some of the most outwardly invested developing economies in the world (map 4.1 and figure 4.5).

What accounts for this dramatic growth? Chinese OFDI has been driven by both push and pull forces. On the one hand, macroeconomic conditions pushed firms out of the domestic market—initially balance-of-payment surpluses and later domestic overcapacity—making investment abroad a policy priority. On the other hand, key inputs to sustain domestic growth pulled firms abroad—initially securing essential commodities and later procuring knowledge and technology—as China's development strategy sought to move the country from a manufacturing-driven to an innovation-driven economy.

The sector breakdown of Chinese OFDI has, as a result, undergone major transformation. During 2003–05, 65 percent of Chinese OFDI flows targeted the primary sector while 18 percent targeted

the services sector. A decade later, these distributions flipped: during 2013–15, 26 percent of Chinese OFDI flows targeted the primary sector while 47 percent targeted the service sector. This reversal can partly be explained by the evolution in Chinese OFDI motivations, moving from initially natural resource–seeking to increasingly market-seeking, efficiency-seeking, and finally strategic asset–seeking. Chinese firms increasingly see OFDI as a means for opening new markets for excess domestic capacity and for acquiring hard-to-develop capabilities faster and more cheaply than developing these indigenously. The goal is to continue domestic upgrading and increase international competitiveness.

This change in OFDI distribution can also be explained partly by differences in OFDI behavior between state-owned enterprises (SOEs) and privately owned enterprises (POEs), and the increasingly important role of POEs in OFDI. Evidence shows Chinese SOEs are willing to invest in politically risky host economies to acquire assets in line with national priorities (for example, securing natural resources) (Amighini, Rabellotti, and Sanfilippo 2013). In contrast, Chinese POEs behave as private firms do in other countries—seeking to maximize profits and minimize risk—and avoid risky investment climates. Reflecting a growing domestic private sector in China, POEs are becoming increasingly important as drivers of OFDI, contributing to growing market and strategic asset–seeking OFDI in developed economies (Dollar 2016; Lardy 2014). In

box continues next page

The Evolving Role of OFDI in China's Economy (continued)

2006, SOEs held 81 percent of China's OFDI stock, while POEs held only 19 percent; 10 years later, China's OFDI stock was almost evenly divided between SOEs (50.4 percent of nonfinancial assets) and POEs (49.6 percent) (Wang 2017). Looking specifically at Chinese OFDI into the United States (the largest destination market for Chinese OFDI), POEs accounted for nearly 80 percent of OFDI in both 2015 and 2016, even as Chinese OFDI into the United States tripled in this single year (Rosen and Hanemann 2017).

These patterns of Chinese OFDI should be understood in the context of an evolving and increasingly sophisticated OFDI regulatory framework. Between 2001 and 2014, China gradually liberalized OFDI regulations, moving from a restrictive to a supportive framework (Sauvant and Chen 2014). In 2014, the regulatory framework matured to embrace corporate social responsibility when investing abroad, such as the environmental and social impact on host economies. Then, at the end of 2016, the government announced plans to tighten the inspection and supervision of Chinese OFDI, especially when not related to the core business of the investing firms, or in areas with limited economic value for the home economy (for example, OFDI in film studios or sports clubs). This also includes plans for identifying industries in which Chinese SOEs cannot invest (a "negative list"), such as heavily polluting industries (China Daily 2017a). Similar to the changes in 2014, which added a quality dimension to the *way* that Chinese OFDI was carried out, Chinese policy has recently added a quality dimension to the *sectors* to which OFDI is targeted.

This recent regulatory tightening has had a large effect on Chinese OFDI. Chinese mergers and acquisitions (M&A) transactions fell by 20 percent in the first six months of 2017 relative to the same period a year earlier (Hanemann, Lysenko, and Gao 2017). By the middle of 2017, the number of transactions had returned to almost the same level as in the pretightening period, yet the average deal size had fallen dramatically owing to greater scrutiny of large transactions. The value of announced OFDI acquisitions averaged more than US$15 billion a month during

2016 but averaged less than US$8 billion a month during January–June 2017 (Hanemann, Lysenko, and Gao 2017). While POE OFDI had been rising as a share of total OFDI, the tightening in regulations seems to favor SOEs, perhaps because they are better able to navigate the changing political context: in the first half of 2017, there were virtually no large private sector M&A deals, and state-related companies accounted for 60 percent of total deals by value, a reversal of the 2016 pattern (Hanemann, Lysenko, and Gao 2017). While M&A OFDI has fallen in most sectors, OFDI into the primary sector, high-tech industries, and modern services (telecom, media, and computing) has proven most resilient, reflecting the strategic importance of these three areas in China's development strategy.

China's increasing use of OFDI to source advanced knowledge and technology has also generated growing political economy tensions with some developed economies, notably the United States and European Union. To give a sense of these growing pressures, in only the first half of 2016, China invested more in Europe than in the previous three years combined and often targeted cutting-edge technology. This sparked European concerns over the long-term impact on host economies. The lack of market-access reciprocity for investment—with developed economies much more open to Chinese OFDI than vice versa—has prompted calls for a more level playing field. In February 2017, Germany, France, and Italy presented the European Commission with a common position on screening foreign investments, implicitly targeting Chinese OFDI and drawing on practices in Australia, Canada, Japan, and the United States (Grieger 2017). In early 2017 China decided to open more sectors to FDI (for example, automation, digitization, financial services, transportation, and renewable energy) (China Daily 2017b). Then, in August 2017, China started requiring that state groups assess political risks to OFDI before proceeding with any deal (FT 2017). It is too soon to tell whether these measures, coupled with implementation of any potential new screening mechanisms, will alleviate political economy tensions.

MAP 4.1   **More Developing Countries Engage in OFDI**

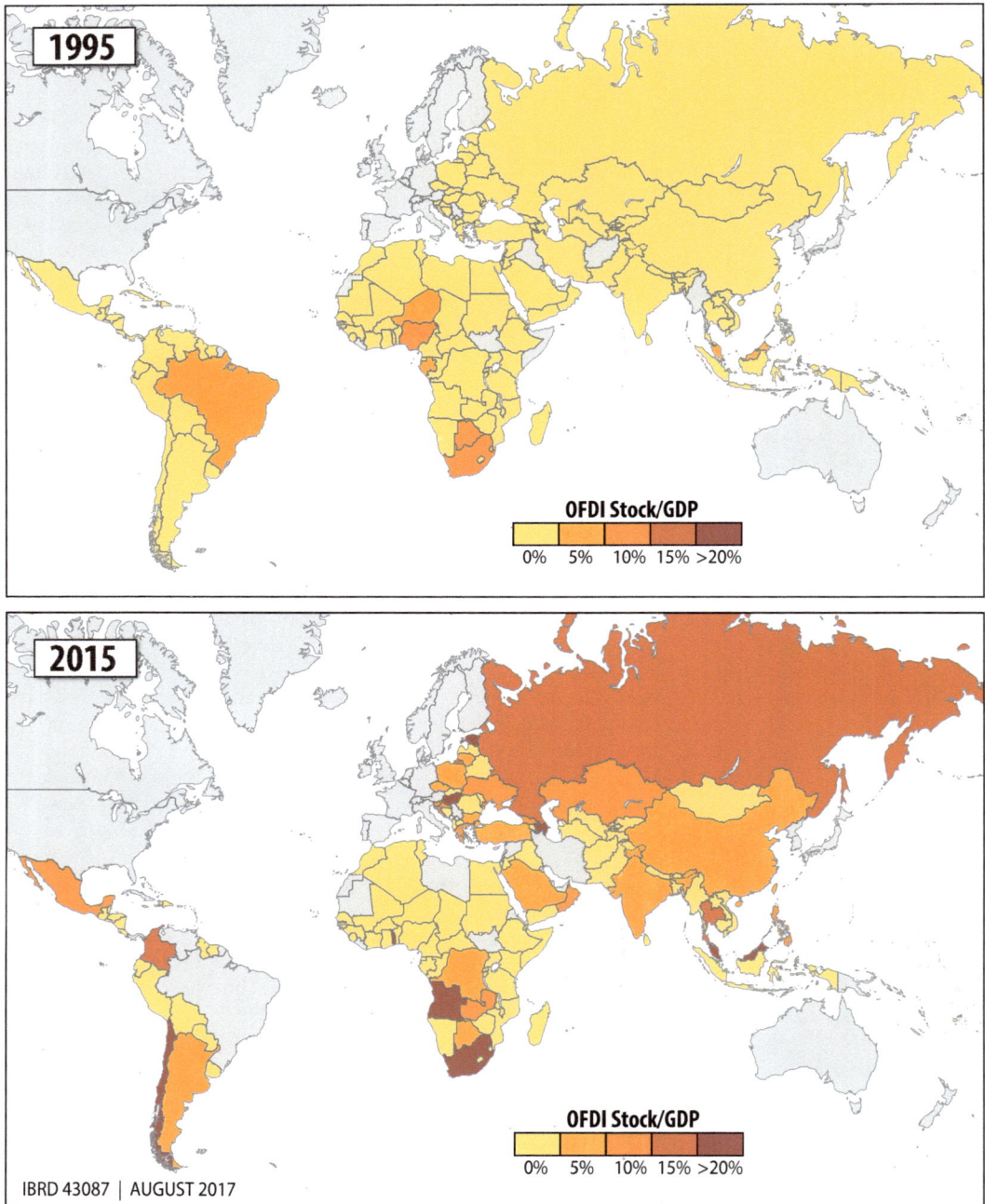

1995

OFDI Stock/GDP

| 0% | 5% | 10% | 15% | >20% |

2015

OFDI Stock/GDP

| 0% | 5% | 10% | 15% | >20% |

IBRD 43087 | AUGUST 2017

Source: Computation based on UNCTAD and World Development Indicators, World Bank.
Note: The five color thresholds correspond to shares of OFDI stock over GDP that are 0–5 percent, 5–10 percent,10–15 percent,15–20 percent, and greater than 20 percent. GDP = gross domestic product; OFDI = outward foreign direct investment.

FIGURE 4.5 **Developing Countries Most Internationalized through OFDI**

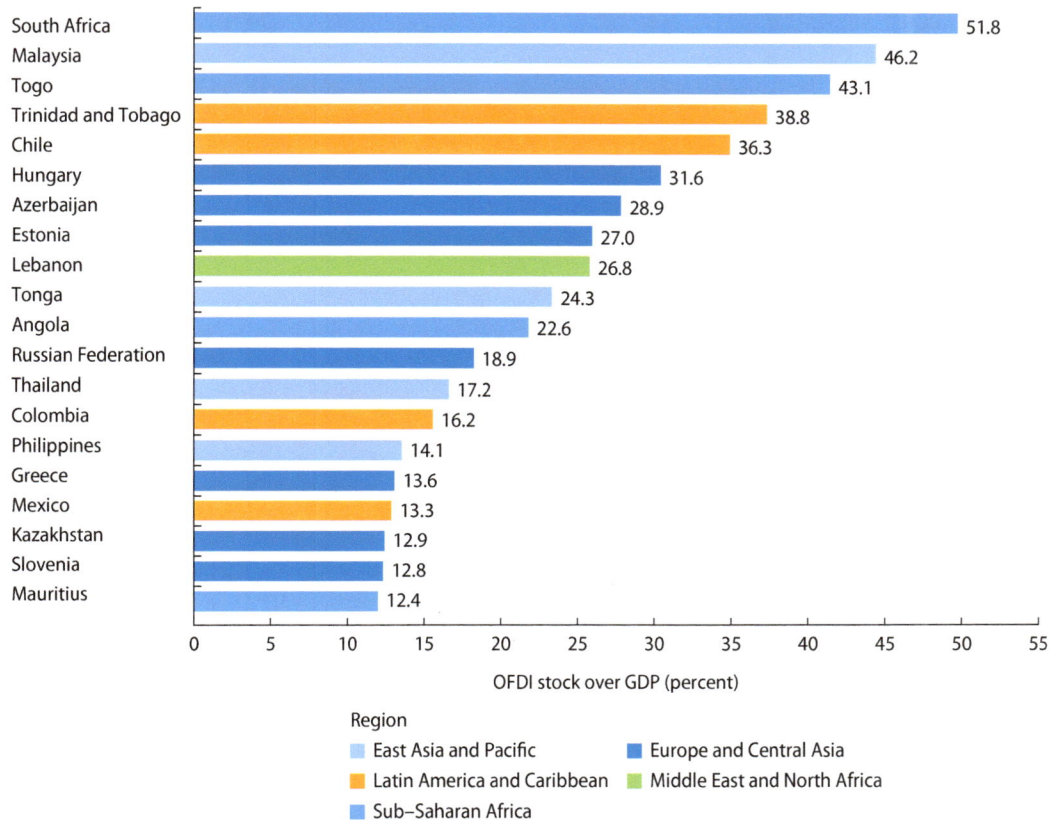

Country	OFDI stock over GDP (percent)
South Africa	51.8
Malaysia	46.2
Togo	43.1
Trinidad and Tobago	38.8
Chile	36.3
Hungary	31.6
Azerbaijan	28.9
Estonia	27.0
Lebanon	26.8
Tonga	24.3
Angola	22.6
Russian Federation	18.9
Thailand	17.2
Colombia	16.2
Philippines	14.1
Greece	13.6
Mexico	13.3
Kazakhstan	12.9
Slovenia	12.8
Mauritius	12.4

OFDI stock over GDP (percent)

Region
- East Asia and Pacific
- Latin America and Caribbean
- Sub–Saharan Africa
- Europe and Central Asia
- Middle East and North Africa

Source: Computation based on UNCTAD and World Development Indicators, World Bank.
Note: GDP = gross domestic product; OFDI = outward foreign direct investment.

more important, with 26 of these countries having an OFDI-to-GDP ratio of 10 percent or greater. The list of countries with the highest values of this ratio (figure 4.5) includes low-, lower-middle-, and upper-middle-income economies, suggesting greater heterogeneity across countries' economic size or development levels. In all, this relative measure reveals a set of economies actively engaged in outward investment that are generally absent from the debate on OFDI, owing to their marginal role in aggregate FDI.

Where? Source–Host FDI Relationships

The rise of OFDI by developing country MNCs has also expanded the number of countries increasingly dependent on this source of external capital. The share of

inward FDI stock from developing countries held by other developing countries (map 4.2)[8] has risen for many economies. In 2001, only 11 developing countries (5 in Sub-Saharan Africa, 5 in Europe and Central Asia, 1 in Latin America and the Caribbean) had half or more of their inward FDI stock owned by other developing countries. In 2012, that number reached 55 countries. Developing countries are a particularly key source of FDI for countries in Sub-Saharan Africa, Europe and Central Asia, and South Asia. With many of these host economies characterized by low economic development,[9] these trends seem to conform with the literature that finds developing country OFDI to be less discouraged by weak institutional and economic environments in host countries (Cuervo-Cazurra 2008; Ma and Van Assche 2011).

MAP 4.2   **Exposure to Developing Country OFDI Rises for Many Developing Host Economies**

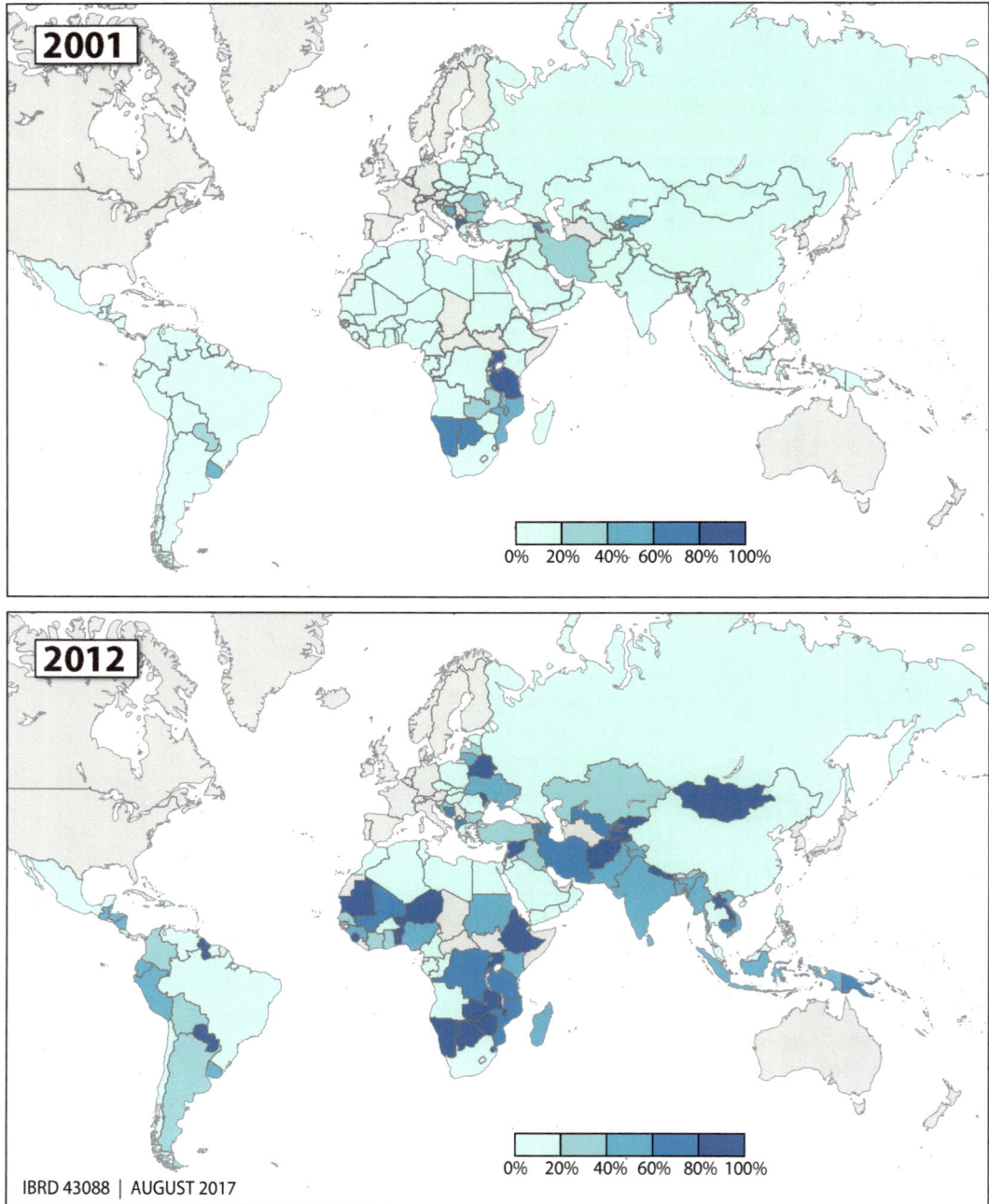

2001

0%   20%   40%   60%   80%   100%

2012

IBRD 43088 | AUGUST 2017

0%   20%   40%   60%   80%   100%

Source: Computation based on UNCTAD.
Note: The five-color thresholds correspond to ratios of inward FDI from developing countries over total inward FDI stocks that are less than 20 percent, 20–40 percent, 40–60 percent, 60–80 percent, and 80–100 percent. OFDI = outward foreign direct investment.

FIGURE 4.6   **The Location of Developing Country OFDI Varies across Regions**

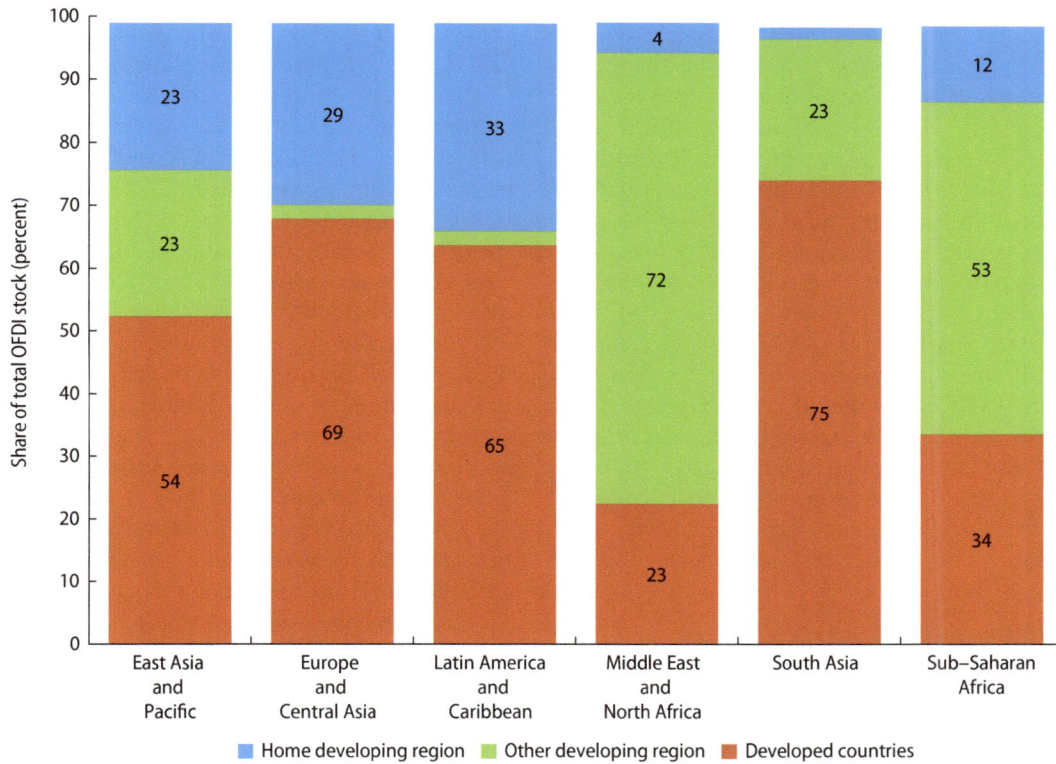

Source: Computation based UNCTAD.
Note: OFDI = outward foreign direct investment.

The geographical distribution of developing country OFDI across regions (figure 4.6) suggests the trade-off that developing country multinationals face when deciding where to locate their investments. For example, OFDI from South Asia, Europe and Central Asia, and Latin America and the Caribbean is relatively concentrated in developed economies. For South Asia, developed economies account for 75 percent of its total 2012 outward stock; for Europe and Central Asia, 69 percent; and for Latin America and the Caribbean, 65 percent. The importance of developed economies as destinations for developing country MNC investments can be attributed to the size and strength of these host markets, a key FDI location determinant (Assunção, Forte, and Teixeira 2011). For Europe and Central Asia

and Latin America and the Caribbean, the share of OFDI remaining in the same region is also relevant. This "regional bias" owes to the preference of such regional MNCs for the lower transaction costs of operating in markets characterized by cultural ties, geographical proximity, or prior trade relations[10] (Aykut and Goldstein 2006). In all, the geographical distribution of developing country OFDI suggests the trade-off that developing country multinationals face when deciding on a location for their subsidiaries—that is, weighing the benefits of investing in close, familiar markets against the cost of weak consumer demand or an inefficient institutional environment.

Is OFDI by developing country firms influenced by this trade-off between market size and strength, and physical and cultural distance? Our econometric analysis (annex 4B) extends the analysis in Gómez-Mera and others (2015), a study that explains the OFDI patterns of four emerging economies (Brazil, India, the Republic of Korea, and South Africa), to a sample of 133 developing countries.[11] Our results show that OFDI by developing country MNCs seeks to balance market attractiveness with the transaction costs associated with distant and unfamiliar markets. On the one hand, measures of host country market size (population, per capita GDP) are significant predictors for the location of OFDI. On the other hand, transaction costs associated with geographical distance and the lack of a shared language or colonial experience between source and host economy limit the prospects of cross-border investments by developing country MNCs.

What and How? Sector and Mode of Entry

The sector distribution suggests an increasingly rich set of investment motivations guiding OFDI patterns. The cumulative OFDI value between 2003 and 2015[12] (annex 4C) is relatively evenly distributed across broad sectors (primary, manufacturing, and services). But service sectors account for a large share of OFDI stock in almost all regions, ranging from 36 percent (Europe and Central Asia) to 41 percent (East Asia and Pacific). Europe and Central Asia and Sub-Saharan Africa also strongly favor extractive industries, which account for about 40 percent of outward stocks. Thus, manufacturing industries[13] tend to be underrepresented in these two regions.

The relatively balanced sectoral distribution suggests that developing country OFDI is increasingly complex. Previous attempts to disentangle OFDI's sector patterns (Gammeltoft 2008) found a particularly high preference for service sectors over manufacturing or natural resources. Such a bias toward services was partly attributed to the wave of privatization of public services

embraced by much of the developing world in previous decades, which attracted FDI into these sectors (Sader 1993). More recently, OFDI into knowledge-intensive industries, both in manufacturing and services (for example, pharmaceuticals, software, and information technology [IT] services) has gained traction (Gammeltoft 2008). OFDI is thus a tool to acquire superior technology and contribute to firms' international competitiveness. All things considered, the rich sectoral distribution of developing country OFDI suggests an equally rich set of investment motivations, with all developing regions participating to some degree in outward natural resource–seeking, efficiency-seeking, market-seeking, and strategic asset–seeking investments.

Based on the number of FDI projects during 2003–15, companies from most developing regions show a slight preference for greenfield FDI rather than for acquisitions.[14] This confirms the same bias found in previous studies (Davies, Desbordes, and Ray 2015; UNCTAD 2015). Yet the pro-greenfield bias is stronger for OFDI from developed economies (figure 4.7): out of 39 industries, OFDI from developed countries accounts for a majority share of greenfield operations in 25 of them, with a median share of 58 percent. On the other hand, developing country OFDI is biased toward greenfield in only 20 industries, with a median share of 50 percent.

The relative preference for M&A in developing country OFDI—when compared to that of advanced economies—is more evident in knowledge-intensive manufacturing industries[15] (figure 4.7): of the nine industries where developing country OFDI shows a pro-M&A difference of 15 percentage points or more (relative to OFDI from developed economies), seven are technology- and knowledge-intensive[16] (automotive components, business machines and equipment, engines, transportation original equipment manufacturer, space and defense, and semiconductors).

The previous trends suggest the importance of OFDI as a mechanism for upgrading in manufacturing by developing country MNCs. A crucial aspect of

FIGURE 4.7 Developing Country Manufacturing MNCs Prefer Investing via M&A

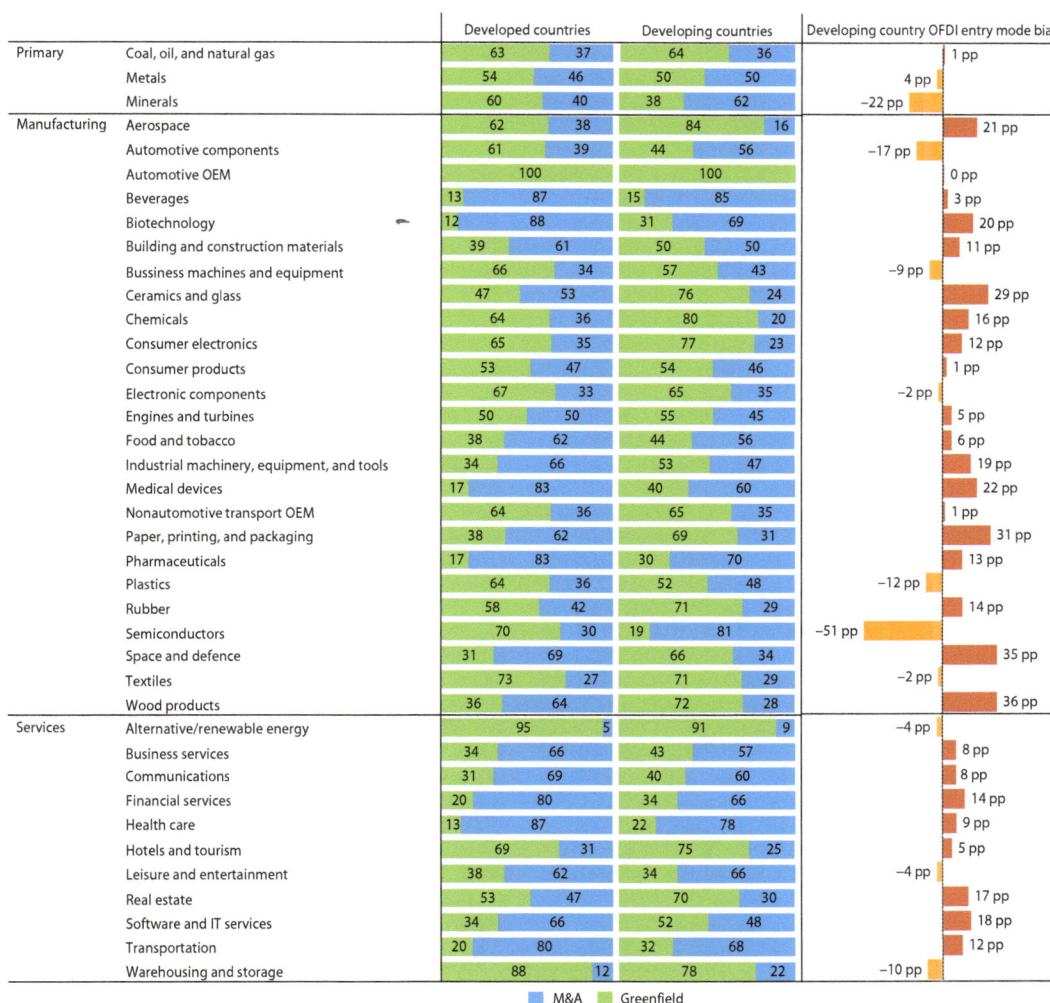

		Developed countries		Developing countries		Developing country OFDI entry mode bias
Primary	Coal, oil, and natural gas	63	37	64	36	1 pp
	Metals	54	46	50	50	4 pp
	Minerals	60	40	38	62	−22 pp
Manufacturing	Aerospace	62	38	84	16	21 pp
	Automotive components	61	39	44	56	−17 pp
	Automotive OEM	100		100		0 pp
	Beverages	13	87	15	85	3 pp
	Biotechnology	12	88	31	69	20 pp
	Building and construction materials	39	61	50	50	11 pp
	Bussiness machines and equipment	66	34	57	43	−9 pp
	Ceramics and glass	47	53	76	24	29 pp
	Chemicals	64	36	80	20	16 pp
	Consumer electronics	65	35	77	23	12 pp
	Consumer products	53	47	54	46	1 pp
	Electronic components	67	33	65	35	−2 pp
	Engines and turbines	50	50	55	45	5 pp
	Food and tobacco	38	62	44	56	6 pp
	Industrial machinery, equipment, and tools	34	66	53	47	19 pp
	Medical devices	17	83	40	60	22 pp
	Nonautomotive transport OEM	64	36	65	35	1 pp
	Paper, printing, and packaging	38	62	69	31	31 pp
	Pharmaceuticals	17	83	30	70	13 pp
	Plastics	64	36	52	48	−12 pp
	Rubber	58	42	71	29	14 pp
	Semiconductors	70	30	19	81	−51 pp
	Space and defence	31	69	66	34	35 pp
	Textiles	73	27	71	29	−2 pp
	Wood products	36	64	72	28	36 pp
Services	Alternative/renewable energy	95	5	91	9	−4 pp
	Business services	34	66	43	57	8 pp
	Communications	31	69	40	60	8 pp
	Financial services	20	80	34	66	14 pp
	Health care	13	87	22	78	9 pp
	Hotels and tourism	69	31	75	25	5 pp
	Leisure and entertainment	38	62	34	66	−4 pp
	Real estate	53	47	70	30	17 pp
	Software and IT services	34	66	52	48	18 pp
	Transportation	20	80	32	68	12 pp
	Warehousing and storage	88	12	78	22	−10 pp

■ M&A   ■ Greenfield

Source: Computation based on fDi Markets database, the Financial Times; and Thomson Reuters.
Note: For both developed and developing countries, the figure shows the mode of entry distribution of the cumulative number of OFDI projects between 2003 and 2015. The last column shows the deviation in percentage points of developing country OFDI modes of entry, with positive (negative) values identifying a greenfield (M&A) bias for the OFDI of developing countries relative to developed economies. IT = information technology; M&A = mergers and acquisitions; MNC = multinational corporation; OEM = original equipment manufacturer; OFDI = outward foreign direct investment.

knowledge-intensive industries is their reliance on intangible assets, involving largely tacit and experiential knowledge in such areas as research and development (R&D), branding, or organizational software. These features make intangible assets difficult to replicate (OECD 2013). M&A is therefore the only means of acquiring the type of knowledge or intangible asset that is inherent to the target firm (Slangen and Hennart 2007).

In sum, our data analysis reveals the following main trends:

- OFDI by developing country firms is an increasingly important source of global investment flows and stocks.
- The main source of developing country OFDI across developing regions is East Asia and Pacific. In absolute terms, BRICS investors are the key drivers of

developing country OFDI, accounting for 62 percent of total developing country OFDI stock in 2015—with China alone accounting for 36 percent.

- The countries with a high OFDI-to-GDP ratio are far more heterogeneous, both across countries' economic sizes and development levels.
- As for regional differences in the geographical location of developing country OFDI: South Asia and Europe and Central Asia channel more than two-thirds of their OFDI stock to developed economies, while the Middle East and North Africa and Sub-Saharan Africa concentrate, respectively, 76 percent and 65 percent of outward stock in developing countries. In general, the geographical distribution of developing country OFDI suggests that developing country MNCs balance the importance of market size with physical and cultural proximity.
- Relative to OFDI from developed countries, developing country OFDI shows greater reliance on M&A when targeting manufacturing industries. This is especially true for knowledge-intensive industries, as developing country MNCs resort increasingly to OFDI to augment capabilities and competitiveness.
- Finally, developing country OFDI is distributed across a rich set of industries, including manufacturing, extractives, and services. It thus covers the full range of investment types (natural resource–seeking, efficiency-seeking, market-seeking, and strategic asset–seeking).

As more developing countries continue to internationalize through OFDI, a pertinent question is the role that OFDI can play in supporting domestic development. Developing countries may be able to leverage OFDI to source technology, increase domestic capacity, upgrade production processes, boost competitiveness, augment managerial skills, and access distribution networks (Amann and Virmani 2014; Driffield and Love 2003, 2007).

The rest of this chapter will address these possibilities by reviewing the literature on OFDI home effects.

Does Development Level Affect OFDI Behavior?

Both the investor survey and the gravity model estimation (annex 4B) suggest that OFDI by developing country MNCs reacts to standard host economy location determinants (for example, market size, income level, distance, common language, colonial links) in much the same way as developed country OFDI: both are attracted to large and growing economies that are geographically close and culturally similar. However, evidence suggests that developing country investors are relatively more willing to target smaller and closer economies (Arita 2013) in a "stepping-stone" strategy. Some of these firms find it difficult to compete in larger, more competitive markets farther away, lacking the networks and experience of developed country firms. Studies of Asia and Latin America find that investors usually expand into large and complex markets only after first successfully expanding in smaller, lower-income economies in the same region (Cuervo-Cazurra 2008; Gao 2005; Hiratsuka 2006).

Differences between developed and developing country outward investment behavior also arise with regard to the role of technology. Developed countries generally exploit existing technological assets in undertaking OFDI. But some developing country MNCs use OFDI to acquire *new* technological assets. Case studies of leading BRICS firms provide examples (Holtbrugge and Kreppel 2012; Rodriguez-Arango and Gonzalez-Perez 2016; UNCTAD 2005). The reason is that most BRICS multinationals face disadvantages in terms of patents, management know-how, or cutting-edge processes, and thus seek to acquire these abroad as part of a strategy of late-comer catch-up. Looking at the econometric evidence, however, this seems to apply mostly to China. Across many studies, a consensus has emerged that Chinese MNCs use OFDI to acquire the knowledge, skills, and technology they lack (Dong and Guo 2013; Huang and Wang 2011; Kang and Jiang 2012; Ramasamy, Yeung, and Laforet 2012; Zhang and Roelfsema 2014).

Developing country investors may also be relatively more willing to target host economies with weaker institutional quality,[17] in view of the "institutional advantage" argument (Cuervo-Cazurra and Genc 2008). This theory suggests that managers of developing country MNCs are more used to uncertainty and may be more flexible in dealing with unpredictable regulatory agencies and corrupt government officials. Several studies support this argument, finding that developing country MNCs are relatively more present in least developed countries (Cuervo-Cazurra and Genc 2008) or by demonstrating an inverse relationship between host political risk and, specifically, Chinese OFDI (Buckley and others 2007; Cui and Jiang 2009; Duanmu and Guney 2009; Kang and Jiang 2012; Quer, Claver, and Rienda 2012).

Does OFDI Matter for Development? Identifying OFDI Home Effects

Developing country OFDI can affect the home economy of investors through different transmission channels. This section first considers these channels and then presents evidence of these effects across two variables: innovation and exports.

A developing country can use OFDI as a catch-up strategy to source technology, increase domestic capacity, upgrade production processes, boost competitiveness, augment managerial skills and access distribution networks (Amann and Virmani 2014; Driffield and Love 2003, 2007). As a result, OFDI can play a major role in a developing country's developmental strategy.[18] The effects of OFDI on the home economy can show up at three different levels. Initially,

only the MNC will directly experience the impact of investing abroad (first-order effect). Later, the firm's enhanced knowledge, capacity, and behavior may affect other domestic firms that are not themselves foreign investors (second-order effect). Finally, the impact may be spread throughout the home economy over time.

OFDI can impact the home economy in at least three ways:

1. *Scale effects:* OFDI allows a firm to grow larger than it would have if limited to operating in its home market. This growth may yield traditional gains based on economies of scale and scope,[19] lowering costs of production and operation.
2. *Competition effects:* Competition with firms in foreign markets where developing country firms invest may force them to improve efficiency and upgrade production processes. Competition in host markets can thus bring efficiencies and expansion of developing country firm activities at home.
3. *Knowledge effects:* OFDI enables firms to acquire knowledge directly, as through M&A, joint ventures, or other forms of partnership. Knowledge can take the form of technology, production techniques, or management skills. Such knowledge transfer initially benefits only the foreign subsidiary. For it to benefit the home economy, it needs to be transferred back to the parent firm—so-called reverse knowledge transfer (for example, through personnel exchanges, production shifting, or management rotation). At the same time, indirect knowledge transfer may occur through knowledge spillovers to other firms in the home economy.

These transmission channels can, however, lead to diverse effects on developing countries' MNCs, as well as on local firms in home markets. Scale and competition effects may push less competitive firms to exit the home market. Knowledge effects may only accrue to those firms with the capacity to integrate such knowledge, causing outward investment to contribute to skills-based inequalities. Rigid factor markets for labor and capital may exacerbate adjustment costs, while undeveloped factor markets may limit the potential benefits of outward investment for the home economy (for example, unskilled labor unable to integrate OFDI-generated knowledge and innovation or capital market imperfections causing OFDI to crowd out domestic investment in the home economy). Appropriate policies are needed to maximize the benefits of outward investment while minimizing its costs.

OFDI Impact on Innovation and Exports

The following review focuses on two key economic benefits where the existing literature provides the most evidence of OFDI impact on the home economy: driving innovation and expanding exports.

OFDI by Developing Country MNCs Can Spur Innovation at Home

OFDI's ability to increase innovation in the home economy is well-documented.[20] The key transmission channels are competition effects that encourage innovation and direct and indirect knowledge effects. Knowledge can take the form of technology, production techniques, or management skills. Disaggregating outward investment by type is especially important, as one particular type of OFDI—knowledge-seeking, which is part of strategic asset–seeking investment[21]—is likely to have the greatest positive effect on home innovation.

Developing country MNCs seem to be using outward investment in innovation-intensive economies to spur home innovation. One study examines OFDI from 20 developing countries into developed countries from 2000 to 2008 (Chen, Li, and Shapiro 2012). It finds that both R&D employment and R&D expenditure in host economies increase

R&D spending by developing country parent companies.[22] Host market R&D intensity therefore seems to be a key element in determining the potential for overseas investment by developing country MNCs to generate innovation spillovers in the home economy (box 4.2).

The evidence also suggests that the effect of outward investment on home innovation is more pronounced in knowledge-intensive sectors.[23] In the auto and chemical and pharmaceuticals industries, evidence reveals that OFDI firms generate reverse technology spillovers to domestic firms that did not invest abroad.[24] The positive effect of OFDI on home R&D is apparent for investments in *both* developed and developing host countries, although it is stronger for developed countries.[25]

South–South OFDI is also showing signs of increasingly becoming a source for home innovation. Whereas previous paradigms considered developed countries as the repository of knowledge and technology, and thus focused on North–North or North–South investment flows, a multipolar global technology network is emerging, with growing South–South innovation-oriented interactions and collaboration.[26] Part of the reason is that knowledge created in developing countries may be more adapted to the needs of other developing countries, and that the level of complexity of that knowledge may be more easily absorbed by other economies at similar levels of development. Evidence from Africa shows that, when the knowledge gap between firms is too great, interactions between firms are less likely to lead to knowledge transfer or spillovers because firms are unable to absorb the knowledge (Boly and others 2014 in Moran, Gorg, and Seric 2016; Deng 2010; Farole and Winkler 2014). Using outward investment to target highly sophisticated knowledge so as to leapfrog to the knowledge frontier may therefore not be an effective strategy until a firm has first increased its absorptive capacity. Different levels of development may thus call for different OFDI knowledge acquisition and innovation strategies depending on

BOX 4.2

Developing Country MNCs Use OFDI to Boost Innovation and Exports

Across the developing world, firms are using outward investment to improve their capabilities and performance. Particularly noteworthy is the breadth of different industries involved. Three industries in three different countries illustrate how outward investment can boost home-firm innovation, exports, and firm growth.

In Turkey, two of the leading household appliance firms have used outward investment to locate R&D activities in foreign markets to increase parent-firm innovation. The leading firm, Arcelik, has seven R&D centers around the world. This emphasis on R&D means that in 2015 the firm had by far the most World Intellectual Property Organization (WIPO) patent applications among all Turkish firms—a staggering eight times more than the second highest Turkish firm—placing Arcelik in the 78th position globally. Another of the top Turkish firms, Vestel, is also using outward investment to tap into foreign technology and boost innovation. It devotes 2 percent of sales revenue to R&D spending, with foreign R&D centers in the United Kingdom and China. As a result, Vestel has also been listed as one of the three Turkish companies among the top 1,000 companies in the world by R&D spending.

Jordan's pharmaceutical sector provides an excellent example of how a relatively smaller developing country can use outward investment to develop a domestic industry's capacity and competitiveness. Al Hikma Pharmaceuticals, Jordan's largest pharmaceutical firm, has led a series of M&A and greenfield investments across the world, in both developed and developing countries, to access technology and markets.

Hikma now has manufacturing facilities approved by the U.S. Food and Drug Administration in Germany, Italy, Jordan, Portugal, Saudi Arabia, and the United States; it also has R&D centers in Algeria, the Arab Republic of Egypt, Jordan, Saudi Arabia, Tunisia, and the United States. Hikma has thus become the third largest generic injectable supplier to the U.S. market. According to the Jordanian Association of Pharmaceutical Manufacturers, about 80 percent of Jordanian production is destined for export to more than sixty countries, with most exports heading to other Arab countries.

China's wind turbine industry illustrates how outward investment can drive innovation in the home market and the key role that supportive policies can play. China's wind power capacity in 2005 was 1,260 megawatts; by the end of 2016, it had grown more than 100-fold to 168,690 megawatts (Global Wind Energy Council 2016). The International Energy Agency estimates that China builds two wind turbines every hour. As a result, China now has more installed wind power capacity than all of the European Union combined, and more than double the capacity of the United States. OFDI has played a key role in facilitating this remarkable growth by helping to access technology. From 2009 to 2014 China made 44 outward investments in the wind energy industry. The Chinese state guided and facilitated this process through policy instruments such as subsidies, tax incentives, R&D spending, technical partnership, and outward investment financial incentives and support. This represents a dramatic example of a developing country using policy measures to leapfrog developed economies.

---

the economy's absorptive capacity (Criscuolo and Narula 2008).

Overseas Investment by Developing Country MNCs Can Expand Home Exports

Empirical evidence confirms that outward investment increases home country exports. The key transmission channels are scale effects and knowledge effects: outward investment may open new markets, creating opportunities for increased export-oriented production of either intermediate or finished goods. Outward investment may also bring back to the home economy knowledge and technology that boost export competitiveness. OFDI may also be used to plug into GVCs through backward and forward supply-chain integration, stimulating exports of intermediate inputs. Yet negative effects may arise if relocating production abroad lowers exports of final goods and services since foreign markets are now being served by local production.

The net effect is therefore theoretically ambiguous, depending on the relative strength of these different effects.

In practice, however, empirical evidence overwhelmingly confirms that outward investment and home exports are complements and not substitutes, and that OFDI increases home exports (box 4.2). For example, looking at Malaysia, the Philippines, Singapore, and Thailand from 1981 to 2013, a recent study finds that in all cases OFDI increases rather than substitutes home country exports.[27] In this study, a 1 percent increase in OFDI leads to a $750 million rise in exports for the Philippines, $72 million for Singapore, $41 million for Thailand, and $31 million for Malaysia.

Time horizon may be an important dimension in determining the effect of OFDI on home-country exports. A longer time horizon may allow more time for adjustments through the different transmission channels, and thereby have larger effects. Evidence for this is provided by European Union exports, where growth in outward investment caused small, positive effects on exports in the short term but with long-run effects that were consistently greater than their short-run equivalents.[28]

When it comes to other potential home country benefits—such as productivity, domestic investment, employment and, ultimately, economic growth—the literature is still inconclusive. While research has found a mostly positive effect of OFDI from developed countries on job growth and economic activity, the literature on developing country OFDI is more nascent and still offers only tentative conclusions, the review of which is beyond the scope of this report.

Absorptive Capacity Is Key

While OFDI can generate benefits for home economies, limitations on firm-level and economy-wide absorptive capacity in developing countries may limit OFDI home effects (box 4.3).

Absorptive capacity can affect the home effects of OFDI in two divergent ways. One view is that firms farthest from the technology frontier may benefit most from spillovers as they are starting from a low base. Another view suggests that these firms may not have the capacity to make the best use of new technologies. Rather, it argues that firms closest to the technology frontier are best placed to adopt cutting-edge technologies available through OFDI.[29] Empirical evidence supports both views, indicating a U-shape function in the relationship between absorptive capacity and OFDI home effects, with simple knowledge at the low range and complex knowledge at the high range being more likely to facilitate these effects (Girma 2005; Girma and Gorg 2007).

The key to positive home effects is a match between the firm's level of absorptive capacity

---

BOX 4.3

Absorptive Capacity Matters at Both Firm and Economy Levels

Absorptive capacity is defined as the "ability to identify, assimilate, and exploit knowledge from the environment" (Cohen and Levinthal 1989). It applies at both the level of the individual firm and the level of the overall economy. At the firm level, absorptive capacity is a function of how effectively a firm can productively integrate knowledge resources. Measures to boost firm-level absorptive capacity can include instituting training programs, increasing R&D spending, and/or developing knowledge management tools. These measures will largely depend on decisions by individual firms.

At the economy level, absorptive capacity depends on whether frameworks and mechanisms exist to help firms integrate knowledge resources and develop linkages and learning between firms. Measures to boost economy-wide absorptive capacity can include establishing institutional partnerships, helping to diffuse information, promoting firm linkages, and designing school curricula. These measures will largely depend on decisions by policy makers.

and the knowledge it seeks to target through OFDI. Firms starting from a more basic level of knowledge can benefit most from exposure to simpler knowledge, giving them potentially a bigger boost to their innovation than if they were to target knowledge at the frontier and not be able to absorb it. In contrast, firms already enjoying more sophisticated knowledge can benefit most from exposure to more complex knowledge at the frontier, giving them a bigger boost to innovation than if they were to target knowledge they already have. In both cases, the ability of the home firm to absorb knowledge and the kind of knowledge being targeted must match. This match will change over time as knowledge is gained and absorptive capacity increases. At some point, the developing country firm should have sufficient absorptive capacity to invest in acquiring knowledge at the frontier. Governments may therefore wish to ensure that their efforts to boost absorptive capacity take into account different needs at both ends of the spectrum of the private sector.[30]

Absorptive capacity may be measured at both the level of the firm and of the economy. When undertaking OFDI decisions, the firm's absorptive capacity is key to determining the appropriate match with target knowledge and technology. But policy interventions to boost absorptive capacity should be considered at the economy level. Officials can adopt measures that boost the absorptive capacity of whole sectors—such as training programs, infrastructure provision, and network creation—rather than try and boost the absorptive capacity of individual firms through subsidies or protectionist measures in order to create national champions (Moran 2015).

Finally, differences in absorptive capacity between developed and developing countries are not caused by structural variables but may simply reflect different stages of development (Ramamurti 2012). Developed countries have been building their absorptive capacity for longer, whether through training, R&D, linkages, or institutional partnerships—all of which can be fostered through policy intervention. Government policies can thus help developing countries catch up by boosting their absorptive capacity to maximize the positive effects of OFDI (box 4.3).

Economies Are Gradually Liberalizing OFDI Regulations

In many developing countries, OFDI policy has shifted gradually from restrictive to more supportive, although restrictions persist (figure 4.8). In 2015, almost half of developing countries (49 percent, or 77 out of 156 countries) had some OFDI restrictions in place. Low-income developing countries[31] were more likely to restrict OFDI than other developing countries. In 2015, 60 percent of low-income developing countries had OFDI restrictions (36 of 60 countries); in contrast, only 43 percent of non-low-income developing countries had OFDI restrictions (41 of 96).[32] This original finding that OFDI restrictions vary with development level accords with earlier work on foreign exchange restrictions to FDI across economies, which found that all high-income countries maintain unrestricted foreign exchange regimes for FDI.[33] Therefore as countries raise their development level, restrictions on outward investment seem to fall, although the direction of this relationship requires further study.

Restrictive regulatory frameworks regarding OFDI stem from concern that capital outflows can worsen the balance of payments and capital availability in the home economy. Measures to restrict OFDI can take the form of approval requirements, reporting requirements, foreign exchange controls, ceilings on investment amounts, or limits on destination sectors or destination economies (Kuźmińska-Haberla 2012). A snapshot of OFDI restrictions in 2011 in 84 developing countries reveals great variation in OFDI restrictiveness, even for countries at similar levels of development (Sauvant and others 2014).

The BRICS provide a representational picture of variation in OFDI regulation:

- *China*, over the course of 2000–14, moved from restricting to encouraging OFDI, although it tightened restrictions again at the end of 2016 (box 4.1).
- *Brazil* has generally favored OFDI, and in 2007 adopted financial incentives to encourage it in specific sectors in which

FIGURE 4.8   **Developing Countries Have a Mixed Record on OFDI Restriction**

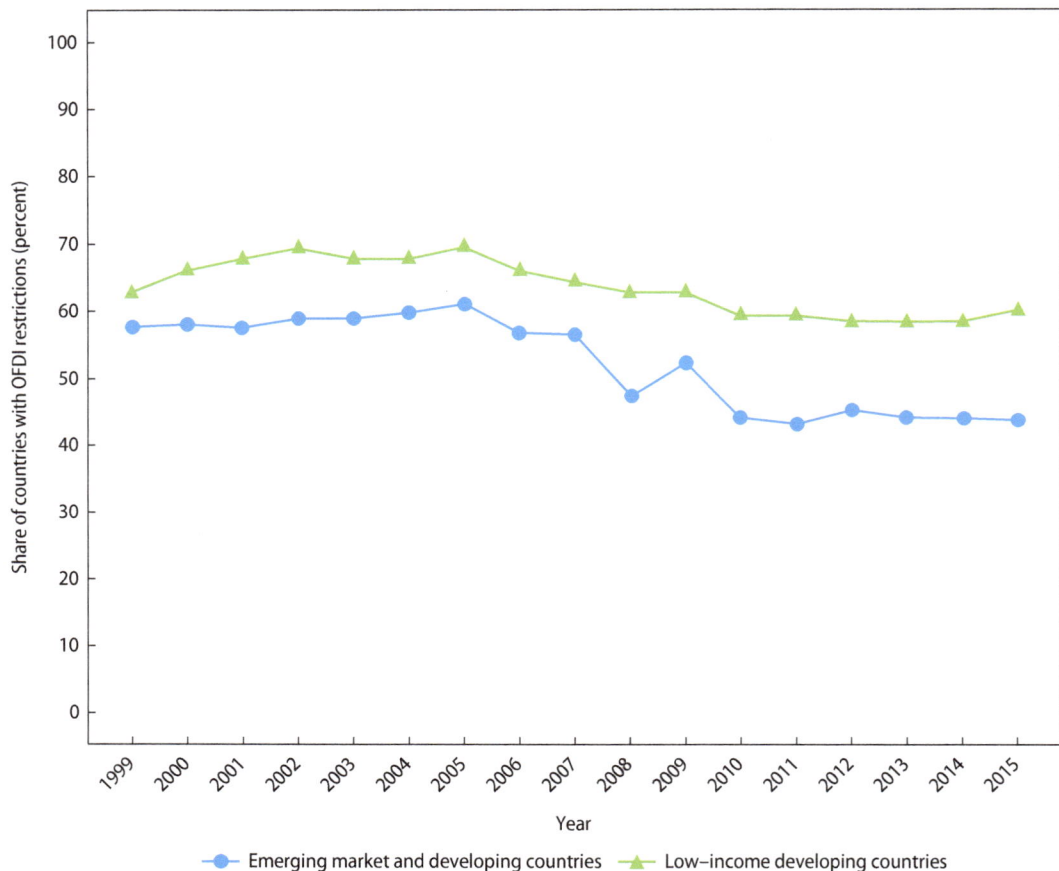

Source: Computation based on IMF Annual Report on Exchange Arrangements and Exchange Restrictions (IMF 2016)
Note: This figure uses IMF country category definitions. The IMF defines low-income developing countries (LIDCs) as those with a level of per capita Gross National Income (GNI) less than the Poverty Reduction and Growth Trust (PRGT) income graduation level for non-small states (that is, twice the International Development Association (IDA) operational threshold, or 2 x IDA-OT) (see IMF 2014). Emerging market and developing countries are all developing countries that are not LIDCs (see IMF 2016). OFDI = outward foreign direct investment.

the Brazilian economy had a comparative advantage (for example, mining, petroleum, pulp and paper, and beef) (Nunes de Alcântara and others 2016).

- *Russia* has also generally welcomed OFDI, mostly in the energy sector, but it has also blocked individual deals (Fortescue and Hanson 2015).
- *India* maintains a relatively restrictive OFDI framework, despite recent liberalization. OFDI in real estate[34] is forbidden, in financial services is quite restricted, and in energy and natural resources,

manufacturing, education, and hospitals requires prior approval by the Reserve Bank of India. Restrictions also apply on how OFDI is carried out in neighboring countries (for example, Bhutan, Nepal, and Pakistan).[35] Quantitative restrictions are also set by the net worth of the Indian firm. If OFDI is approved, the firm must submit annual performance reports on each OFDI deal.[36]

- *South Africa* also restricts OFDI, although with its own particular regulatory conditions. Firms face a limit of 1 billion rand per calendar year for OFDI, above which they must formally apply to the South African Reserve Bank and ensure that at least 10 percent of the target entity's voting rights are obtained through the investment. Even for deals under the 1 billion rand limit, restrictions remain, such as the net sale proceeds being repatriated to South Africa and South African-owned intellectual property not being sold without prior approval.[37]

Given the potential benefits of OFDI to home economies, developing country governments with OFDI restrictions may wish to carefully weigh their costs and benefits.

Conclusion

From the empirical evidence, developing country OFDI clearly has the potential to contribute substantially to development in home markets. Evidence suggests that OFDI increases home innovation and exports, but conclusive evidence is not yet available regarding productivity, domestic investment, employment, and economic growth. One reason may be that it is relatively easier to detect effects for variables at the firm or sector level and more difficult to do so at the economy level.

Even within a single variable, the effect of outward investment can vary across sectors, factors of production, investment types, and over time. OFDI may, in fact, simultaneously exhibit positive and negative effects across these different dimensions. For example, it may benefit high-skilled labor while hurting low-skilled labor; or it may force less competitive home firms to exit the market, while boosting the productivity and profits of more competitive home firms that seize opportunities or adjust to new realities. Differences may also arise concerning the time horizon. In the short term, the impact of outward investment on the home economy may be more limited but over time different transmission channels

(scale effects, competition effects, and knowledge effects) may play out, augmenting and accentuating effects on the home economy. To understand OFDI, we need to move beyond thinking of it as having simply a positive or negative impact on home economies and disaggregate its effects across different dimensions.

OFDI policy should therefore adopt a holistic approach. It should consider both the effects on single variables and on the set of variables that policy makers care about. Just as with trade, OFDI will create winners and losers, but overall the positive effects on the home economy may outweigh the negative effects. Concretely, our study suggests the following policy considerations:

Given the growing importance of developing country OFDI, governments can *target investment promotion activities* not only to traditional sources of FDI from developed economies, but also to new sources from developing economies. South–South and intraregional developing country OFDI represent a sizable share of total FDI flows. IPAs may therefore wish to court developing country OFDI from regional neighbors and developing economies in other regions as a potential source of investment. This source holds considerable promise but has been largely underemphasized in many investment promotion strategies.

Governments may also want to *review any restrictions on OFDI*, weigh their costs and benefits, and ensure that these are based on sound policy goals.[38] Several of the largest source markets of developing country OFDI have recently eased restrictions on OFDI, although restrictions do remain. These controls may be based on macroeconomic objectives such as securing financial stability or promoting domestic investment. But the evidence suggests source countries can also benefit from OFDI, and restrictions may only be constraining positive home effects.

Governments can maximize the potential positive home effects from OFDI by adopting measures that *strengthen economy-wide absorptive capacity*. Given that empirical evidence indicates that absorptive capacity is a U-shape function—with simple knowledge at one end and complex knowledge at the other—governments may wish to first identify the size of the technology gap to tailor the type of policy intervention accordingly. Measures to consider include boosting R&D expenditure, providing training programs, promoting firm linkages, establishing institutional partnerships, helping to disseminate information, and redesigning school curricula.

Given that OFDI by developing country firms has only boomed in the last decade, current research is fairly limited and many questions remain. More work is needed regarding how home effects vary across OFDI type,

whether natural resource–seeking, efficiency-seeking, market-seeking, or strategic asset–seeking. The effect on the home economy is likely to depend on the motivation for undertaking OFDI, but no work has yet disentangled these dynamics.

In addition, more evidence is needed regarding developing country OFDI's effect on home economy productivity, employment, growth, and domestic investment.

Finally, developing country governments need to better understand how investment incentives and other policies affect their firms' OFDI decisions. A clearer understanding of the dynamics in these three areas would allow policy makers to better design and implement OFDI policy interventions.

Annex 4A. Developing Country OFDI by Income Category

FIGURE 4A.1   **Distribution of Developing Country OFDI across Income Categories**

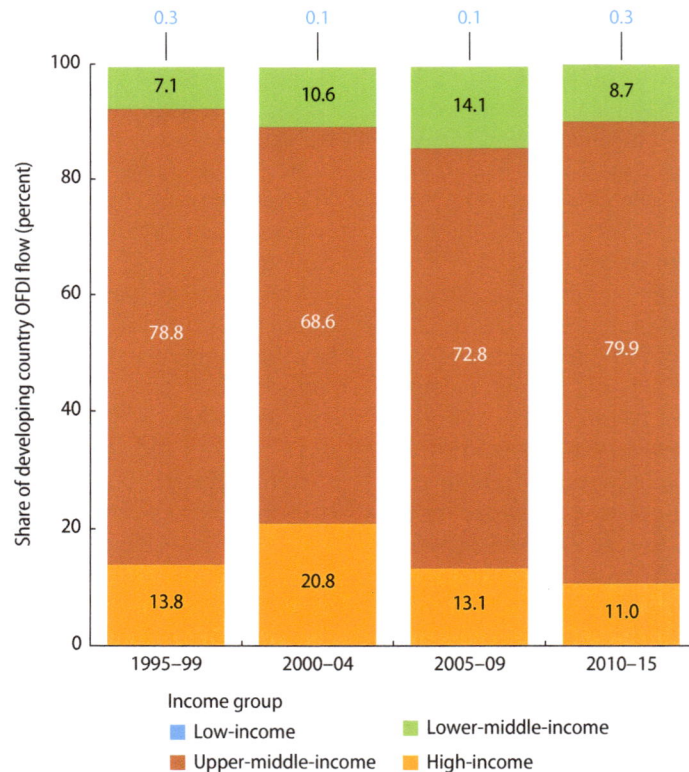

Source: Computation based on UNCTAD and World Development Indicators, World Bank.
Note: OFDI = outward foreign direct investment.

Annex 4B. Estimation of a Gravity Model on Developing Country FDI Determinants

This annex presents the details and results of a gravity model that evaluates the strength of standard FDI location determinants in guiding developing country OFDI. Gravity models have become a widely used framework for explaining economic relations between countries. Early empirical applications, dating back to the decade of the 1960s, largely focused on explaining patterns of bilateral trade (Linneman 1966). One of the most robust findings of this research strand is the significance of relative market size, geographical distance, and common cultural and institutional features, such as language, colonial experience, or trade agreements, as predictors of trade between two countries. Taking advantage of the increasing availability of bilateral economic data, the gravity specification has eventually been applied to the study of capital flows, and FDI in particular (Bevan and Estrin 2004; Talamo 2007).

This gravity exercise follows the empirical inquiry of Gómez-Mera and others (2015), a study that explains OFDI patterns of four emerging economies (Brazil, India, Korea, and South Africa) through a gravity specification. Such specification includes standard location determinants on host market size (GDP per capita, population) and some of the standard bilateral variables (for example, distance, common language, colonial links). Thus, it arrives at the following conclusions: First, the market size of the host economy is a significant predictor of the outward investments of these emerging economies. Second, the lower transaction costs derived from sharing the same language or colonial heritage are significant determinants of the probability of investing. Third, physical distance between countries reduces the probability of investing. Fourth, the existence of bilateral investment treaties (BITs) between source and host economy is a predictor of OFDI for these countries, reducing also the cost derived from geographical distance.

The present analysis departs from Gómez-Mera and others (2015) in two main ways. First, the use of the United Nations Conference on Trade and Development FDI bilateral dataset allows for creation of a panel dataset that covers developing countries engaged in OFDI between 2001 and 2012. Second, having a panel dataset influences the choice for the Poisson Pseudo-Maximum Likelihood method[39] (PPML), which offers several advantages for estimating panel datasets with gravity variables (Santos Silva and Tenreyro 2006). The following equation illustrates the baseline econometric specification.

$$FDI_{ijt} = \alpha + \beta_1 \, GDPPC_{jt} + \beta_2 POP_{jt}$$
$$+ \beta_3 DISTCAP_{ij} + \beta_4 Contig_{ij}$$
$$+ \beta_5 Commlang_{ij} + \beta_6 Colony_{ij}$$
$$+ \beta_7 BIT_{ijt} + \beta_8 DIST_{ij} * BIT_{ijt}$$
$$+ \beta_9 X_{ijt} + \beta_{10} D_i + e_{ijt},$$

where the dependent variable is the flow of FDI between source i and host j in year t. The specification model includes a categorical variable controlling for fixed effects of the source country[40] (D). The host market attractiveness variables include per capita GDP in purchasing power parity in current international dollars ($GDPPC$) and population (POP). The standard gravity variables are the distance between source and host country capitals ($DISTCAP$), a dummy variable for source and host country sharing the same border ($Contig$), the same language ($Commlang$), and the same colonial history ($Colony$). In line with Gómez-Mera and others (2015), exports from source to host (X) are included to control for the complementarities between trade and FDI. In addition, a dummy for a ratified BIT is included, both independently and interacted with distance (data definitions and sources are included in table 4B.1). The use of these variables and data sources allows for the creation of a panel for 133 developing source countries and 147 host countries (developed and developing), across the 2001–12 interval.

TABLE 4B.1 **Variables and Data Sources**

Variable	Definition	Source
FDI	Bilateral flow of FDI ($)	UNCTAD FDI bilateral dataset
GDPPC	GDP per capita, PPP (current international $)	World Development Indicators
POP	Total population (million)	World Development Indicators
DISTCAP	Capital-to-capital distance	CEPII
Contig	Dummy variable for source and host country sharing a common border.	CEPII
Commlang	Dummy variable for source and host country sharing the same official language	CEPII
Colony	Dummy variable for source and host country sharing the same colonial history.	CEPII
BIT	Existence of a ratified bilateral investment treaty between two countries.	ICSID (2017)
X	Export value from origin to destination, 3-year moving average of t-2, t-1, t	UN Comtrade

TABLE 4B.2 **Poisson Pseudo-Maximum Likelihood Estimation Results**

Variables	PPML coefficients (1)	PPML coefficients (2)
GDPPC	0.0220***	0.0219***
	(9.98)	(9.72)
POP	0.00084***	0.00083***
	(3.17)	(3.14)
DISTCAP	−0.00019***	−0.00021***
	(−7.49)	(−6.93)
Contig	0.3014	0.2967
	(1.42)	(1.40)
Commlang	0.9148***	0.9069***
	(4.04)	(4.01)
Colony	0.7181**	0.7063**
	(2.25)	(2.27)
BIT	0.9210***	0.7700***
	(4.48)	(2.82)
X	0.0166***	0.0169***
	(6.14)	(5.98)
DISTCAP*BIT		0.0000348
		(0.88)
Year	0.2058***	0.2059***
	(12.45)	(12.45)
Constant	−421.40***	−421.51***
	(−12.70)	(−12.70)
Observations	216,009	216,009

Source: Computation using data sources in table 4B.1.
Note: ***$p<0.01$; **$p<0.05$; * $p<0.1$. Z statistics in parentheses. The Poisson Pseudo-Maximum Likelihood estimation specifies robust standard errors and origin-destination clustering to allow for clustered standard errors within pairs.

The results of the PPML estimation, with and without interaction term (table 4B.2), show that the trade-off between host market strength and physical and cultural proximity remains when the analysis is extended to a comprehensive sample of developing country FDI sources. The results largely corroborate the ones found in Gómez-Mera and others (2015): both host market attractiveness variables (*GDPPC, POP*) and the reduced transaction costs derived from shared cultural links (*Commlang, Colony*) are significant predictors of FDI flows from developing countries. Distance, on the other hand, acts as a significant inhibitor of these flows. Thus, BITs are found to be an enabler of FDI flows. All things considered, the only result that is in dissonance with those found in Gómez Mera and others (2015) is the role of BITs in reducing the deleterious effect of distance over FDI flows, with the interaction term between both variables not being significant across any specification.[41]

Annex 4C. Developing Country OFDI by Industry

FIGURE 4C.1   Distribution of Developing Country OFDI across Industries

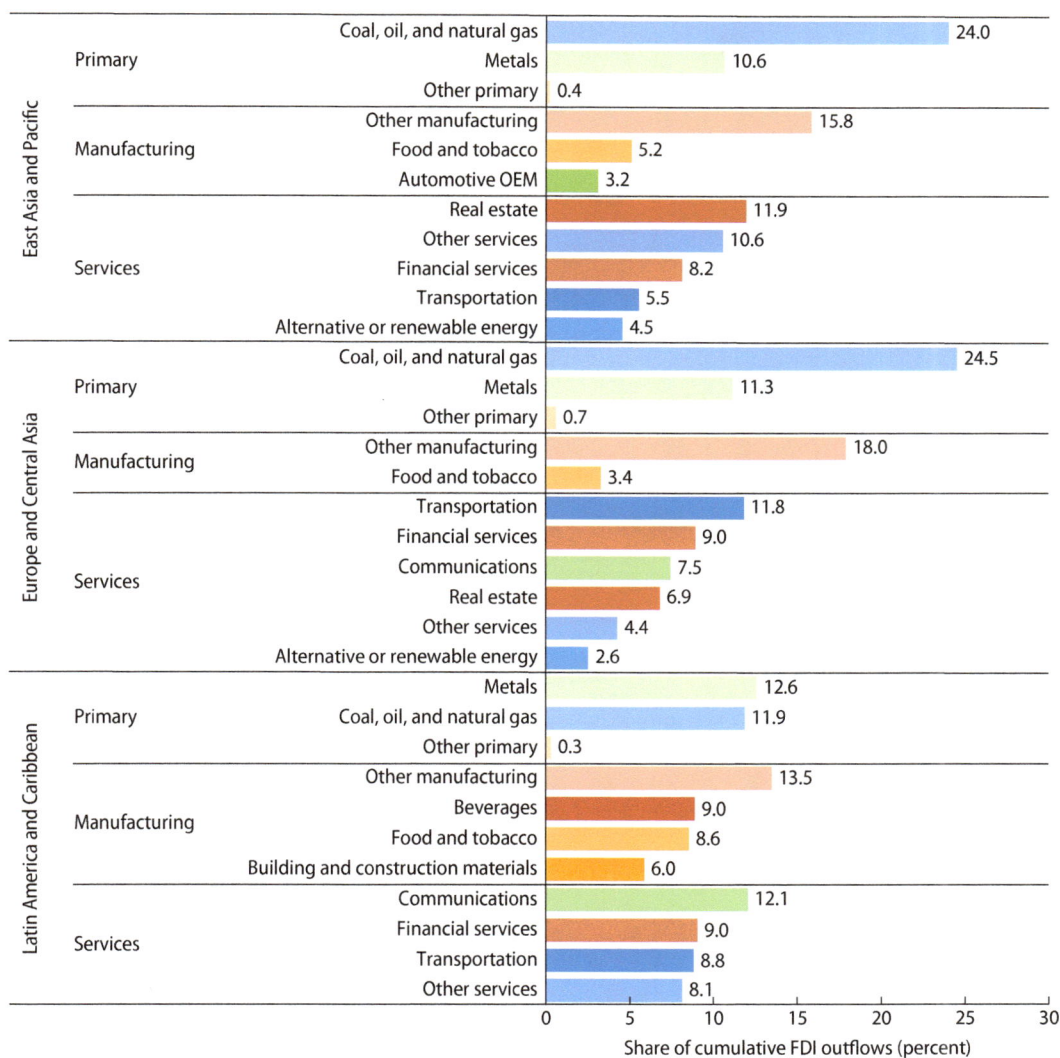

Share of cumulative FDI outflows (percent)

figure continues next page

FIGURE 4C.1   **Distribution of Developing Country OFDI across Industries (continued)**

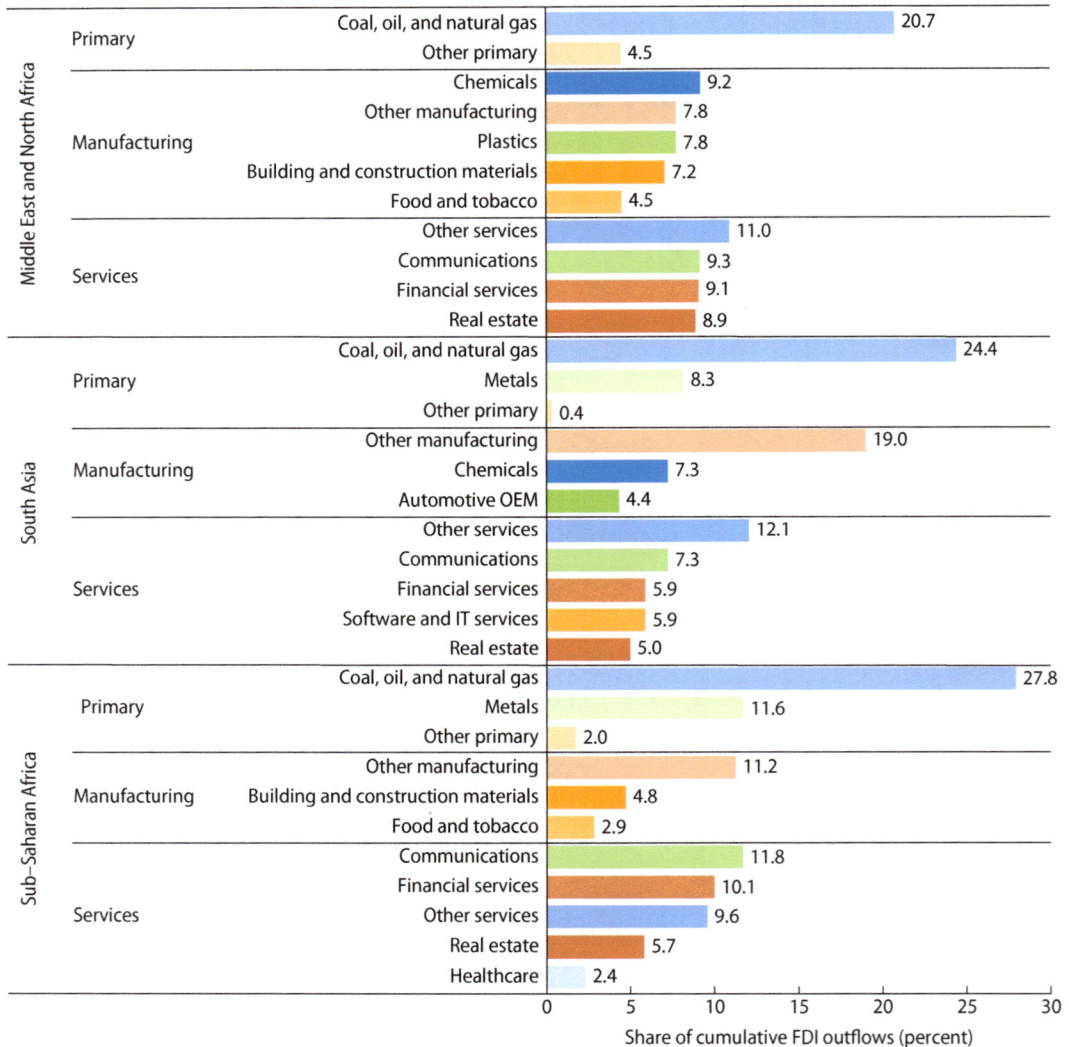

Source: Computation based on fDi Markets database, the Financial Times; and Thomson Reuters.
Note: For each developing region, the figure shows the relative share of the cumulative value of OFDI projects across sectors between 2003 and 2015.
IT = information technology; OEM original equipment manufacturer; OFDI = outward foreign direct investment.

Notes

1. A country is considered developed or developing according to the World Bank income classification. With 1995 as the initial year for the descriptive analysis, the group of developing countries includes all that were low- or middle-income that year. For consistency, these countries remain in the developing country group even if they eventually

exceed the high-income threshold. These economies include Argentina (2014–15), Chile (2012–15), Croatia (2008–15), the Czech Republic (2006–15), Estonia (2006–15), Equatorial Guinea (2007–14), Greece (1996–2015), Hungary (2007–15), Latvia (2009; 2012–15), Lithuania (2012–15), Mauritius (1998–2015), Oman (2007–15), Poland (2009–15), the Russian Federation (2012–14), Saudi Arabia (2004–15), the Slovak Republic

(2007–15), Slovenia (1997–2015), Trinidad and Tobago (2006–15), Uruguay (2012–15), and República Bolivariana de Venezuela (2014). Two additional adjustments have been made. First, the sample disregards 38 tax and financial havens, following an OECD list available at http://www.oecd.org/countries /monaco/jurisdictionscommittedtoimprovin gtransparencyandestablishingeffectiveexcha ngeofinformationintaxmatters.htm. Second, Hong Kong SAR, China, is also removed, given its intermediary role for Chinese OFDI.

2. The literature uses a four-part typology to disaggregate FDI flows by investor motivation: natural resource–seeking, efficiency-seeking, market-seeking, or strategic asset–seeking (Dunning 2000).

3. In value terms, the region's OFDI increases from $32 billion in 2000–04 to $788 billion in 2010–15.

4. These shares correspond to $33 billion and $242 billion, respectively.

5. Equivalent to $51 billion during 2000–04 and $399 billion in 2010–15.

6. An example is the contribution of these countries to global GDP growth. During 1995–2000, the BRICS accounted for half the GDP growth generated in the developing world. This contribution has increased further in recent years, reaching 60 percent during 2010–15.

7. The heat map establishes discrete thresholds at lower than 5 percent, 5–10 percent, 10–15 percent, 15–20 percent, and greater than 20 percent.

8. This figure is based on the UNCTAD FDI bilateral dataset, which maps investment flows and stocks across both home and host economy, between the years 2001 and 2012.

9. The correlation between the share of inward developing country OFDI and per capita GDP (PPP) is -0.51.

10. Another dimension by which to study this regional bias is that across regional trade blocks. In this regard, the relative importance of FDI between members varies markedly across different customs unions and regional trade agreements. As an example, and relying on the UNCTAD bilateral FDI dataset, the share of the intra-agreement stock of OFDI (for example, the share of OFDI stock from member countries located in another member of the agreement) is virtually zero in the Caribbean Community (CARICOM), 10 percent in the Mercado Común del Sur

(Mercosur), 22 percent in the West African Economic and Monetary Union (WAEMU), 36 percent in the Association of Southeast Asian Nations (ASEAN), and 76 percent in the East African Community (EAC).

11. The sample of developing countries is the same used for the descriptive analysis in this chapter (for example, the countries below the high-income threshold in 1995).

12. To illustrate FDI trends across sectors, the analysis relies on information from two transaction-level data sources on FDI projects. First, the fDi Markets dataset tracks media announcements of firm-level greenfield FDI projects. Second, the Thomson Reuters dataset provides the value of individual M&A transactions. The matching methodology detailed in Kierkegaard (2013) is used to merge both datasets. In all, the information from these two datasets allows us to create a single FDI dataset covering the years 2003–15 and including both greenfield and M&A.

13. The groups "Other Manufacturing" and "Other Services" are residual categories that include manufacturing and service industries with shares smaller than the sectors included for each region. For example, all the industries included in "Other Manufacturing" in East Asia and Pacific hold an OFDI share that is smaller than Communications (3.7 percent). Therefore, the industries included in these residual categories may differ by region. The manufacturing industries that are always included in "Other Manufacturing" are aerospace, automotive components, biotechnology, business machines and equipment, consumer electronics, consumer products, electronic components, engines and turbines, industrial machinery, medical devices, nonautomotive transport original equipment manufacturer, and pharmaceuticals. Service industries that are marginal enough to be included in the "Other Services" category are business services, leisure and entertainment, and warehousing and storage.

14. The preference for greenfield is most evident in South Asia and Europe and Central Asia, with 60 percent of South Asia and 55 percent of Europe and Central Asia projects channeled this way. The only exception is Latin America and the Caribbean, where 54 percent of projects are through M&A. When measured by cumulative project value (versus

the number of projects), the share of green-field projects in total OFDI is 68 percent in South Asia, 62 percent in Middle East and North Africa, 60 percent in East Asia and Pacific, 59 percent in Europe and Central Asia, and 58 percent in Sub-Saharan Africa. Again, the only exception is Latin America and the Caribbean, where the share of green-field projects in total OFDI is 33 percent.

15. This information is conveyed in the last column of figure 4.7, which shows the deviation in percentage points of the greenfield share of developing country OFDI relative to developed economies.

16. Eurostat (2017) identifies those industries with high or medium-high technology intensity.

17. Institutional quality embraces several attributes. The World Bank's World Governance Indicators (WGI) give it six dimensions: Voice and Accountability, Political Stability and Absence of Violence, Government Effectiveness, Regulatory Quality, Rule of Law, and Control of Corruption.

18. Countries can also play a significant role in giving their firms incentives to undertake OFDI, through what has alternatively been called "home country measures" or "home determinants." For a comprehensive discussion of the measures that economies can enact in support of their firms undertaking OFDI, see Sauvant and others (2014). These measures can take the form of information, support services, financial measures, and fiscal measures. The relationship between home determinants and home effects is a rich and unexplored area that merits future investigation.

19. While economies of scale arise from lower average costs attributable to an increase in the size of the operation, economies of scope arise from lower average costs owing to production of similar goods or services.

20. Innovation is generally examined through R&D measures (expenditures, employment) and patent measures (registration, citation).

21. Dunning's classic typology for FDI motivations includes strategic asset–seeking FDI (Dunning 2000); more recently, scholars have used the term knowledge-seeking FDI (Meyer 2015). The former type is broader than the latter: all knowledge-seeking FDI is strategic asset–seeking, but not all strategic asset–seeking is knowledge-seeking. For example, acquiring a brand for brand-name

recognition is strategic asset–seeking but not knowledge-seeking. Knowledge-seeking OFDI aims to augment firm-specific advantage owned by the firm to improve its competitiveness by acquiring new knowledge (Chen, Li, and Shapiro 2012). This chapter is mostly concerned with knowledge-seeking OFDI and not other forms of strategic asset–seeking as this type of investment is more likely to generate home effects. In this chapter, the term "knowledge" is used to subsume different forms of knowledge, including technology and management know-how.

22. Chen, Li, and Shapiro (2012) investigate the explanatory power of three host economy knowledge-related independent variables (R&D employment, R&D expenditures, and patents) for variation in home technological ability (proxied by home economy firm-level R&D expenditure).

23. See earlier section "What and How? Sector and Mode of Entry" for a discussion of knowledge-intensive industries.

24. For the chemical and pharmaceutical sectors, see Criscuolo (2009). For the auto industry, see Mani (2013).

25. Looking at the Indian automotive industry, Pradhan and Singh (2008) examine OFDI from 1988 to 2008 and find a positive effect on home in-house R&D intensity for investments in *both* developed and developing host economies, although it is stronger for OFDI in developed economies.

26. For a discussion of the growing importance of South–South technology networks, see Nepelski and De Prato (2015).

27. The coefficients of OFDI are positive and statistically significant at the 5 percent level for all countries, indicating that the OFDI and exports are complementary (Ahmad, Draz, and Yang 2016).

28. The study looked at the effect of outward investment stocks on bilateral exports among the 15 countries of the European Union from 1986 to 1996 (Egger 2001).

29. For a discussion of the implications of different levels of absorptive capacity, see Tang and Altshuler (2015).

30. Other studies have suggested that the export intensity of a firm, its size, governance structures, and R&D spending all may affect absorptive capacity. First, firms that are exporters have more knowledge of, and experience with, foreign markets, which may make them more capable of understanding

and absorbing foreign technologies (Tang and Altshuler 2015). Second, small firms may enjoy more spillovers as they are less bureaucratic, making it easier to adjust to new technologies (Sinani and Meyer 2004); nonetheless, small firms may not be able to compete as effectively with foreign firms (Aitken and Harrison 1999). Third, large, family-owned conglomerates have emerged in many developing countries to address market failures linked to weak property rights, contract enforcement, and widespread corruption. Yet studies have found such relation-based governance to be associated with lower levels of innovation— as innovation makes the sunk costs invested in relationships less valuable—suggesting lower levels of absorptive capacity (Li, Park, and Li 2003). Fourth, R&D spending may improve recipients' absorptive capacity, while also helping transform pure knowledge into inputs for productive innovation (Chen, Li, and Shapiro 2012).

31. The International Monetary Fund defines low-income developing countries as those with a level of per capita gross national income less than the Poverty Reduction and Growth Trust (PRGT) income graduation level for non-small states (IMF 2014).

32. Looking at the share of countries at different income levels that maintain some form of OFDI restrictions does not, however, capture the relative intensity of restrictions. On the basis of individual country examples, OFDI restrictions seem to be getting less restrictive over time even if some form of OFDI restriction today remains in place in many countries. Future work will explore the relative intensity of OFDI restrictions across countries at different levels of development, and across time.

33. See Anderson (2013) for a World Bank Group report on "Converting and Transferring Currency: Benchmarking Foreign Exchange Restrictions to Foreign Direct Investment across Economies."

34. The Government of India specifies that real estate is the "buying and selling of real estate or trading in Transferable Development Rights (TDRs) but does not include development of townships, construction of residential/commercial premises, roads or bridges" See Question 4 "Can overseas direct investment be made in any activity? What are the prohibited activities for overseas direct investment?" in *Frequently Asked Questions*,

Overseas Direct Investments, Reserve Bank of India (updated April 12, 2017), available at https://www.rbi.org.in/Scripts/FAQView.aspx?Id=32.

35. See Question 12 "Are overseas investments freely allowed in all the countries and are there any restrictions regarding the currency of investment?" in *Frequently Asked Questions*, Overseas Direct Investments, Reserve Bank of India (updated April 12, 2017), op cit.

36. See full list of 61 *Frequently Asked Questions*, Overseas Direct Investments, Reserve Bank of India (updated April 12, 2017), op cit.

37. See *Guidelines to Authorised Dealers in respect of genuine new foreign direct investments of up to R1 billion per company per calendar year* (2016-05-10), published by the Financial Surveillance Department of the South African Reserve Bank. Available at https://www.resbank.co.za/RegulationAndSupervision/FinancialSurveillanceAndExchangeControl/Guidelines/Guidelines%20and%20public%20awareness/Guidelines%20-%20FDI.pdf.

38. For discussion of how developing economies in Asia have successfully reformed their OFDI regulatory frameworks, see Rasiah, Gammeltoft, and Jiang (2010).

39. Gómez-Mera and others (2015) devise a cross-sectional econometric specification with two steps: a logit model to determine the probability of investment, and a zero-truncated negative binomial model to determine the drivers of the positive count of investments. With our dependent variable being the flow of FDI between two countries at a given year, our analysis adopts a Poisson Pseudo-Maximum Likelihood Estimator (PPML). Under weak assumptions, Santos Silva and Tenreyro (2006) find that the PPML provides consistent estimates, circumventing the problem of heteroscedasticity in standard nonlinear gravity specifications. Thus, the PPML estimator is also consistent in the presence of fixed effects. It is also better suited to include zero observations, eliminating the possibility of sample selection bias.

40. The gravity equation under PPML does not specify bilateral country-pair fixed effects controlling for unobserved time-invariant heterogeneity, due to problems of collinearity with explanatory variables. Instead, the specification includes single source fixed effects.

41. The CEPII dataset includes alternative variables to test for shared colonial history and language. Specifically, a dummy variable for source and host having the same colonizer after 1945 (comcol) and a dummy that takes the value of 1 if a language is spoken by at least 9 percent of the population in both countries (comlang-ethno). The use of these alternatives did not change any of the results, except for comcol, which is insignificant as a proxy for shared colonial history.

Bibliography

Ahmad, F., M. U. Draz, and S. C. Yang. 2016. "A Novel Study on OFDI and Home Country Exports: Implications for the ASEAN Region." *Journal of Chinese Economic and Foreign Trade Studies* 9 (2): 131–45.

Aitken, B. J., and A. E. Harrison. 1999. "Do Domestic Firms Benefit from Direct Foreign Investment? Evidence from Venezuela." *American Economic Review* 89 (3): 605–18.

Amann, E., and S. Virmani. 2014. "Foreign Direct Investment and Reverse Technology Spillovers." *OECD Journal: Economic Studies* 3 (1): 129–53.

Amighini, A. A., R. Rabellotti, and M. Sanfilippo. 2013. "Do Chinese State-Owned and Private Enterprises Differ in Their Internationalization Strategies?" *China Economic Review* 27: 312–25.

Anderson, J. 2013. "Converting and Transferring Currency: Benchmarking Foreign Exchange Restrictions to Foreign Direct Investment across Economies." World Bank, Washington, DC.

Arita, S. 2013. "Do Emerging Multinational Enterprises Possess South-South FDI Advantages?" *International Journal of Emerging Markets* 8 (4): 329–53.

Assunção, S., R. Forte, and A. Teixeira. 2011. "Location Determinants of FDI: A Literature Review." FEP Working Papers 433, Faculdade de Economia, Universidade do Porto, Portugal.

Aykut, D., and A. Goldstein. 2006. "Developing Country Multinationals: South–South Investment Comes of Age." Working Paper 257, OECD Development Centre, Paris, France.

Aykut, D., and D. Ratha. 2004. "South-South FDI Flows: How Big Are They?" *Transnational Corporations* 13 (1): 149–76. UNCTAD, Geneva.

Barba Navaretti, G., and D. Castellani. 2004. "Investments Abroad and Performance at Home: Evidence from Italian Multinationals."

CEPR Discussion Paper 4284, Centre for Economic Policy Research, London.

Bevan, A.A. and S. Estrin. 2004. "The Determinants of Foreign Direct Investment into European Transition Economies." *Journal of Comparative Economics* 32 (4): 775–87.

Bitzer, J., and H. Görg. 2009. "Foreign Direct Investment, Competition and Industry Performance." *The World Economy* 32 (2): 221–33.

Boly, A., N. D. Coniglio, F. Prota, and A. Seric. 2014. "Diaspora Investments and Firm Export Performance in Selected Sub-Saharan African Countries." *World Development* 59: 422–33.

———. 2015. "Which Domestic Firms Benefit from FDI? Evidence from Selected African Countries." *Development Policy Review* 33 (5): 615–36.

Braconier, H., K. Ekholm, and K. H. M. Knarvik. 2001. "In Search of FDI-Transmitted R&D Spillovers: A Study Based on Swedish Data." *Review of World Economics* 137 (4): 644–65.

Buckley, P. J., L. J. Clegg, A. R. Cross, X. Liu, H. Voss, and P. Zheng. 2007. "The Determinants of Chinese Outward Foreign Direct Investment." *Journal of International Business Studies* 38 (4): 499–518.

Chen, V. Z., J. Li, and D. M. Shapiro. 2012. "International Reverse Spillover Effects on Parent Firms: Evidences from Emerging Market MNEs in Developed Markets." *European Management Journal* 30 (3): 204–18.

Chen, W., and H. Tang. 2015. *Chinese Investment in Africa Is More Diverse and Welcome than You Think.* Quartz Africa. https://qz.com/488589/chinese-investment-in-africa-is-more-diverse-and-welcomed-than-we-give-it-credit/.

China Daily. 2017a. "SOEs Face 'Red Line' on Investment." *China Daily*, January 19. http://english.gov.cn/state_council/ministries/2017/01/19/content_281475545487067.htm.

———. 2017b. "Making China FDI-friendly again." *China Daily*, February 20. http://english.gov.cn/news/top_news/2017/02/20/content_281475572940524.htm.

Cohen, W. M., and D. A. Levinthal. 1989. "Innovation and Learning: The Two Faces of R&D." *The Economic Journal* 99 (397): 569–96.

Criscuolo, C. 2009. "Innovation and Productivity: Estimating the Core Model across 18 Countries." In *OECD, Innovation in Firms: A Microeconomic Perspective*, 111–38. Paris: OECD Publishing.

Criscuolo, P., and R. Narula. 2008. "A Novel Approach to National Technological Accumulation and Absorptive Capacity: Aggregating Cohen and Levinthal." *The European Journal of Development Research* 30 (1): 56–73.

Cuervo-Cazurra, A. 2008. "The Multinationalization of Developing Country MNEs: The Case of Multilatinas." *Journal of International Management* 14 (2): 138–54.

Cuervo-Cazurra, A., and M. Genc. 2008. "Transforming Disadvantages into Advantages: Developing-Country MNEs in the Least Developed Countries." *Journal of International Business Studies* 39 (6): 957–79.

Cui, L. and F. Jiang. 2009. "FDI Entry Mode Choice of Chinese Firms: A Strategic Behavior Perspective." *Journal of World Business* 44 (4): 434–44.

Deng, P. 2009. "Why Do Chinese Firms Tend to Acquire Strategic Assets in International Expansion?" *Journal of World Business* 44 (1): 74–84.

———. 2010. "Absorptive Capacity and A Failed Cross-Border M&A." *Management Research Review* 33 (7): 673–82.

Davies, R., R. Desbordes, and A. Ray. 2015. "Greenfield versus Merger & Acquisition FDI: Same Wine, Different Bottles?" Working Paper Series, UCD Centre for Economic Research, No 15/03.

Dollar, D. 2016. "China as a Global Investor." *China's New Sources of Economic Growth: Vol. 1: Reform, Resources and Climate Change.* Edited by Ligang Song, Ross Garnaut, Cai Fang and Lauren Johnston. Australia National University Press, Acton.

Dong, B. and G. Guo. 2013. "A Model of China's Export Strengthening Outward FDI." *China Economic Review* 27: 208–26.

Driffield, N., and J. H. Love. 2003. "Foreign Direct Investment, Technology Sourcing and Reverse Spillovers." *The Manchester School* 71 (6): 659–72.

———. 2007. "Linking FDI Motivation and Host Economy Productivity Effects: Conceptual and Empirical Analysis." *Journal of International Business Studies* 38: 460–73.

Driffield, N., J. H. Love, and K. Taylor. 2009. "Productivity and Labour Demand Effects of Inward and Outward Foreign Direct Investment on UK Industry." *Manchester School* 77 (2): 171–203.

Driffield, N., and P. C. (Michelle) Chiang. 2009. "The Effects of Offshoring to China: Reallocation, Employment and Productivity in Taiwan." *International Journal of the Economics of Business* 16 (1): 19–38.

Duanmu, J.-L. and Y. Guney. 2009. "A Panel Data Analysis of Locational Determinants of Chinese and Indian Outward Foreign Direct Investment." *Journal of Asia Business Studies* 3 (2): 1-15.

Dunning, J. H. 2000. "The Eclectic Paradigm as an Envelope for Economic and Business Theories of MNE Activity." *International Business Review* 9 (2): 163–90.

Dunning, J. H., C. S. Kim, and D. H. Park. 2008. "Old Wine in New bottles: A Comparison of Emerging-Market TNCs Today and Developed-Country TNCs Thirty Years Ago." In *The Rise of Transnational Corporations from Emerging Markets: Threat or Opportunity?*, edited by K. P. Sauvant, 158–78. Cheltenham, UK: Edward Elgar Publishing.

Echandi, R., J. Krajcovicova, and C. Z. W. Qiang. 2015. "The Impact of Investment Policy in a Changing Global Economy." Policy Research Working Paper 7437, World Bank, Washington, DC.

Egger, P. 2001. "European Exports and Outward Foreign Direct Investment: A Dynamic Panel Data Approach." *Weltwirtschaftliches Archiv* 137 (3): 427–49.

Eurostat. 2017. "Statistics Explained." http://ec.europa.eu/eurostat/statistics-explained/index.php/Main_Page.

Farole, T., and D. Winkler, eds. 2014. *Making Foreign Direct Investment Work for Sub-Saharan Africa: Local Spillovers and Competitiveness in Global Value Chains.* Directions in Development. World Bank, Washington, DC.

FT (Financial Times). 2017. "China Tightens Rules on State Groups' Foreign Investments." August 3. *Financial Times.* https://www.ft.com/content/3251987c-7806-11e7-90c0-90a9d1bc9691.

Fortescue, S., and P. Hanson. 2015. "What Drives Russian Outward Foreign Direct Investment? Some Observations on the Steel Industry." *Post-Communist Economies* 27 (3): 283–305.

Gammeltoft, P. 2008. "Emerging Multinationals: Outward FDI from the BRICS Countries." *International Journal of Technology and Globalisation* 4 (1): 5–22.

Gammeltoft, P., H. Barnard, and A. Madhok. 2010. "Emerging Multinationals, Emerging Theory: Macro- and Micro-Level Perspectives." *Journal of International Management* 16 (2): 95–101.

Gao, T. 2005. "Foreign Direct Investment from Developing Asia: Some Distinctive Features." *Economics Letters* 86 (1): 29–35.

Garcia-Herrero, A., L. Xia, and C. Casanova. 2015. "Chinese Outbound Foreign Direct Investment: How Much Goes Where after Roundtripping and Offshoring?" BBVA Working Paper 15/17, Hong Kong SAR, China.

Girma, S. 2005. "Absorptive Capacity and Productivity Spillovers from FDI: A Threshold Regression Analysis." *Oxford Bulletin of Economics and Statistics* 67 (3): 281–306.

Girma, S., and H. Gorg. 2007. "Evaluating the Foreign Ownership Wage Premium using A Difference-in-Differences Matching Approach." *Journal of International Economics* 72 (1): 97–112.

Global Wind Energy Council. 2016. "Global Wind Report: Annual Market Update." http://www.gwec.net/publications/global-wind-report-2/global-wind-report-2016/.

Gómez-Mera, L., T. Kenyon, Y. Margalit, J. G. Reis, and G. Varela. 2015. *New Voices in Investment: A Survey of Investors from Emerging Countries*. World Bank Studies. Washington, DC: World Bank.

Grieger, G. 2017. "Foreign Direct Investment Screening: A Debate in Light of China-EU FDI flows." EPRS (European Parliamentary Research Service) Document PE 603.941. http://www.europarl.europa.eu/thinktank/en/document.html?reference=EPRS_BRI%282017%29603941

Hanemann, T., A. Lysenko, and C. Gao. 2017. "Tectonic Shifts: Chinese Outbound M&A in 1H 2017." Rhodium Group Report. June 2017. http://rhg.com/notes/tectonic-shifts-chinese-outbound-ma-in-1h-2017.

Herzer, D. 2011. "The Long-Run Relationship between Outward FDI and Total Factor Productivity: Evidence for Developing Countries." *Journal of Development Studies* 47 (5): 767–85.

———. 2012. "How does Foreign Direct Investment Really Affect Developing Countries' Growth?" *Review of International Economics.* 20 (2): 396–414

Hiratsuka, D. 2006. "Outward FDI from and Intraregional FDI in ASEAN: Trends and Drivers." Discussion Paper 77, Institute of Developing Economies, JETRO, Chiba

Holtbrügge, D. and H. Kreppel. 2012. "Determinants of Outward Foreign Direct Investment from BRIC Countries: An Explorative Study." *International Journal of Emerging Markets* 7 (1): 4–30.

Huang, Y. and B. Wang. 2011. "Chinese Outward Direct Investment: Is There a China Model?" *China & World Economy* 19 (4): 1–21.

ICSID (International Centre for Settlement of Investment Disputes). 2016. *Annual Report on Exchange Arrangements and Exchange Restrictions.* Washington, DC.

———. 2017. Database of Bilateral Investment Treaties. https://icsid.worldbank.org/en/Pages/resources/Bilateral-Investment-Treaties-Database.aspx.

IMF (International Monetary Fund). 2014. "Proposed New Grouping in WEO Country Classifications: Low-Income Developing Countries." IMF Policy Paper, Washington, DC.

———. 2016. *Annual Report on Exchange Arrangements and Exchange Restrictions.* Washington, DC: IMF.

Kalotay, K., and A. Sulstarova. 2010. "Modelling Russian Outward FDI." *Journal of International Management* 16 (2): 131–42.

Kang, Y. and F. Jiang. 2012. "FDI Location Choice of Chinese Multinationals in East and Southeast Asia: Traditional Economic Factors and Institutional perspective." *Journal of World Business* 47: 45–53.

Kierkegaard, J. 2013. "New Avenues for Empirical Analysis of Cross-Border Investments: An Application for the ASEAN Members and Middle and Low Income Country Outward Investments." PhD dissertation, Johns Hopkins University, Washington, DC.

Kimura, F., and K. Kiyota. 2006. "Exports, FDI, and Productivity: Dynamic Evidence from Japanese Firms." *Review of World Economics (Weltwirtschaftliches Archiv)* 142 (4): 695–719.

Kuźmińska-Haberla, A. 2012. "The Promotion of Outward Foreign Direct Investment—Solutions from Emerging Economies." Working Paper, Institute of International Business, University of Gdansk no. 31, Poland.

Lardy, N. R. 2014. *Markets over Mao.* Peterson Institute for International Economics, Washington, DC.

Lee, C., C. G. Lee, and M. Yeo. 2016. "Determinants of Singapore's Outward FDI." *Journal of Southeast Asian Economies* 33 (1): 23–40.

Li, S., S. H. Park, and S. H. Li. 2003. "The Great Leap Forward: The Transition from Relation-Based Governance to Rule-Based Governance." *Organizational Dynamics* 33 (1): 63–78.

Linneman, H. 1966. "An Econometric Study of International Trade Flow." North-Holland, Amsterdam, 77.

Luo, Y., Q. Z. Xu, and B. J. Han. 2010. "How Emerging Market Governments Promote Outward FDI: Experience from China." *Journal of World Business* 45 (1): 68–79.

Ma, A. C., and A. Van Assche. 2011. "Product Distance, Institutional Distance and FDI." Mimeo, University of San Diego, School of Business Administration.

Mani, S. 2013. "Outward Foreign Direct Investment from India and Knowledge Flows, the Case of Three Automotive Firms." *Asian Journal of Technology Innovation* 21: 25–38.

Meyer, K. E. 2015. "What Is 'Strategic Asset-Seeking FDI'?" *Multinational Business Review* 23 (1): 57–66.

MOFCOM. 2015. *Belt and Road Helps China Become Net Capital Exporter: Report* (accessed May 5, 2017), http://english.mofcom.gov.cn/article/zt_beltandroad/news/201511/20151101156468.shtml.

Moran, T. 2015. "The Role of Industrial Policy as a Development Tool: New Evidence from the Globalization of Trade-and-Investment." CGD Policy Paper 071. Center for Global Development, Washington, DC. http://www.cgdev.org/publication/role-industrial-policy-development-tool-new-evidenceglobalization-trade-and-investment

Moran, T., H. Gorg., and A. Seric. 2016. "Quality FDI and Supply-Chains in Manufacturing." Kiel Centre for Globalization Policy Paper 1, Kiel.

Narula, R. 2004. "Understanding Absorptive Capacity in an 'Innovation System' Context: Consequences for Economic and Employment Growth." MERIT-Infonomics Research Memorandum Series 3, Maastricht.

Nepelski, D., and G. De Prato. 2015. "International Technology Sourcing between a Developing Country and the Rest of the World. A Case Study of China." *Technovation* 35: 12–21.

Nguyen, H. T., G. Duysters, J. H. Patterson, and H. Sander. 2009. "Foreign Direct Investment Absorptive Capacity Theory." Paper presented at GLOBELICS 2009, 7th International Conference, Dakar, Senegal, October 6–8.

Nunes de Alcântara, J., C. M. P. Paiva, N. C. P. Bruhn, H. R. de Carvalho, and C. L. L. Calegario. 2016. "Brazilian OFDI Determinants." *Latin American Business Review* 17 (3): 177–205.

OECD (Organisation for Economic Co-Operation and Development). 2013. *Interconnected Economies: Benefiting from Global Value Chains*. Paris.

Pradhan, J. P., and N. Singh. 2008. "Outward FDI and Knowledge Flows: A Study of the Indian Automotive Sector." *International Journal of Institutions and Economies* 1 (1): 155–86.

Quer, D., E. Claver, and L. Rienda. 2012. "Political Risk, Cultural Distance, and Outward Foreign Direct Investment: Empirical Evidence from Large Chinese Firms." *Asia Pacific Journal of Management* 29 (4): 1089–1104.

———. 2015. "Chinese Outward Foreign Direct Investment: A Review of Empirical Research." *Frontiers of Business Research in China* 9 (3): 326–70.

Ramamurti, R. 2009. "What Have We Learned about Emerging-Market MNEs?" In *Emerging Multinationals in Emerging Markets*, edited by Ravi Ramamurti and Jitendra V. Singh, 399–426. Cambridge, U.K.: Cambridge University Press.

———. 2012. "What is Really Different About Emerging Market Multinationals?" *Global Strategy Journal* 2 (1): 41 –7.

Ramasamy, B., M. Yeung, and S. Laforet. 2012. "China's Outward Foreign Direct Investment: Location Choice and Firm Ownership." *Journal of World Business* 47: 17–25.

Rasiah, R., P. Gammeltoft, and Y. Jiang. 2010. "Home Government Policies for Outward FDI from Emerging Economies: Lessons from Asia." *International Journal of Emerging Markets* 5 (3/4): 333–57.

RBI (Reserve Bank of India). "Frequently Asked Questions, Overseas Direct Investments" (accessed April 12, 2017), https://www.rbi.org.in/Scripts/FAQView.aspx?Id=32.

Rodriguez-Arango, Liliana and Maria Alejandra Gonzalez-Perez. 2016. "Giants from Emerging Markets: The Internationalization of BRIC Multinationals." In *The Challenge of BRIC Multinationals*, edited by Rob Van Tulder, Alain Verbeke, Jorge Carneiro, and Maria Alejandra Gonzalez-Perez, 195–226. Progress in International Business Research, Vol. 11. Emerald Group Publishing Limited.

Rosen, D. H., and T. Hanemann. 2017. "New Neighbors 2017 Update: Chinese FDI in the United States by Congressional District." Rhodium Group Report.

Sader, F. 1993. "Privatization and Foreign Investment in the Developing World. 1988–92." World Bank Policy Research 1202, Washington, DC.

Santos Silva, J. M. C., and S. Tenreyro. 2006. "The Log of Gravity." *The Review of Economics and Statistics* 88 (4): 641–58.

Sauvant, K. P. 2008. "The Rise of TNCs from Emerging Markets: The Issues." In *The Rise of Transnational Corporations from Emerging Markets: Threat or Opportunity?* edited by

K. P. Sauvant, 3–14. Cheltenham, U.K.: Edward Elgar Publishing.

Sauvant, K. P., and V. Z. Chen. 2014. "China's Regulatory Framework for Outward Foreign Direct Investment." *China Economic Journal* 7 (1): 141–63.

Sauvant, K. P., P. Economou, K. Gal, S. W. Lim, and W. Wilinski. 2014. "Trends in FDI, Home Country Measures and Competitive Neutrality." In *Yearbook on International Investment Law & Policy 2012–2013*, edited by Andrea Bjorklund, 3–107. New York: Oxford University Press.

Sinani, E., and K. E. Meyer. 2004. "Spillovers of Technology Transfer from FDI: The Case of Estonia." *Journal of Comparative Economics* 32 (3): 445–66.

Slangen, A., and J. F. Hennart. 2007. "Greenfield or Acquisition Entry: A Review of the Empirical Foreign Establishment Mode Literature." *Journal of International Management.* 13 (4): 403–29.

South African Reserve Bank. 2016. "Guidelines to Authorised Dealers in Respect of Genuine New Foreign Direct Investments of Up to R1 billion per Company per Calendar Year (2016-05-10)." South African Reserve Bank, Pretoria.

Talamo, G. 2007. "Institutions, FDI, and the Gravity Model." In *Workshop PRIN 2005 SU, Economic Growth; Institutional and Social Dynamics*, 25-27.

Tang, J. T., and R. Altshuler. 2015. "The Spillover Effects of Outward Foreign Direct Investment on Home Countries: Evidence from the United States." Unpublished. http://dx.doi .org/10.2139/ssrn.2545129.

Turkish Household Appliances Suppliers. 2017. "Turkish Household Appliances Supply Industry Sector in Turkey." http://www.turkhas .org/upload/statistics.pdf.

UNCTAD (United Nations Conference on Trade and Development). 2005. "Case Study on Outward Foreign Direct Investment by South African Enterprises." TD/B/COM.3 /EM.26/2/Add.5. Geneva. http://unctad.org/en /Docs/c3em26d2a5_en.pdf.

———. 2013. *World Investment Report 2013: Global Value Chains: Investment and Trade for Development.* Geneva.

———. 2015. *World Investment Report 2015: Reforming International Investment Governance.* Geneva.

———. 2017. *World Investment Report 2017: Investment and the Digital Economy.* Geneva.

Vahter, P., and J. Masso. 2007. "Home versus Host Country Effects of FDI: Searching for New Evidence of Productivity Spillovers." *Applied Economics Quarterly* 53 (2): 165–96.

Wang, M. 2017. "Chinese Overseas Investment." Unpublished (3/19/17).

Wang, P., and Z. H. Yu. 2014. "China's Outward Foreign Direct Investment: The Role of Natural Resources and Technology." *Economic and Political Studies* 2 (2).

Wells, L. T., Jr. 2009. "Third World Multinationals: A Look Back." In *Emerging Multinationals in Emerging Markets*, edited by R. Ramamurti and J. V. Singh, 23–41. Cambridge, UK: Cambridge University Press.

Zhang, Y. and H. Roelfsema. 2014. "Unravelling The Complex Motivations Behind China's Outward FDI." *Journal of the Asia Pacific Economy* 19 (1): 89–100.

Zheng, N., Y. Wei, Y. Zhang, and J. Yang. 2016. "In Search of Strategic Assets through Cross-Border Merger and Acquisitions: Evidence from Chinese Multinational Enterprises in Developed Economies." *International Business Review* 25 (1): 177–86.

FDI in Fragile and Conflict-Affected Situations | 5

Alexandros Ragoussis and Heba Shams

Foreign direct investment (FDI) in fragile and conflict-affected situations (FCS)[1] represents just 1 percent of global flows, more than five times less per capita than the world average, according to latest estimates. Despite increasing tenfold over the last two decades, FDI is still mostly concentrated in a handful of fragile countries, all middle-income or resource-rich or both. Furthermore, differences in FDI potential and dependence within the FCS group are also stark: FDI inflow as a share of gross national income (GNI) ranges from more than 40 percent in Liberia to virtually zero in South Sudan.

In response to the proliferation of conflicts and forced displacements in this decade to date, the development community has committed itself to doing more for fragile countries. Foreign investment is a central part of that commitment, yet consensus on the facts, drivers, and imperatives surrounding it has not yet been achieved. Better understanding is key for the development community to design the right interventions.

But can FDI support stabilization and prevent violent conflicts? FDI can create jobs, generate wealth and tax income, and thereby affect what fragile societies risk losing by engaging in conflict (that is, the opportunity cost of war). Yet, while the argument makes intuitive sense, the empirical evidence on the direct relationship between foreign investment and conflict remains inconclusive. Some argue that a foreign presence can generate grievances by adversely affecting income distribution and worsening political unrest in low-income countries (Gissinger and Gleditsch 1999), while others contend that trade and FDI complement each other in reducing conflict risk (Polachek and Sevastianova 2012). More nuanced effects have been acknowledged, too, such as that FDI reduces the duration of civil wars but not the likelihood of their onset (Barbieri and Reuveny 2005).

Clearly, not all FDI has the same effects on host countries. The sectoral distribution of FDI, especially amid distorted conditions, can potentially reinforce opposite trends. This is partly why policy discussions have focused on dilemmas surrounding "good" and "bad" FDI in fragile contexts, often related to the exploitation of natural resources (International Dialogue for Peace-Building and State-Building 2016). Recognizing the limitations of econometrics in addressing the question is also critical. The pro-cyclical movement of foreign investment,[2] and the indirect channels through which it affects

135

the opportunity cost of conflict, complicate the identification of its effect on peace and stability.

The purpose of this chapter is to take a step back from this discussion and fill in a gap in understanding FDI across these sensitive environments. The discussion rests on a fundamental notion of FDI's *potential* to generate jobs, increase wealth, and improve public goods—all of which are essential for a stable and prosperous society. The chapter considers the *where, who,* and *how* of foreign investment in FCS before delving into difficult questions of *why* and of ways to support investment through policies that, in principle, would also enhance stability.

Foreign investment in fragile situations has the potential to deliver good results. Apart from resource-seeking investment, the structure of economic activity in these countries reveals a strong potential for FDI-driven value creation in sectors with low domestic competition or others experiencing growth attributable to postconflict reconstruction. But investors are cautious: outside natural resource sectors, they concentrate their investment in a limited number of capital-intensive activities. They also tend to commit to smaller projects, create fewer jobs, and avoid geographical exposure to security risks. FCS pose unique conditions and risks at both the operational and institutional levels where investment climate reforms could make a difference.

Investment climate reforms that unlock opportunities for the private sector and create jobs are necessary to consolidate peace and move from fragility to resilience. Broad and deep changes to the rules of the game are essential. An investment climate reform strategy requires proper sequencing and prioritizing and must take into account the country's conflict dynamics, economic opportunity, institutional capacity, and willingness to reform. The strategy must be implemented in a balanced way to secure short-term gains while building the momentum for deep institutional transformation. The key elements of the strategy should be reducing risks to investors while maximizing investment opportunities and rewards.

The Where, Who, and How of Foreign Investment in FCS

Foreign sources of income sustain a large part of economic activity in fragile and conflict-affected situations. Yet international investors do not typically consider FCS as hosts, owing to economic fundamentals and fragility, which are mutually reinforcing. While fragile situations are remarkably heterogeneous (box 5.1), commonalities do exist: investment opportunities arise in capital-intensive activities sustained by foreign demand, particularly during transitions from conflict to peace. But investors are cautious in how they leverage these opportunities. Those who understand the context do better.

FCS Depend Heavily on Foreign Sources of Income

Foreign investment, along with other sources of income sustains a large part of economic activity in fragile and conflict-affected situations. The combination of remittances from the diaspora, official development assistance (ODA), official aid, and foreign investment often exceed a third of national income at varying degrees of dependence (figure 5.1).

Diaspora income, ODA, and FDI interact in a variety of complementary ways in fragile states. For example, although remittances are largely used for consumption, they are increasingly seen as a resource for investment.[3] And while a lot of debate has been had on the relationship between ODA and FDI, conventional wisdom and empirical evidence point to the catalyzing effects of ODA on FDI. The composition of ODA matters in this respect: Assistance used to finance complementary inputs, such as public infrastructure and human capital investments, has been shown to draw in FDI, while assistance in the form of pure physical capital transfers may crowd out investment (Selaya and Sunesen 2012).

The prevalence of FDI among foreign sources of income reflects to a large extent heterogeneous conditions among FCS.

BOX 5.1

FCS Are Highly Heterogeneous in Terms of Risks and Opportunities for Investment

Although encountered mainly in low-income countries, fragile and conflict-affected situations (FCS) persist also in middle-income countries where opportunities for investment are markedly different. Abundant natural resources explain the middle-income status of such FCS as Iraq or Libya, but not exclusively. The former Yugoslavia and Lebanon are examples of middle-income countries with a history of violent conflict. Investment opportunities in this group are associated not only with greater purchasing power of the population and market growth, but also with existing industrial structures, skills, and government capacity that allow working toward more ambitious targets in terms of investment climate.

The risks facing investors also vary across FCS, affecting investor decisions as well as the scope and depth of necessary reforms. Along the so-called fragility chain, conflict-affected situations include territories under severe risk of conflict, others experiencing active conflicts, and states in postconflict transitions.

Countries at risk of conflict suffer substantial economic marginalization, political polarization, and external stresses, which heighten uncertainty and point to the need for prevention of conflict-related situations, including through foreign direct investment (FDI).

Subnational conflict within otherwise stable countries means that foreign investment can take place on a large scale in stable parts of the territory, and that government capacity for reform exists.

Active large-scale conflict and crisis situations are distinct in that investment no longer takes place and priority is given to political solutions and basic stabilization.

Finally, *states in postconflict or frequent conflict-to-peace transitions* typically suffer from weak institutions with poor governance but offer the greatest opportunities for economic transformation through investment, as well as momentum for reform.

FIGURE 5.1 FCS Depend on Income from ODA, the Diaspora, and Foreign Investors, 2015

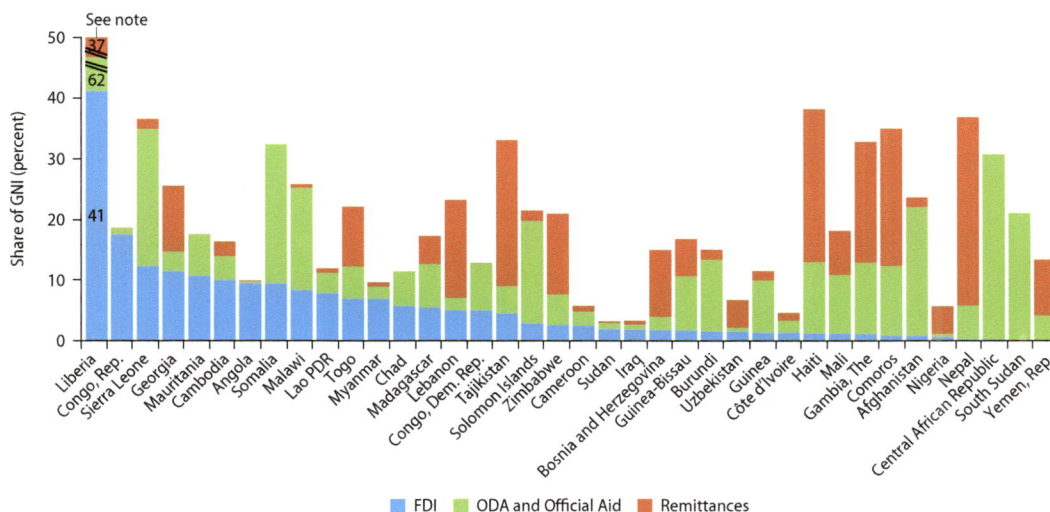

Source: Computation based on World Development Indicators, World Bank.
Note: The figures for ODA and official aid and remittances for Liberia have been scaled, and the actual figures are noted in the graph. The Central African Republic and South Sudan have missing values for remittances. FCS = fragile and conflict-affected situations; FDI = foreign direct investment; GNI = gross national income; ODA = official development assistance.

Remittances, for example, are important for a few fragile states with large diaspora populations (for example, Haiti, Lebanon, Liberia, and Nepal). Foreign investment represents a substantial share in such resource-rich countries as the Republic of Congo and Sierra Leone, while smaller low-income states (for example, island territories) rely far more on ODA and official aid. Unstable territories in transition fall under this category too: Afghanistan, the Central African Republic, Libya, Somalia, and South Sudan depend heavily on aid for reconstruction and less on FDI despite their wealth of natural resources.

Investment in Many FCS Is below Potential

Economic fundamentals alone—such as current size of the market, growth, and savings—in addition to remoteness, trade openness, and natural resources would suggest lower levels of expected investment in FCS than in the rest of the world (annex 5B). Among emerging economies, the bottom quartile of investment predicted by economic fundamentals is populated mostly by FCS (figure 5B.1). This result is not surprising because fragile and conflict-affected situations represent small and remote markets

that trade less with the rest of the world than other emerging economies.

Fragility also takes a heavy toll: the distance between expected and actual investment is considerable (map 5.1), highlighting the extent to which investment opportunities remain unleveraged. Considering that fragility affects existing economic fundamentals that are used to form expectations, the distance between actual investment and what would likely have taken place under stability and peace is likely even greater. Only a few countries had high levels of both expected and actual investment in recent years: Iraq, Lebanon, Bosnia and Herzegovina, Sudan, Côte d'Ivoire, and others. Countries currently experiencing high levels of violence, such as Libya, the Syrian Arab Republic, and the Republic of Yemen, also presented high expected values at points of their latest available data (that is, before conflicts escalated).

All the countries with higher expected values within the group are either middle-income with developed local markets that can attract market-seeking investment or countries possessing natural resources with high potential for investment. Remoteness to large industrial economies makes even fewer of them attractive for export-oriented, efficiency-seeking FDI; notable examples being Bosnia and

MAP 5.1   FDI Flows to FCS Remain below Potential, 2008–14

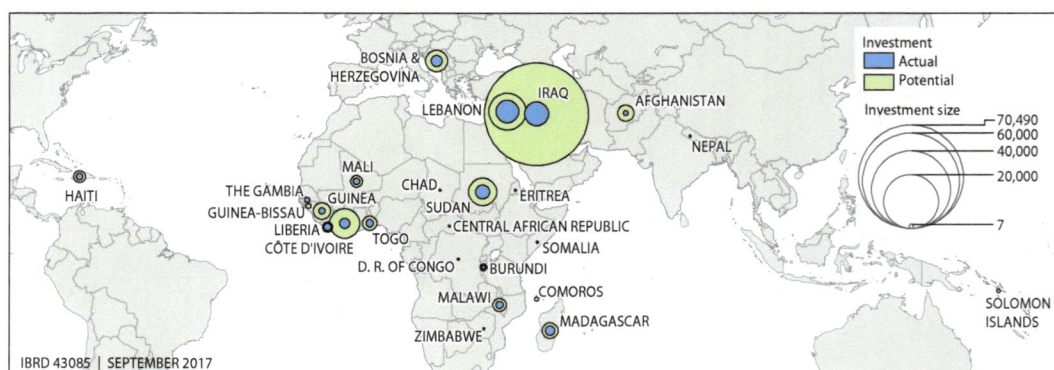

Source: Computation based on Investment Map Database, International Trade Centre; World Development Indicators, World Bank. CEPII Database; Fragile States Index (2014), the Fund for Peace.
Note: Investment expectations based on economic fundamentals, represented with green circles, shed light on how much FDI can be expected nett of the effect of fragility. Separating the negative impact of fragility from the predicted inflow (that is, fitted value) from a regression on FDI determinants yields this estimate. Actual Investment flows are represented with a blue circle for comparison. Data are only presented for selected countries officially designated as FCS (in millions of US dollars). Countries with latest data from before 2012, or significantly changed circumstances since the latest data point, are excluded. FCS = fragile and conflict-affected situations; FDI = foreign direct investment.

Herzegovina, Lebanon, and to a lesser extent, Haiti. The gap between expected and actual investment is the highest in Iraq, a country suffering from protracted instability and violence for more than two decades. Most FCS have many disadvantages—as in market size, growth, connectivity, openness, and natural resources—making them less appealing to investors. Burundi is typical of FCS, with low expectations for market-seeking, efficiency-seeking, and resource-seeking investments, all of which are almost entirely unrealized.

Investment Is Concentrated in Capital-Intensive Activities

Opportunities for investment vary considerably from one fragile situation to another since the group is highly variable in economic development terms. While most are low-income, middle-income countries in the group (for example, Angola, Bosnia and Herzegovina, and Iraq) offer different opportunities and development prospects.

Furthermore, economies in active conflict present dynamics that differ sharply from what is experienced in pre- or postconflict cases (see box 5.1).

However imperfect,[4] the available evidence broadly confirms the scarcity of capital-intensive activities in FCS, except for mining, and oil and gas in some resource-rich states. One can argue that it is precisely in these capital-intensive sectors where large business opportunities lie, given the lack of local competition. Yet this is not always so because fragility discourages financial market development, which in turn creates barriers to growth. Labor-intensive activities, especially services and agriculture, are essential for the survival of much of the population and hence dominate the economy. However, variation within the group is pronounced: for example, the share of services ranges from 17 percent in Liberia to 90 percent in Lebanon, and in agriculture, from 1 percent in Libya to 64 percent in Liberia (figure 5.2).

FIGURE 5.2   **Agriculture Dominates Highly Fragile Economies**

Share of agriculture in GDP of FCS, 2014 or latest year

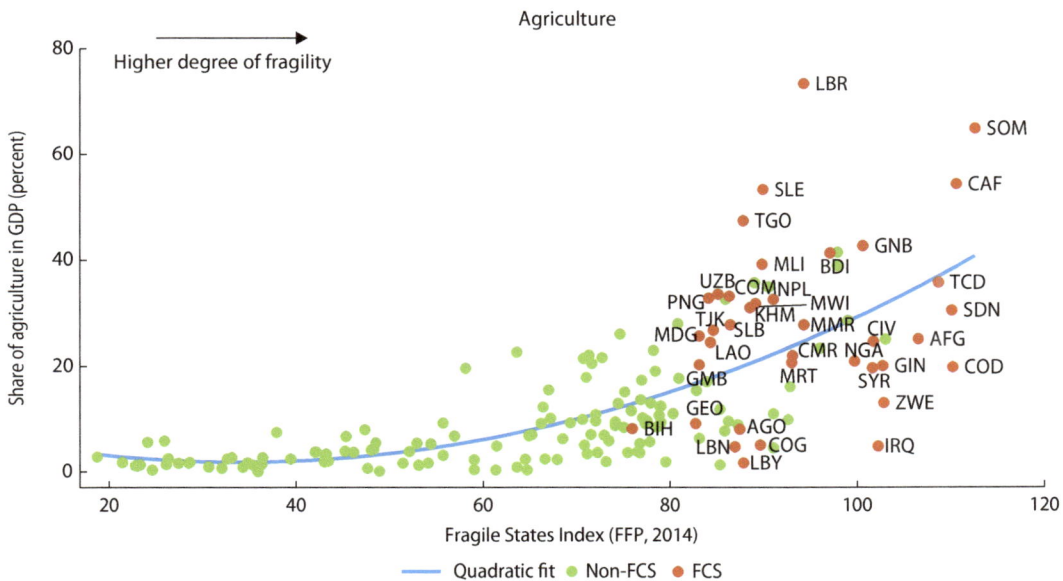

Source: Computation based on the United Nations Statistics Division database on gross value added across sectors; Fragile States Index, the Fund for Peace.
Note: Not all countries at high degree of fragility, according to FFP, are officially classified as FCS by the World Bank. The latter group is designated with red and labeled. FCS = fragile and conflict-affected situations; GDP = gross domestic product.

The agricultural sector itself is highly fragmented. The bulk of employment in FCS is in the small farmer and household enterprise[5] sectors, driven by necessity and resilience rather than growth.

Whether a country is at a high risk of conflict, is in conflict, or is postconflict matters for how prevalent different economic activities are, explaining at least partly the variation within the group. For example, construction accounts for a large share of economic activity in such FCS as Lebanon, which are not in full-blown conflict, or countries where large reconstruction efforts are taking place, such as Afghanistan or Angola. The weight of the sector in countries with deep fragility and frequent peace-to-conflict transitions like Somalia or Sudan is significantly smaller. More capital-intensive activities, such as manufacturing, exhibit reverse linear relationships with the levels of fragility—specifically because of the capital flight in the face of fragility (IFC 2017).

Opportunities Grow during Transitions from Conflict to Peace

Within the group of FCS, postconflict economies offer significant new business opportunities. The reestablishment of peace is associated with renewed investment confidence and growth. In fact, evidence points to distinct episodes of high growth in the wake of conflicts and many opportunities for investment. Recent evidence shows that, a year after the end of conflict, FDI increases dramatically, and, three years after the end of conflict, inflows about double relative to the last years of conflict (Mueller, Piemontese, and Tapsoba 2017). By sector, construction and services experience high growth and pull labor out of agriculture in postconflict years. An illustration of the average share each activity gains or loses over a 12-year period after peace is established (figure 5.3) suggests common trends across postconflict countries[6] and time periods. For example, the weight of agriculture in gross domestic

FIGURE 5.3   Postconflict Growth Clocks
Median change in shares of GDP by sector 1–12 years postconflict, 1990–2014

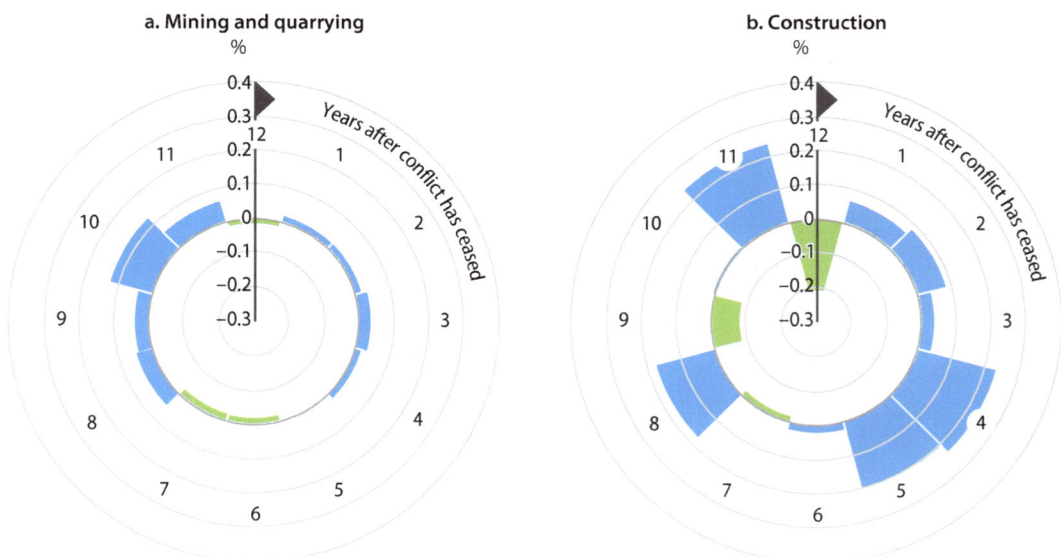

a. Mining and quarrying

b. Construction

figure continues next page

FIGURE 5.3   **Postconflict Growth Clocks (continued)**

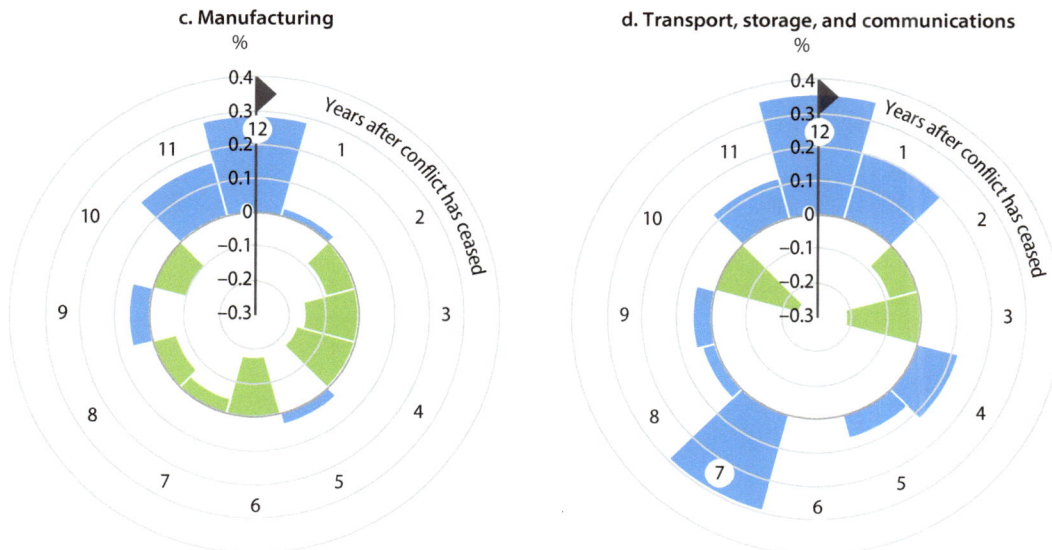

c. Manufacturing

d. Transport, storage, and communications

Source: Computation based on United Nations Statistics Division database on gross value added across sectors on selected postconflict economies; Uppsala Conflict Dataset (1990–2014).
Note: "Growth clocks" present for each sector the median year-to-year change in shares of gross domestic product (GDP) across economies that have recently transitioned from conflict to peace. The bars for each of the 1–12 years postconflict are illustrated at the positions of hours in a hypothetical clock. The inner circle represents zero growth, the blue bars represent a positive change, and the green bars a negative change. The exact year the conflict has ceased is identified using the Uppsala Conflict dataset, and the sample covers postconflict economies for the period 1990–2014.

product (GDP) gradually declines after the cessation of hostilities.[7]

Of all economic sectors, construction shows the most pronounced growth in the aftermath of conflicts. The sector grows in the short run in response to reconstruction efforts and fluctuates around a steady state over the medium term. Much of this growth represents an opportunity for foreign firms (box 5.2). Higher rates of growth in telecommunications and transport are apparent over the medium term—infrastructural weaknesses possibly explaining the time lag in growth. The necessary conditions for diversification only materialize after a substantial period. Manufacturing, for example, tends to exhibit slower growth in postconflict economies, specifically because conditions for its growth take more time to materialize.[8] In contrast, mining and other sectors that rely on natural resources remain stable throughout, possibly because of the sectors'

resilience during conflict, which translates into little transformation in the aftermath of conflicts.

Foreign Investors Are Cautious

Investment opportunities exist in fragile and postconflict situations but are generally hard for foreign investors to exploit. Multinational corporations (MNCs) will choose to do business in FCS only when the reward outweighs, by a sufficiently large margin, the risk. In addition, MNCs will tend to concentrate in activities where there is limited domestic competition, owing to advantages enjoyed by domestic firms in markets where the political economy is distorted.

High rewards and low competition occur simultaneously only for selected natural resource and other capital-intensive activities, which depend on high demand outside FCS. This exact pattern is confirmed by comparing the distribution of sectoral shares in aggregate

BOX 5.2

Postconflict Growth in Construction and FDI Opportunities

Construction opportunities abound in postconflict countries, where sizable funds are available from donors. For example, in the first decade after conflict ended in Lebanon, the country received about $10 billion for reconstruction, while Bosnia and Herzegovina received $5.4 billion in the same period. How much of this activity actually benefits foreign firms and investors? A disproportionally large part. Local firms are at a disadvantage in seizing these opportunities for several reasons: they lack the capacity and skills to carry out large, complex projects,

and they do not have prior experience with such contracts or how to bid for them. A snapshot of reconstruction efforts in Haiti in 2012 shows that, of the billions spent by the U.S. Agency for International Development, more than 99 percent went to foreign firms. The extent to which the local private sector benefits from the presence of multinational firms depends on supply linkages, the development of which remains a priority in many postconflict contexts.

Sources: Bray 2005; Porter Peschka 2011; Ramachandran and Walz 2012.

investment inflows across FCS and non-FCS low-income countries. While countries in these two groups show significant variation, FCS exhibit systematically different shares in four broad industries: extractives (mining, petroleum, mineral products), construction, forestry and fishing, and food and beverages. Of those, only construction, and food and beverages rely largely on local demand, supplemented in some cases by foreign aid. The opportunity is presumably generated by the absence of downstream value-chain development and capital scarcity for large-scale production. All these sectors are relatively capital-intensive (figure 5.4).

But investors are more cautious when they enter FCS markets, as revealed by greenfield investment patterns across countries (figure 5.5). In natural resource sectors, the range of their choices on scale and location are bound by the location and volume of reserves. By contrast, in sectors other than extractives, the more fragile a country, the less investors will tend to commit to large projects. Avoiding financial exposure at the beginning makes sense where there is significant uncertainty. Investors also tend to commit to fewer jobs for every dollar they invest in FCS. These patterns are probably due to the concentration of projects in capital-intensive

industries coupled with the difficulty of bringing in skilled expatriate staff. Finally, investors tend to concentrate their investment spatially in the most stable territory of the fragile countries.

Understanding the Context Helps in Seizing Opportunities

From capturing local demand and mitigating operational risks to avoiding unintentional consequences, a deep understanding of the local context is necessary for successful foreign investment. While this applies for international business in any context, it is particularly relevant for investment in FCS. Firms employ many strategies in doing so.

Engaging with the local private sector in domestic supply chains features prominently among strategies of foreign firms. Local firms tend to have a higher risk tolerance, know the local market and political economy, and have contacts with the authorities that mitigate risks faced by MNCs (USAID 2016). Some of the risk borne by these entrants can be shared with local suppliers, for example, through license agreements or "contract manufacturing," both of which are safer for MNCs than joint ventures (Campbell 2002).

Operating in a so-called conflict-sensitive manner is another strategy deeply rooted in understanding the local context. Firms in a fragile context stand to aggravate local tensions unintentionally by disproportionally employing staff from one community or another, providing revenue for authorities that engage in human rights violations, or training security forces that can later be deployed in conflicts. To avoid such pitfalls, and the associated risks to their businesses, large MNCs increasingly add to their operational policy such concepts as "do-no-harm" or "conflict sensitivity," which originated in the development and humanitarian community. Adopting a conflict-sensitive approach means that a company invests in understanding the context in which it operates, becomes aware of potential positive and negative effects it may have on a conflict environment, and takes all the necessary steps to avoid causing, or worsening, conflict.

On all these accounts, regional MNCs may have a comparative advantage in these challenging contexts relative to global firms. This category includes, for example, companies

FIGURE 5.4 **Foreign Investors Concentrate in Natural Resources and a Few Other Capital-Intensive Activities**

Distribution of sector shares in inward FDI flows across FCS, 2008–14

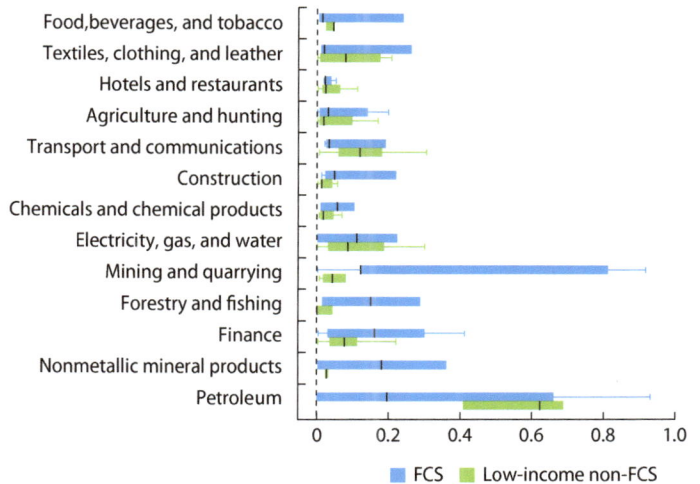

Source: Computation based on Investment Map Database, International Trade Centre; World Development Indicators, World Bank.
Note: The distribution of shares of sectors in total FDI inflows across all FCS (in blue) is compared with the same distribution across all low-income and lower-middle-income non-FCS countries (in green) for which data exist after 2008. Each horizontal box illustrates the median of the distribution across the two groups with a black line; the box delimits the 25th percentile (left) and 75th percentile (right) of each distribution—i.e., the top and bottom quartile; and the lines extending from the box illustrate the full range of shares. FCS = fragile and conflict-affected situations; FDI = foreign direct investment.

FIGURE 5.5 **Outside of Natural Resource Sectors, Investors Are Cautious**

Characteristics of greenfield FDI project announcements, nonextractives, 2008–16

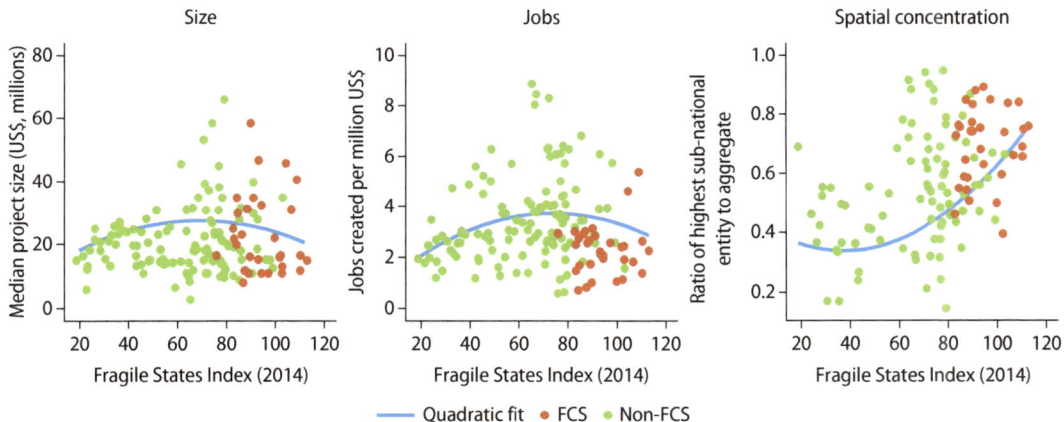

Source: Computation based on fDi Markets database, the Financial Times; Fragile States Index (2014), the Fund for Peace.
Note: The sample does not include extractive industries. Not all countries that are highly fragile according to FFP are officially classified as FCS by the World Bank. The latter group is designated with red. Green represents all other countries. FCS = fragile and conflict-affected situations; FDI = foreign direct investment.

from Lebanon investing in other countries in the Middle East and companies from Morocco and Nigeria expanding into places in West Africa. These firms leverage the fact that they are "local" in a particular area of the world, and have sufficient affinity with their target markets because of the similarity with their home market. Lower risks resulting from this affinity would tend to make investors, in principle, commit to larger projects, and lower information asymmetries for local recruitment that can make a greater difference in terms of stability and in catalyzing further investment. These firms deserve special attention from the development community.

But how much of greenfield investment comes from regional firms? The evidence suggests that it represents a considerable amount (figure 5.6). While the footprint of France and the United Kingdom remains large in Africa and the Middle East, greenfield investment, for example, from the Russian Federation to Uzbekistan, Malaysia to Cambodia, South Africa to Nigeria, Japan and Thailand to Myanmar, and the United Arab Emirates to Iraq confirm that intraregional investment takes place in FCS on a large scale.

Barriers to Investment: Risks and Obstacles

The previous sections have painted a clear picture of the investment potential for most fragile and conflict-affected situations. Even at its lowest benchmark, this potential remains unfulfilled. The data also show that investors are cautious and keep a small footprint, creating fewer jobs relative to similar investments in less risky environments and concentrating in capital-intensive sectors. Understanding the reasons for these trends will help create deeper and more inclusive markets in FCS and expand their investment opportunities.

Several global data sources document what investors and businesses perceive to be the biggest obstacles hindering their ability to expand their investment in a given market. Among these sources are the World Bank Group's Enterprise Surveys[9] and the World Economic Forum's (WEF) Executive Opinion Surveys.[10] Surveys of business executives such as these are frequently used to measure *perceptions* about problems whose severity can be compared across countries and over time. These surveys are particularly appealing when quantitative data are either unavailable or difficult to gather, as in many FCS.

This section looks into the recent findings of the Executive Opinion Survey and the Enterprise Surveys to examine what they tell us about the obstacles and risks that limit the willingness to invest in FCS. Building on these findings, the section analyzes the institutional realities in FCS to understand the scope for

FIGURE 5.6   **Regional Investment Occurs on a Large Scale**
Origins of greenfield FDI project announcements in FCS, 2008–16

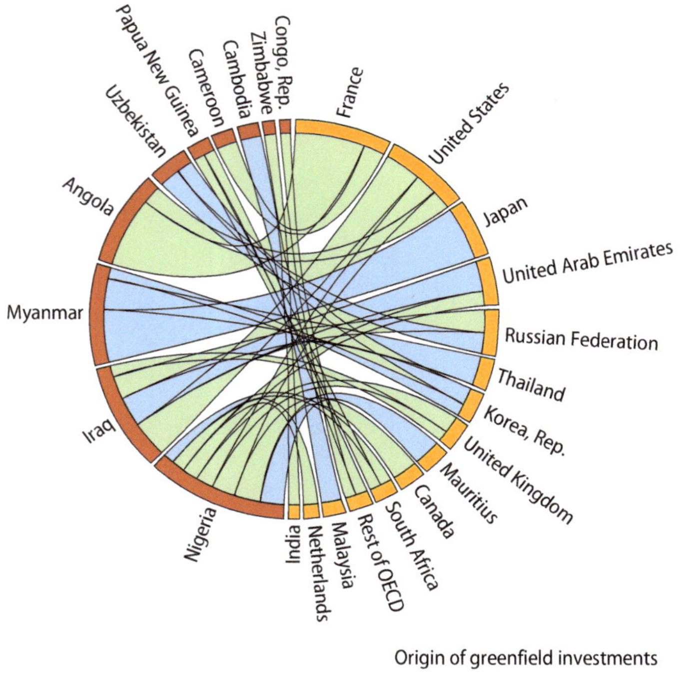

Source: Computation based on Financial Times FDI Markets database, the Financial Times.
Note: Origins (on the right side of the chord diagram, in orange) and FCS destinations (on the left side, in red) of greenfield projects exceeding $3 billion since 2008. Blue chords indicate intraregional investment. FCS = fragile and conflict-affected situations; FDI = foreign direct investment; OECD = Organisation for Economic Co-operation and Development.

government action to promote foreign investment.

Charting the Obstacles Facing Investors

The fundamental questions that arise from the analysis of market conditions and risks facing businesses in fragile situations are:

- How pervasive the challenges are (that is, how disruptive risks and market conditions can be for business), and
- How specific they are to FCS (that is, how distinct they are to fragility and conflict rather than a specific level of development).

However imperfect, the WEF Executive Opinion Survey offers answers to both questions. Average *perceptions* on the intensity of constraints across fragile states shed light on the major challenges. And the difference in averages between FCS and non-FCS low-income countries determines how FCS-specific a problem is. By charting these two variables on a scatter plot (figure 5.7, severity on the horizontal axis and FCS specificity on the vertical axis), four groups of challenges can be distinguished: those that are both severe and FCS-specific (top-right hand corner of the panel); those that are severe but similar to what is experienced in other low-income countries (bottom right); those that are FCS-specific but not severe (top left); and the remaining variables, which are less relevant on both dimensions (bottom left).

Operational Constraints Are Most Pervasive

Operational constraints are high on the mind of surveyed businesses as an obstacle to growth, affecting the opportunity for investment in fragile environments (figure 5.7). The quality of electricity is at the top of this list, followed by constraints related to the size of markets (domestic and foreign), transport infrastructure, and access to finance. The results are hardly surprising: frequent and prolonged power outages, as well as shortages in the supply of water, are more common in FCS than in non-FCS, according to several surveys (Speakman and Rysova 2015). In the Republic of Yemen, for example, three out of four firms surveyed by the World Bank in 2013 reported power outages as a major constraint on their operations. Because of similar power grid failures, in South Sudan two-thirds of all power consumed by firms in 2014 was produced by privately owned generators, imposing added costs of operations, an upper limit to their scale, and narrower returns to investment (Speakman and Rysova 2015). The numbers are equally striking in other domains and countries. Banking penetration in Guinea-Bissau, for example, remained below 1 percent of the population in 2013, and access to finance was cited by three out of four businesses as an important constraint for business operations, on par with electricity (Arvanitis 2014). The constraints identified by executives are also interrelated. Low local demand, for example, boils down to widespread poverty, limiting the volume of business activity that the local population can sustain, while foreign markets often remain out of reach because of the poor quality of transport infrastructure.

Institutional Constraints Are Severe and Diverse

Business executives also identify a number of institutional constraints that hinder business expansion in FCS. Two clusters of institutional concerns can be identified: one relates to property rights and the means for their enforcement, and the second concerns the quality of public governance. Executives responding to the survey identified weaknesses in intellectual property rights, judicial independence, and hence dispute settlement as severe obstacles in FCS. Weakness in property right regimes was given a score of severity below the median, which may be more reflective of the small footprint that investors keep in FCS and the coping mechanisms they deploy (including political risk insurance).

FIGURE 5.7 **Perceptions on Severity and FCS-Specificity of Challenges, 2016**

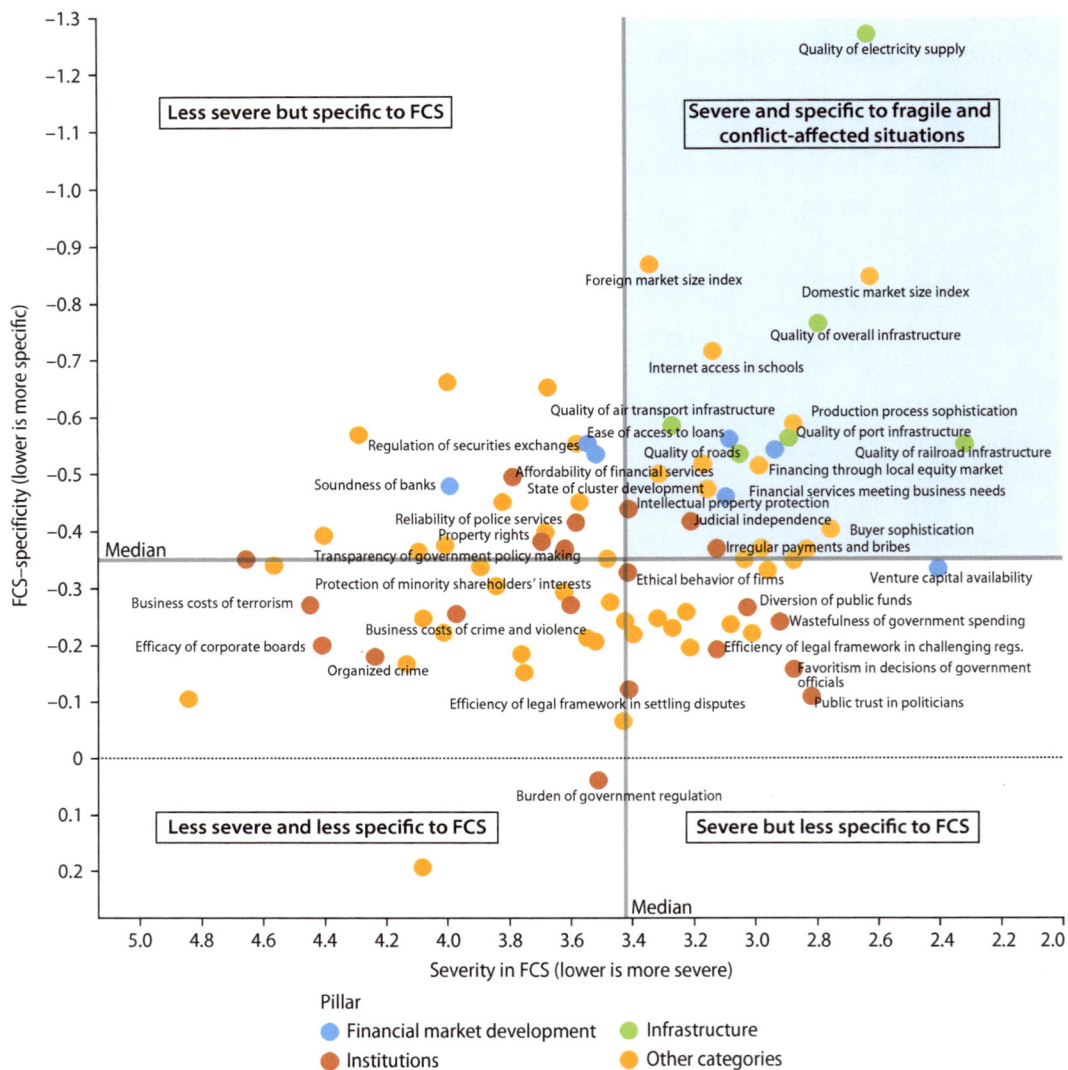

Source: Computation based on Global Competitiveness Index database, World Economic Forum.
Note: FCS = fragile and conflict-affected situations.

The quality of public governance is also a major obstacle to private investment in FCS. Issues of irregular payments and bribes, weak public trust in politicians, and favoritism in decision making by government officials were perceived as severe obstacles.

The analysis of the WEF Executive Opinion Survey Data points to another element that strongly influences the choice of

approach to private sector development in FCS. Executives operating in FCS rank the burden of government regulations below average in terms of severity. It also ranks very low in terms of FCS-specificity. This is corroborated by the findings of the Enterprise Surveys, which show that the amount of time that senior management spent on dealing with government regulations is lowest on average in FCS, at 8.6 percent, rising to 11 percent in past-FCS (figure 5.8). Thus, the problem in FCS may be less one of regulatory burden and more the absence of needed market regulation.

The Link between Operational and Institutional Constraints

The analysis now turns to the state of public institutions in FCS using global indicators. It aims to illustrate that, while institutional weaknesses are a defining feature of FCS, cross-country variations are significant for the design of private sector development approaches in FCS.

Institutional weaknesses in FCS are partly the cause of operational constraints that worry foreign investors. Government capacity, regulatory effectiveness, and institutional quality are fundamentally interconnected with market conditions that constrain businesses. Infrastructure projects, for example, require a minimum government capacity to deliver[11] but also basic regulation and enforcement to protect investor property rights.

Examples of the relationship between institutional and operational constraints abound. Successful power projects in Afghanistan, Côte d'Ivoire, Guinea, Iraq, Mali, Myanmar, and Nepal all involved extensive work developing regulations and government sector plans, building the relevant government capacity, providing up-front advisory resources in project development, and supporting complementary government investments (for example, electricity distribution and provision of co-financing support and risk guarantees) (Mills and Fan 2006, 29; USAID 2009, 45, 48).

The same applies to development of financial services to address the scarcity of capital. Banks avoid setting up operations in territories without viable banking laws and foreign exchange regulations (Bray 2005). Initially, they tend to concentrate on international customers—such as diplomats and aid

FIGURE 5.8 **Senior Management Spent Less Time Dealing with Government Regulations in FCS**

Average share of senior management time spent dealing with the requirements of government regulation (percent)

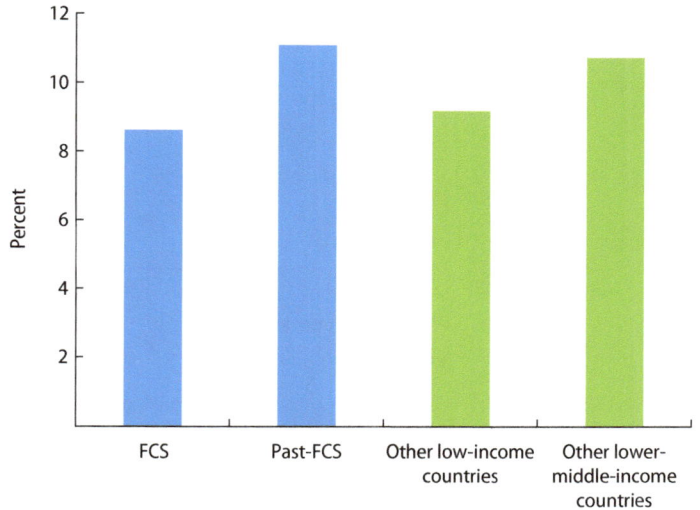

Source: Computation based on Enterprise Surveys, World Bank.

workers—and may not develop a retail market for several years after the end of the conflict, until such regulatory conditions are met. In addition, a key reason that foreign market access is prohibitively expensive for firms, including MNCs, in fragile countries is the logistical burden of certification requirements, corruption in customs authorities, and other failures directly related to institutional and governance weaknesses (Hoeffler 2012).

To conclude, investors and businesses face severe challenges in FCS. The obstacles range from market characteristics to infrastructure and access to finance constraints combined with a myriad of institutional constraints. Institutions in FCS are weak and the weakness has persisted over the years. There are, however, significant variations in weaknesses among these countries (figure 5.9). These variations matter in determining the best approach to facilitating and attracting investment in a particular country.

FIGURE 5.9 Varying Levels of Fragility and Government Effectiveness among FCS

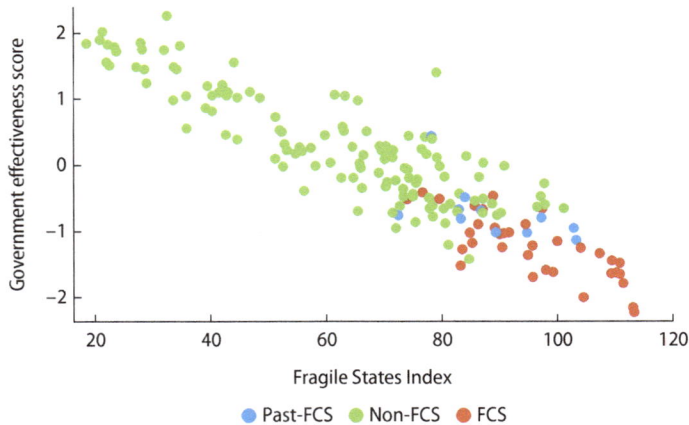

Source: Worldwide Governance Indicators, World Bank; Fragile States Index, the Fund for Peace.
Note: Government effectiveness is an aggregate indicator that reflects perceptions of the quality of public services, the quality of the civil service and its independence from political pressures, the quality of policy formulation and implementation, and the credibility of the government's commitment to such policies. This is part of the Worldwide Governance Indicators dataset.

Investment Climate Reforms Can Create Markets and Maximize Investment

Investment climate reforms are essentially legal, regulatory, procedural, and institutional reforms that enhance a country's investment competitiveness. Such reforms can affect, in different ways, the risk–return equation that investors use to make their investment decisions. Some reforms reduce risk to investors by improving the transparency and predictability of investment policy making. Other investment climate reforms contribute to increasing investment opportunity and maximizing the return on investment by facilitating access to the market or by encouraging clustering and interfirm linkages.

Analysts agree that investment climate reforms are *necessary* but *insufficient* for private sector development in fragile countries. Where they diverge is on the appropriate timing and sequencing of reforms (box 5.3) and the balance between broad-based interventions and direct interventions that benefit specific communities, firms, sectors, economic spaces, or identified value chains.

As the challenges in FCS mount and the pressure for short-term returns on reforms increases, policy makers tend to de-emphasize broad-based deep reforms in favor of interventions with quicker yields in terms of job creation and investment flows. This tendency, however, poses some risks. The transformation from a conflict economy to a peace economy, and from a fragile market to a resilient and inclusive one, is not possible without changing the rules of the game. A targeted approach that strengthens the institutional foundation for the market is therefore the way to go.

This section analyzes the limits of traditional approaches to investment climate reform and outlines a path forward to successfully de-risk investment and expand investment opportunity through reforms that take into account countries' institutional capacity, the investment opportunities that they offer, and the nature of conflict and instability.

Traditional Approaches to Investment Climate Reforms Have Their Limits

Private investment attracted attention as an area of focus in FCS development only in the early 2000s. A 2013 review conducted by the World Bank Group's Independent Evaluation Group (IEG) of the investment climate portfolio identified some 120 projects implemented in FCS with an average of 12 active projects a year. This indicates significant attention paid to private sector issues in FCS in the past decade.

Traditional investment climate reforms in FCS have tended to focus mostly on business licensing, permitting, and administrative barriers to the growth of the private sector, as well as investment promotion and public–private dialogue. Many FCS have used *Doing Business*[12] indicators to map and frame their strategy for business environment reform, focusing initially on simplifying burdensome administrative processes (IEG 2015).

BOX 5.3

Prioritizing Economic Reforms

The *World Development Report 2011* on *Conflict, Security and Development* (World Bank Group 2011) identifies legitimate institutions as the common "missing factor" in countries affected by violence relative to those that do not slide into violence despite comparable threats and stresses. The 2011 Report found that countries with good governance indicators have 30 to 40 percent lower risk of civil war than their peers with weaker governance indicators. Therefore, the path to resilience must be through institutional transformation. Yet institutional reform is difficult, even more so in countries starting from a low base. Prioritization, thus, is a central theme of the path out of violence as envisioned by the WDR.

The Report advocates prioritizing "ending and preventing violence" as the main impact that all interventions in fragile and conflict-affected situations should aim to achieve. Armed by research and analysis, the Report identified three key outcomes as essential to achieving this ultimate objective: security, justice, and jobs. It also showed how the three outcomes are interlinked. In Kosovo, for example, creating jobs by encouraging regional trade depended on securing the main road connecting Kosovo to neighboring countries. In Mozambique, providing livelihood opportunities to ex-combatants was essential to achieving security.

As far as economic reform is concerned, the Report defines job creation as the priority outcome that all efforts should be geared toward. As such, this outcome determines the sequencing path identified by the Report. It argues for starting the process by *building confidence* through signaling change and achieving short-term results and moving from that to *transforming institutions*. It also stresses that this process is a repeated one with transition being an ever-expanding spiral of change.

Regulatory simplification and removing barriers to investment entry were identified by the Report as good confidence-building signals that can yield early results. In the same vein, addressing infrastructure constraints, such as access to electricity and transit, were also identified as good early confidence-building interventions that can stimulate the private sector. The Report also highlighted the importance of value chain development through skills building, access to finance and technology, and connecting producers to markets as a second stage of intervention suitable for fragile environments. Deeper institutional reform such as, privatization, may take longer and may not be suitable for early-stage interventions.

The Report stresses, however, that prioritization should be based on the local context. Priorities should be identified not based on a prototypical prescription but rather on the basis of assessment of the reality in each country. The Report indicates that countries with a long tradition of strong institutions, such as some of the middle-income countries affected by conflict, may be able to take on more ambitious institutional transformations at an early stage that other countries affected by conflict may be unable to do.

The central message of the Report is that strengthening legitimate institutions that can provide citizens with security, justice, and jobs is crucial for breaking the cycle of violence. This institutional transformation, however, should adopt "best-fit" not "best practices" approaches. Institutional transformation takes time. It took the fastest reforming countries in the 20th century 20 years to achieve a functioning bureaucratic quality. So, proceed with realism and recognize that the "scope and speed of reforms are themselves risk factors."

Evaluations of these reforms did not find clear evidence of the relationship between simplification and investment flows or job creation. They also questioned the realism of such reform efforts considering the low levels of institutional capacity and political commitment found in many FCS. It is now clear that investment climate reforms must go well beyond simplifying procedures and must respond more clearly to the challenges and characteristics of FCS.

There is value in prioritizing the simplification of business regulations over revamping and expansion at the early stages of reform in FCS. The rationale for this approach is that such reforms give the necessary signal of friendliness toward business and mark a departure from the past. They have also been seen to produce short-term results needed to build confidence in the reforms (World Bank Group 2011, 157–66).

It therefore bears noting, before outlining an approach that takes into account the limits of traditional approaches to reform, the continued relevance of such approaches as part of a more targeted package of reforms:

1. Improving the business environment with the guidance of the *Doing Business* indicators gives reformers in FCS the quick wins needed to sustain the momentum for reform.
2. *Doing Business* reforms cut across government agencies and, when implemented effectively, they can be an opportunity for building a coalition of reformers.
3. Simplifying regulations and removing obsolete rules is a key step toward freeing the capacity of government to regulate effectively and reduce opportunities for rent-seeking.

New Approaches to Investment Climate Reforms Create Markets

The agenda for investment climate reform in fragile countries is long, yet institutional capacity is typically low and patience for results limited. Thus, such reforms must be designed for the long-term goal of institution building with an eye on the short-term goal of creating jobs and attracting investment. The long-term effort of building institutions and developing regulatory capacity should be combined with faster-yielding reforms that target priority sectors and support value chains.

Sectors offering the most immediate promise should have priority in long-term interventions. For example, in postconflict construction booms, construction permit reforms and removal of entry barriers that benefit the construction sector, among other

sectors, should get priority. Targeted approaches to reform, thus, can be seen to have a greater influence on reforms in FCS.

A market-creation approach to investment climate reform would focus on reducing the risk to investment in fragile countries, and on expanding the investment opportunity and maximizing its rewards. Moreover, the risk–return equation differs by type of investor. Investors with affinity for the jurisdiction—such as local investors, diaspora investors, or investors from neighboring countries with cultural ties to fragile countries—are equipped with local knowledge that may offset some of the risks precluding other investors. Noting this distinction is important for designing policies that remove obstacles to investment faced by this amenable group of investors.

De-Risking: Reducing Risks Faced by Investors

The defining risks of a fragile country for investors, domestic or foreign, are:

- Security risks arising from political conflict or private criminal violence, and
- Political risk arising from institutional fragility.

Investment climate reforms that better protect investments, improve transparency, and encourage rule-based decision making reduce the perception of political risk among investors. Spatial solutions that create secure zones for investors to operate also contribute to reducing the security risk and make investment opportunities more accessible.

Existing investors are the first category of investors that should be targeted by de-risking interventions. As noted earlier, FCS attract their own pioneer investors, albeit at a lower rate. When the return to investment exceeds the cost of risk, investors come. They often initially invest mainly in the extractive sector, but also in telecommunications, finance, and construction. The first step for investment climate reform in fragile countries is to identify the pool of existing investors and to set up systems for investor aftercare and grievance redress so that these investors remain. This approach works for all FCS regardless of their level of institutional capacity.

Government services that seek to retain investors should also target domestic investors. These investors, especially high-growth ones, also leave the country if the risks exceed rewards. So investor retention interventions that reduce the risks to investment can also be used to prevent this type of capital flight and protect domestic private sector capacity.

Recent unpublished investor surveys conducted as part of the World Bank Group's engagement in FCS have revealed that investors in these economies are well acclimated to the risks of violence and terrorism but are less willing or able to handle the challenges posed by adverse regulations or cumbersome processes. In one case, investors indicated that the number one reason for considering divestment and relocation out of a particular market was regulatory and procedural constraints.[13]

Investor aftercare systems and grievance redress mechanisms should take into account the government's institutional capacity. They should also reflect the political economy of the country. In FCS, investors' grievances are as likely to arise from formal government action as they are from informal rules and institutions such as customary laws and tribal authorities. Any mechanism set up to identify and address such grievances should be able to influence formal and informal decision making (Echandi 2013).

Targeting investment climate reforms to subnational regions that demonstrate higher levels of security and stability is another way of lowering the risk to investors and creating safer spaces for economic activity. This approach can be combined with special economic zones (SEZs) or other types of spatial solutions to reassure investors in FCS. In addition to minimizing geographical exposure to conflict, SEZs can help address several other problems, such as infrastructural, regulatory, or skills deficiencies. At a critical mass of companies, the zones can also foster knowledge and skills transfer along local value chains. Variations of these approaches have been tried in fragile states with mixed results. A key difficulty is the requirement for sufficient state capacity in formulating and implementing a coherent, responsive, and reasonable SEZ package, without either failing to do so or being captured by vested interests (AfDB 2015).

In Iraq, where more than 50 percent of the population were affected by conflict in 2016, private investment flowed to more stable regions, such as Basra in the South and the Kurdish region in the north. Institutional reforms to encourage private sector development were undertaken at the subnational level. In Iraq, with natural resources, large population, high GDP per capita, and long institutional tradition, severe and widespread conflict did not preclude opportunities for both investment and reform.

Maximizing Investment Opportunities

Encouraging Formalization and Supporting Firms with High Growth Potential

One of the key effects of conflict and insecurity is excessive business informality. In response to conflict and fragility, high-potential domestic firms tend to flee the country while small firms tend to be informal and "go under the radar" to avoid harassment or extortion by public authorities. These trends reduce the size and productivity of economic activities, and undermine market development. They increase the cost of operations as they mandate reliance on foreign input. In some cases, where needed inputs cannot be secured, they may render the investment opportunity unrealizable. Encouraging formalization and supporting domestic firms with high growth potential is therefore a key component of a private sector development strategy in fragile states.

While not all economic activities have to be formalized, a high degree of formality is necessary for markets to be created and for investment to flow. Domestic firms cannot attract equity investment and foreign investors cannot enter the market by partnering with domestic firms without formalization.

Investment climate reforms that help high-growth economic activity shift to the formal sector are key to this process. Depending on the degree of fragility, the demand for reform can be as basic as setting up a well-functioning company registration process and introducing appropriate company laws. In other contexts, other incentives to formalization may be needed.

Linking Domestic Firms to Foreign Direct Investors

Another cost of conflict and fragility is the fragmentation of the market and the loss of firm clusters and cross-sectoral linkages. The underdevelopment of business clusters poses a severe constraint specifically for fragile countries. This, combined with the typically small size of the local market, underscores the importance of focusing on investment climate reforms that target the development of local suppliers and link them to foreign investors operating in the country.

Since investment in fragile states concentrates reforms in a small number of sectors—such as extractives, construction, and telecommunication, with variations across countries—to support the development of linkages, they should focus on sectors that attract investment in the specific countries.

Targeted Investment Promotion Efforts

In addition to conflict and fragility, one of the key inhibitors of investment flows to FCS is the lack of reliable and accessible country-level information important for investor decision making. Better access to information may help offset the adverse impact of poor country image and reputation that result from media reporting of conflict and fragility. For this reason, reforms must build the capacity of the country's institutions to carry out *targeted* investment promotion. The country must also be able to map its investment opportunities and identify sectors with potential for investment attraction.

Finally, as noted earlier, highly skilled labor and large domestic investors tend to flee the country during conflict. This potential pool of diaspora investors also demands a strategy of targeted investment promotion and attraction. The political economy of diaspora engagement varies from country to country, and tailored strategies that take the reality of conflict into account are critical.

Taking a Regional Approach

Many FCS are characterized by small domestic markets and weak institutional capacity, which limits their ability to attract investment and mitigate risks for investors. For this reason, a regional approach to investment climate reform can enhance the market-creation potential of the intervention. Interventions can benefit from a regional dimension in several ways:

1. The investment opportunity for some FCS may lie in a large neighboring market. Investment opportunity derived from market size is measured not just by the size of the domestic market, or by access to the global market, but also by the size of the regional market bordering the fragile country. A small fragile state, such as Bosnia and Herzegovina or Kosovo, secures significant investment opportunities through its proximity to affluent regional markets. Investment climate reforms that aim to develop the domestic private sector and attract foreign investment must be designed with this potential in mind.

2. One of the key reasons for fragile and conflict-affected situations' low growth and weak trade is a lack of investor confidence and a high perception of risk. Commitment mechanisms are needed for these countries to signal commitment to change that assures investors and raises their confidence (World Bank Group 2011, 283–84). Regional integration agreements with market access commitments and legal harmonization initiatives offer fragile states an opportunity to signal commitment by participating in such agreements and in their mutual monitoring mechanisms.

3. Cooperation among regional actors to pool technical and administrative resources can compensate for lack of

institutional capacity in FCS (World Bank Group 2011, 283–84). Such approaches may be considered a part of investment climate reform. For example, neighboring countries can set up national quality infrastructure and standards necessary for implementing them as shared regional institutions. Good and well-enforced product quality standards are a prerequisite for market access and competitiveness in foreign markets.

Neighboring countries and countries within the same regional block have an incentive to support fragile states in transitioning out of fragility. Conflict dynamics do not stay within borders and both reputational and conflict risk tend to spill over to neighboring countries. Regional organizations thus have a growing role to play in reducing fragility within their regions.

In summary, investment climate reforms are necessary for markets to move from conflict to peace, and from fragility to resilience. Deep changes to the rules of the game are essential. The limited capacity of governments in FCS, combined with the urgent need for quick and positive returns on reform efforts, require a balanced strategy that substantially enhances the investment climate in the country. De-risking and retaining investment, targeting investment promotion toward realistic investment opportunities, and optimally formalizing the economy to promote linkages between foreign and domestic investment are key elements of such a strategy.

Conclusion

Investors in fragile countries face a wide range of adverse market conditions, although some are similar to what they face in other developing markets—such as shortages of skilled labor, capital scarcity, and infrastructure shortcomings. The severity of these conditions in FCS, combined with security risks and lack of institutional capacity and legitimacy, create a seriously deficient investment climate in FCS.

Investment in FCS is thus well below potential. It is also concentrated in a limited number of capital-intensive sectors and creates fewer jobs than it would in less fragile environments. Investors are naturally cautious. If a firm decides to invest, the rewards must outweigh the risks. But the high risks in fragile states render many investment opportunities unviable.

Firms operating in FCS have several options for responding to the obstacles they face and to minimizing costs, risks, and challenges. Strategic choices of multinationals in terms of scale, staffing, and location often aim to address multiple challenges and risks at once. For example, hiring local staff provides access to local intelligence that helps mitigate security risks, as well as engage the local community. Some of the strategies documented by interviews with investors (IFC 2017) include integrated management and due diligence systems; strategically locating warehouses and production sites; tiered investments; international standards; flexibility in scale, supply, and business plans; and supporting government functions.

Investors with more knowledge of the local context, such as regional investors and diaspora investors, have still other mechanisms for coping in fragile states. Such investors familiar with the FCS environment tend to be able to cope better, take more risk, and accept lower returns. Data show that intraregional investment flows to fragile states are growing. These trends underscore the importance of regional sources of investment and regional approaches in transitioning out of fragility.

As development assistance becomes more constrained relative to the demands of reconstruction and development in FCS, the role of private investment in moving countries out of fragility will continue to grow. This underscores the need for active strategies for attracting investment and for developing the private sector in FCS.

The central message of this chapter is that, considering the centrality of the economic underpinnings of conflict, graduating from fragile status requires serious modifications to conventional methods of economic development. Market-creating investment climate reforms that reduce the risk to investors and maximize the opportunity are crucial to success.

Firm-specific strategies are clearly limited in what they can achieve. And, although they can keep a company out of harm's way, they cannot address the risks associated with fragility holistically or permanently. Given that many risks are inherently part of the definition of fragile states, even a large company's strategies can go only so far in addressing them. Investment climate reform tailored to the FCS context can go a long way toward reducing investors' risks and creating markets for investment.

Annex 5A. Definitions of FCS

The World Bank Group's (WBG) Fragile, Conflict and Violence Group (formally the Center on Conflict, Security and Development, CCSD) annually releases the Harmonized List of Fragile Situations. The first such list was compiled in fiscal year 2006 and has had a series of classification changes from the *Low-Income Countries Under Stress* List (LICUS) (2006–09), to the *Fragile States* List (2010), to the current *Harmonized List of Fragile Situations* (2011–15). The concept and the list have evolved as the WBG's understanding of the development challenges in countries affected by violence and instability has matured (see World Bank Group 2016).

"Fragile Situations" have either a harmonized average Country Policy and Institutional Assessment (CPIA) country rating of 3.2 or less or the presence of a UN or regional peacekeeping or peace-building mission during the past three years. This list includes only IDA-eligible countries and non-members or inactive territories/countries without CPIA data. Countries in the International Bank for Reconstruction and Development (IBRD) with CPIA ratings below 3.2 do not qualify for this list owing to nondisclosure of CPIA ratings; IBRD countries included here qualify only by the presence of a peacekeeping, political, or peace-building mission—and their CPIA ratings are thus not quoted here.

The 2017 list of FCS includes Afghanistan, Burundi, the Central African Republic, Chad, the Comoros, the Democratic Republic of Congo, Côte d'Ivoire, Djibouti, Eritrea, The Gambia, Guinea-Bissau, Haiti, Kiribati, Kosovo, Liberia, Madagascar, Mali, the Marshall Islands, the Federated States of Micronesia, Myanmar, Papua New Guinea, Sierra Leone, the Solomon Islands, Somalia, South Sudan, Sudan, Togo, Tuvalu, and the Republic of Yemen. Territories: West Bank and Gaza. Blend: Zimbabwe; IBRD only: Iraq, Lebanon, Libya, and Syria.

Countries that have appeared in the World Bank list since the first compilation include Angola, Bosnia and Herzegovina, Cambodia, Cameroon, the Republic of Congo, Georgia, Guinea, the Lao People's Democratic Republic, Lebanon, Malawi, Mauritania, Nepal, Nigeria, São Tomé and Príncipe, Tajikistan, Timor-Leste, Tonga, Uzbekistan, and Vanuatu.

Annex 5B. Investment Expectations Based on Economic Fundamentals

Predicted values of FDI and deviations to actual investment are used in the literature to form expectations based on specific questions of academic or policy interest (For examples, see Bellak, Leibrecht, and Stehrer 2008; Brenton and Di Mauro 1999; Demekas and others 2007). Non-econometric estimations in the form of composite indexes have also been published for the same purposes (see Maza and Villaverde 2015; Rodríguez, Gómez, and Ferreiro 2009; UN 2012), although they do not map directly onto flows of foreign investment.

These exercises have clear limitations: they depend on assumptions about the drivers of foreign investment, on past records rather than forecasts, and they are designed to answer questions that vary from one study to another. In addition, estimations are constrained by data availability for specific countries. Data constraints are particularly acute for FCS, most of which lack a complete and up-to-date set of drivers. As such, the estimates serve only to illustrate the cost of fragility at some specific point in time, and are not suitable for forward-looking country-specific policy advice, nor for country rankings.

In this exercise, predicted values of FDI flows are calculated to determine how much FDI inflows would be expected, based on recorded economic fundamentals *nett* of an estimated effect of fragility. Separating the negative impact of fragility from the predicted inflow (that is, fitted value) of this

TABLE 5B.1 Regression Coefficients

Variables	OLS Estimation				
	I	*II*	*III*	*IV*	*V*
GDP growth (percent)	0.023***	0.026	0.026		0.052***
	(0.008)	(0.017)	(0.017)		(0.012)
GDP (log)	1.136***	0.876***	0.909***	0.919***	0.938***
	(0.035)	(0.053)	(0.022)	(0.021)	(0.029)
	−0.207***	0.042			
Population (log)	(0.034)	(0.061)			
Trade openness ((X+M)/GDP)	0.011***	0.011***	0.011***	0.011***	0.010***
	(0.001)	(0.001)	(0.001)	(0.001)	(0.001)
Natural resources (percentage of GDP)	0.003	0.008***	0.008***	0.008***	0.014***
	(0.002)	(0.003)	(0.002)	(0.002)	(0.004)
Landlocked (=1)	−0.113	−0.261***	−0.253***	−0.203**	−0.339***
	(0.071)	(0.092)	(0.095)	(0.087)	(0.116)
Proximity to world markets	0.111	0.115	0.098	0.091	0.275***
Σ (Foreign GDP/distance)	(0.079)	(0.093)	(0.094)	(0.093)	(0.094)
Fragile States Index		−0.016***	−0.014***	−0.013***	−0.019***
		(0.003)	(0.003)	(0.003)	(0.003)
					−0.014***
Savings (percent of GDP)					(0.004)
Country fixed effects	No	No	No	No	No
Time (year) fixed effects	Yes	Yes	Yes	Yes	Yes
N = Number of observations	2074	882	882	884	738
R^2	0.753	0.766	0.765	0.761	0.771

Source: Computation based on data sources in the note.
Note: Standard errors are provided in parentheses under the estimated coefficients.
***$p < 0.01$; **$p < 0.05$; *$p < 0.1$.

Data sources for the table are as follows:

Variable	Source
FDI inflows (log)	Investment Map Database, International Trade Centre
Fragile States Index	The Fund for Peace (2014)
GDP (log)	World Development Indicators (2016), World Bank
GDP growth	World Development Indicators (2016), World Bank
Population	World Development Indicators (2016), World Bank
Savings	World Development Indicators (2016), World Bank
Trade openness	World Development Indicators (2016), World Bank
Distance to world markets	CEPII (2012)
Landlocked	CEPII (2012)
Natural resources	CEPII (2012); World Development Indicators (2016), World Bank

FIGURE 5B.1 **Expected Inward Investment Varies across FCS**

Fragility and predicted FDI flows, 2008–14

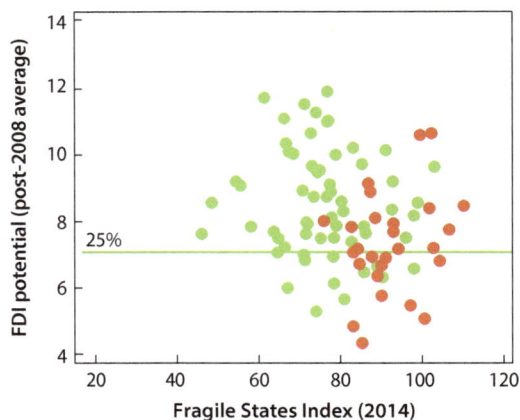

Source: Computations based on Investment Map Database, International Trade Centre.
Note: The green line crossing the panel indicates the upper threshold of the bottom quartile. The scatterplot shows predicted FDI and levels of fragility with FCS indicated in red and other developing countries in green. FCS = fragile and conflict-affected situations; FDI = foreign direct investment.

regression would yield an estimate of that expectation.

Investment is modeled using the following log-linear equation:

$$I_{it} = a + y_{it}\beta + f_{it}\gamma + d_t + \varepsilon_{it}, \quad I_{it} \in \mathbb{R}^+,$$

where the dependent variable I_{it} corresponds to the logarithm of investment inflows of country i at year t; y_{it} is a vector of country characteristics (table 5B.1); f_{it} corresponds to the FFP's Fragile States Index; d_t are fixed-effects for year t; and ε_{it} is the error term. The sample comprises all but the high-income countries of the world and standard errors are heteroscedasticity-consistent (robust estimation). In addition, the sample is not bilateral, hence the presence of few zeros, not warranting regressions based on special distributions.

Among five variants, the preferred specification used for the investment presented corresponds to the last column of table 5B.1, without population as a measure of size, but includes savings as share of GDP. Fixed effects are only includes for years but not for

countries, to avoid the absorption of the effect of fragility by the idiosyncratic effect.

The prediction is decomposed into two vectors: (a) a vector of covariates unrelated to fragility, and (b) the estimated impact of fragility and the error. The Structural Prediction corresponds to the first vector for country i at year t only:

$$\hat{I}_{it} = \left(a + y_{it}\hat{\beta} + \hat{d}_t\right) + f_{it}\hat{\gamma}$$

$$= structural\ prediction + f_{it}\hat{\gamma}$$

Granular FDI flows by origin or sector of activity are available for some of the FCS, but information based on investment potential at that level reduced the sample enormously and was not preferred.

Notes

1. See annex 5A for definition of FCS and list of economies.
2. Capital flees uncertainty and conflict (Knight, Loayza, and Villanueva 1996; Fielding 2004); and foreign firms are frequently targeted during insurgencies (Czinkota and others 2010; Lutz and Lutz 2014).
3. The *Liberian Diaspora Fund* is an example, with remittances from Liberians abroad pooled and matched to investments in a variety of sectors.
4. National Accounts data do not include the informal economy, which can be substantial in fragile and conflict-affected situations. Latest estimates of the size of the informal economy for the period 2005–2010 reveal very high numbers: 69 percent in Chad, 77 percent in DRC, 86 percent in Nepal, and 87 percent in Mozambique (see Charmes 2012). The numbers on the formal economy also likely suffer from errors due to the resource constraints of statistical agencies (inadequately trained staff; absence of resources for surveys; obsolete monitoring systems) also preventing regular updates. Conflict, lastly, brings about shocks to demographic and economic structures that statistical agencies are only able to capture years after violence has ceased. In Eritrea, Libya, and Syria, for example, GDP figures have not been updated for the last six years.

5. Household enterprises can include various service activities (for example, hairdressing, repairs, selling of goods), as well as industrial activities (for example, making of charcoal, bricks, iron work, grain processing), and artisanal activities (for example, woodworking, dressmaking, construction). Household enterprises in manufacturing tend to be replaced over time by factories, so they disappear faster over time than household enterprises in services (see Filmer and Fox 2014).

6. Post-conflict countries, for the purposes of this chart, include the subgroup of FCS where conflict has occurred since 1990, in addition to 11 outside the official list: Algeria, Colombia, Ethiopia, Guatemala, Mozambique, Nicaragua, Peru, Rwanda, Sri Lanka, Uganda, and Ukraine.

7. Afghanistan, the Central African Republic, the Republic of Congo, Sudan, and Zimbabwe are where the growth of services as a result of the associated shift of labor from agriculture to other sectors has been most pronounced.

8. Growth in manufacturing is only experienced in small countries such as Lebanon, the Federated States of Micronesia, Timor-Leste, or Tuvalu for reasons that are probably unrelated to transition along the postconflict continuum.

9. An Enterprise Survey is a firm-level survey of a representative sample of an economy's private sector. The surveys cover a broad range of business environment topics including access to finance, corruption, infrastructure, crime, competition, and performance measures. Since 2002, the World Bank has collected this data from face-to-face interviews with top managers and business owners in over 155,000 companies in 148 economies. See www.enterprisesurveys.org.

10. The World Economic Forum's (WEF) Executive Opinion Survey is one of the most comprehensive datasets that provides detailed insights into the challenges that firms face across countries. In its most recent version for 2016, 14,723 business executives from 141 countries assessed their domestic markets and countries on more than 80 variables.

11. In Liberia, for example, government's consistent underinvestment in infrastructure resulted in a poorly maintained public road network and energy infrastructure, much of which was subsequently destroyed during the prolonged conflict. Despite the reconstruction in the wake of the conflict, ports and other essential infrastructure could not satisfy local demands.

12. The Doing Business project by the World Bank Group provides objective measures of business regulations for local firms in 190 economies and selected cities at the subnational level. See http://www.doingbusiness.org/.

13. Such surveys are often conducted as part of the diagnostics necessary for advising governments on the best way to improve the investment climate. They are not published and, thus, specifying the country where such survey was conducted is not possible.

Bibliography

AfDB (African Development Bank). 2015. *Special Economic Zones in Fragile Situations—A Useful Policy Tool?* Abidjan: African Development Bank.

Arvanitis, Y. 2014. "Providing Efficient Banking Services in a Fragile Environment—Structure, Performance and Perspectives of the Banking Sector in Guinea-Bissau." West Africa Policy Note No. 1, Abidjan: African Development Bank.

Barbieri, Katherine, and Rafael Reuveny. 2005. "Economic Globalization and Civil War." *Journal of Politics* 67 (4): 1228–47.

Bray, J. 2005. "International Companies and Post-Conflict Reconstruction—Cross-Sectoral Comparisons." Social Development Papers, Conflict Prevention and Reconstruction Series no. CPR 22, World Bank, Washington, DC.

Bellak, C., M. Leibrecht, and R. Stehrer. 2008. "Policies to Attract Foreign Direct Investment: An Industry-Level Analysis." Presentation at the OECD Global Forum on International Investment, Paris, France, March 2008.

Brenton, Paul, and Francesca Di Mauro. 1999. "The Potential Magnitude and Impact of FDI Flows to CEECs." *Journal of Economic Integration* 14: 59–74.

Campbell, A. 2002. "The Private Sector and Conflict Prevention Mainstreaming: Risk Analysis and Conflict Impact Assessment Tools for Multinational Corporations." Mimeo. Carleton University.

Charmes, Jacques. 2012. "The Informal Economy Worldwide: Trends and Characteristics." *Margin: The Journal of Applied Economic Research* 6 (2): 103–32.

Collier, Paul. 2009. "Post-Conflict Recovery: How Should Strategies Be Distinctive?" *Journal of African Economies* 18 (1): 99–131.

Czinkota, M. R., G. Knight, P.W. Liesch, and J. Steen. 2010. "Terrorism and International Business: A Research Agenda." *Journal of International Business Studies* 41 (5): 826–43.

Demekas, D. G., H. Balász, E. Ribakova, and Y. Wu. 2007. "Foreign Direct Investment in European Transition Economies—The Role of Policies." *Journal of Comparative Economics* 35 (2):369–86.

Echandi, R. 2013. "Complementing Investor-State Resolution: A Conceptual Framework for Investor-State Conflict Management." In *Prospects in International Investment Law and Policy*, edited by R. Echandi and P. Sauvé, 270–306. Cambridge: Cambridge University Press.

Fielding, D. 2004. "How Does Violent Conflict Affect Investment Location Decisions: Evidence from Israel During the Intifada." *Journal of Peace Research* 41 (4).

Filmer, D., and L. Fox. 2014. *Youth Employment in Sub-Saharan Africa*. Africa Development Series. Washington, DC: World Bank.

Fund for Peace. 2016. "Fragile States Index." http://fundforpeace.org/fsi/.

Gissinger, R., and N. P. Gleditsch. 1999. "Globalization and Conflict. Welfare, Distribution, and Political Unrest." *Journal of World-Systems Research* 5 (2): 274–300.

Hallward-Driemeier, M., and L. Pritchett. 2015. "How Business Is Done in the Developing World: Deals versus Rules." *Journal of Economic Perspectives* 29 (3): 121–40.

Hoeffler, A. 2012. "Exporting from Fragile States: Challenges and Opportunities." OECD Working Paper 4, OECD, Paris.

IFC (International Finance Corporation). 2017. *Private Enterprise in Fragile and Conflict Situations*. Washington, DC.

IEG (Independent Evaluation Group). 2015. *Investment Climate Reforms: An Independent Evaluation of World Bank Group Support to Reforms of Business Regulations*. Washington, DC: World Bank.

International Dialogue for Peace-Building and State-Building. 2016. *International Standards for Responsible Business in Conflict-Affected and Fragile Environment*. Paris: OECD.

Knight, M., N. Loayza, and D. Villanueva. 1996. "The Peace Dividend: Military Spending Cuts and Economic Growth." Policy Research Working Paper 1577, World Bank, Washington, DC.

Liu, C., and E. Harwit. 2016. "The Effectiveness of Private Sector Development in Fragile and Conflict Affected Situations: Evidence from Evaluations." IFC, Washington, DC.

Lutz, B. J., and J. M. Lutz. 2014. "Terrorism and Its Impact on Foreign Economic Activity in Sub-Saharan Africa." *Journal of Business and Economics* 5 (4): 249–58.

Maza, A., and J. Villaverde. 2015. "A New FDI Potential Index: Design and Application to the EU Regions." *European Planning Studies* 23 (12): 2535–65.

Mills, R., and Q. Fan. 2006. "The Investment Climate in Post-Conflict Situations." Policy Research Working Paper 4055. World Bank, Washington, DC.

Mueller, H. F., L. Piemontese, and A. Tapsoba. 2017. "Recovery from Conflict: Lessons of Success." Policy Research Working Paper 7970, World Bank, Washington, DC.

Polachek, S. W., and D. Sevastianova. 2012. "Does Conflict Disrupt Growth? Evidence of the Relationship between Political Instability and National Economic Performance." *The Journal of International Trade and Economic Development* 21 (3): 361–88.

Porter Peschka, M. 2011. "The Role of the Private Sector in Fragile and Conflict-Affected States." Background Paper for the World Development Report, The World Bank, Washington, DC.

Ramachandran, V., and J. Walz. 2012. "Haiti: Where Has All the Money Gone?" CGD Policy Paper 004. Center for Global Development, Washington, DC.

Rodríguez, C., C. Gómez, and J. Ferreiro. 2009. "A Proposal to Improve the UNCTAD's Inward FDI Potential Index." *Transnational Corporations* 18 (3): 85–114.

Selaya, P., and E. R. Sunesen. 2012. "Does Foreign Aid Increase Foreign Direct Investment?" *World Development* 40 (11): 2155–76.

Speakman, J., and A. Rysova. 2015. *The Small Entrepreneur in Fragile and Conflict-Affected Situations*. Washington, DC: World Bank.

UN (United Nations). 2012. *World Investment Report, 2012*. Geneva: UN.

USAID (United States Agency for International Development). 2009. "Diaspora Direct Investment (DDI): The Untapped Resource for Development." Washington, DC.

———. 2016. *Local Private Sector Partnerships: Assessing the Sate of Practice.* Washington, DC: USAID.

WEF (World Economic Forum). 2016. *The Global Competitiveness Report 2016.* Geneva: WEF Publishing.

World Bank Group. 2009. *The Costs of Violence.* Washington, DC: World Bank.

———. 2011. *World Development Report 2011: Conflict, Security and Development: 2011.* Washington, DC: World Bank.

———. 2014. "Promoting Foreign Investment in Fragile and Conflict-Affected Situations." Investment Climate in Practice No. 22. World Bank, Washington, DC.

———. 2016. "Information Note: The World Bank Group's Harmonized List of Fragile Situations." http://pubdocs.worldbank.org /en/586581437416356109/FCS-List-FY16 -Information-Note.pdf.

Glossary

Behavioral incentives. Investment incentives intended to encourage certain investor behaviors, such as hiring local staff, investing in innovation, or using local suppliers to establish linkages.

Bilateral investment treaty. An agreement between two countries establishing the terms and conditions for private investment by an entity of one country in another country.

Competition effects. Competition between foreign firms and domestic firms that can lead to firms improving efficiency and upgrading production processes.

Demonstration effects. A type of spillover from FDI to the host economy in which domestic firms increase productivity by replicating foreign technologies or managerial practices either through observation or by hiring workers trained by foreign firms.

Developed countries. Developed countries refer to high-income countries as defined in this text.

Developing countries. Developing countries include low-, lower-middle-, and upper-middle-income countries as defined in the text. For the chapter on outward foreign direct investment (OFDI), these economies are classified according to the income category for 1995 and remain in the developing category even if they eventually surpass the high-income threshold in later years. They include Argentina, Chile, Croatia, Czech Republic, Estonia, Equatorial Guinea, Greece, Hungary, Latvia, Lithuania, Mauritius, Oman, Poland, the Russian Federation, Saudi Arabia, Slovak Republic, Slovenia, Trinidad and Tobago, Uruguay, and República Bolivariana de Venezuela.

Doing Business. This WBG project provides objective measures of business regulations and their enforcement across 190 economies and selected cities at the subnational and regional level. Launched in 2002, the project looks at domestic small and medium-sized companies and measures the regulations applicable to them throughout their life cycle.

East Asia and Pacific (EAP). The World Bank Group (WBG) region that includes the economies of American Samoa, Australia, Brunei Darussalam, Cambodia, China, Fiji, French

Polynesia, Guam, Hong Kong SAR China, Indonesia, Japan, Kiribati, the Democratic People's Republic of Korea, the Republic of Korea, Lao People's Democratic Republic, Macao SAR China, Malaysia, the Marshall Islands, the Federated States of Micronesia, Mongolia, Myanmar, Nauru, New Caledonia, New Zealand, Northern Mariana Islands, Palau, the Philippines, Samoa, Singapore, the Solomon Islands, Taiwan China, Thailand, Timor-Leste, Papua New Guinea, Tonga, Tuvalu, Vanuatu, and Vietnam. For the purposes of this report, the countries surveyed for the region may be a smaller subset of the actual regional grouping.

Efficiency-seeking FDI. One of the four motivations for FDI, efficiency-seeking FDI is when investors seek to increase cost efficiency of production by taking advantage of location-specific factors. These investors are also known as "cost-competitive investors." In this report and the Global Investment Competitiveness (GIC) survey, they are respondents who identified "lower production costs" or "establish a new base for exports" as a motivation to invest.

Enterprise Survey. A firm-level survey conducted by the WBG of a representative sample of an economy's private sector. The survey covers a broad range of business environment topics including access to finance, corruption, infrastructure, crime, competition, and performance measures. Since 2002, the WBG has collected this data via face-to-face interviews with top managers and business owners in more than 155,000 companies in 148 economies.

Europe and Central Asia (ECA). WBG region that includes the economies of Albania, Andorra, Armenia, Austria, Azerbaijan, Belarus, Belgium, Bosnia and Herzegovina, Bulgaria, Channel Islands, Croatia, Cyprus, Czech Republic, Denmark, Estonia, Faroe Islands, Finland, France, Georgia, Germany, Gibraltar, Greece, Greenland, Hungary, Iceland, Ireland, Isle of Man, Italy, Kazakhstan, Kosovo, Kyrgyz Republic, Latvia, Liechtenstein, Lithuania, Luxembourg, the former Yugoslav Republic of Macedonia, Moldova, Monaco, Montenegro, the Netherlands, Norway, Poland, Portugal, Romania, Russian Federation, San Marino, Serbia, Slovak Republic, Slovenia, Spain, Sweden, Switzerland, Tajikistan, Turkey, Turkmenistan, Ukraine, the United Kingdom, and Uzbekistan. For the purposes of this report, the countries surveyed for the region may be a smaller subset of the actual regional grouping.

Export share by sector. Calculated as non-host country sales divided by total sales based on the U.S. Bureau of Economic Analysis (BEA).

FDI inflow. All liabilities and assets transferred between resident direct investment enterprises and their direct investors into the reporting economy for the reporting period, usually for one year.

FDI outflow. All liabilities and assets transferred outward between resident direct investors and their direct investment enterprises away from the reporting economy for the reporting period, usually for one year.

FDI spillover. The impact of foreign firms' presence on domestic firms' economic performance. Positive FDI spillovers indicate that domestic firms acquire foreign technology and frontier knowledge through direct and indirect interactions with MNCs.

FDI stock. According to the Organisation for Economic Co-operation and Development (OECD), FDI stock measures total direct investment at a given point in time, usually at the end of a quarter or of a year. It represents the value of the resident investors' equity in and net loans to enterprises resident in the reporting economy.

Foreign affiliates. Generic term to describe various types of entities that a foreign investment might take. Affiliates may be subsidiaries, branches, or any other enterprise resident in a host country that is controlled by a nonresident institutional unit.

Foreign direct investment (FDI). According to the International Monetary Fund (IMF), FDI is a category of international investment made by a resident entity in one economy with the goal of establishing a lasting interest in an enterprise, resident in an economy other than the investor's. A lasting interest refers to the existence of a long-term relationship between the direct investor and the enterprise, and a significant degree of influence by the direct investor on the management of the direct investment enterprise. Components of FDI include equity, intra-company debt, and reinvested earnings.

Fragile and conflict-affected situations (FCS). Group of economies that have either a harmonized average Country Policy and Institutional Assessment (CPIA) country rating of 3.2 or less; or the presence of a United Nations or regional peacekeeping or peace-building mission during the past three years. The group of countries includes IDA-eligible countries and nonmember or inactive territories or countries without CPIA data. For fiscal year 2017, FCS include the following states and territories: Afghanistan, Burundi, Central African Republic, Chad, Comoros, the Democratic Republic of Congo, Côte d'Ivoire, Djibouti, Eritrea, The Gambia, Guinea-Bissau, Haiti, Iraq, Kiribati, Kosovo, Lebanon, Liberia, Libya, Madagascar, Mali, the Marshall Islands, the Federated States of Micronesia, Myanmar, Papua New Guinea, Sierra Leone, the Solomon Islands, Somalia, South Sudan, Sudan, the Syrian Arab Republic, Togo, Tuvalu, West Bank and Gaza, the Republic of Yemen, and Zimbabwe.

Government effectiveness. Part of the WBG's Worldwide Governance Indicators, government effectiveness is an aggregate indicator that reflects perceptions of the quality of public services, the quality of the civil service and the degree of its independence from political pressures, the quality of policy formulation and implementation, and the credibility of the government's commitment to such policies.

Global value chains (GVCs). International fragmentation of production where a single finished product results from manufacturing and assembly in multiple countries, with each step in the process adding value to the end product.

Gravity model. Economic model used to estimate bilateral effects between two geographic points, based usually on economic sizes and distance between the two locations.

Greenfield. Investment in which the investor builds its business operations from the ground up. In this report, greenfield refers to a mode of entry for FDI, where a foreign investor builds its operations in a host economy.

Herfindahl–Hirschmann Index (HHI). A measure of market concentration. In this report, the HHI for geographic concentration is defined as the sum of the squares of all countries' shares in the total number of FDI projects for a given sector. It would hence take the value of 1 in a hypothetical case where all FDI projects in a given sector went to one country. As the scale approaches 0, FDI projects are more dispersed among countries and the sector less geographically concentrated.

High-income countries. For fiscal year 2017, high-income economies are defined as those with a GNI per capita of $12,476 or more in 2015. For the chapter on OFDI, in 1995, these countries are defined as those with a gross national income (GNI) per capita of $9,386 or more.

High-growth firms. Firms that have a disproportionately large role in job creation in the economy.

Home economy. Country of origin of the foreign investment.

Horizontal FDI. Investment abroad by a company in the same industry in which the company operates in in the home economy.

Host economy. Country that receives the foreign investment.

International investment agreement (IIA). A type of treaty between states that addresses issues on cross-border investments. IIAs exist in three levels: bilateral (such as bilateral investment treaties), regional or preferential (such as regional customs unions and free trade areas or preferential trade agreements), and multilateral (such as applicable rules in World Trade Organization agreements and other international investment conventions).

Investment incentives. Measurable economic advantages that governments offer to specific enterprises or groups of enterprises with the goal of steering investments into preferred sectors or locations. These benefits can be fiscal (for example, tax concessions) or nonfiscal (for example, loans or rebates).

Investment protection guarantees. Guarantee or insurance provided for by law, government, multilateral agency, or any party for an investment made.

Investment promotion agency (IPA). Government agency or nonprofit organization whose job is to attract investment to the host economy.

Knowledge effects. Acquisition of knowledge, through FDI, either directly by the investor or investee firm, or indirectly through spillovers to other firms. Knowledge can take the form of technology, production techniques, or management skills.

Knowledge-seeking FDI. Type of FDI that aims to augment firm-specific advantage owned by the investor to improve its competitiveness by acquiring new knowledge. All knowledge-seeking FDI is strategic asset–seeking but not all strategic asset–seeking is knowledge-seeking.

Latin America and the Caribbean (LAC). WBG region that includes the economies of Antigua and Barbuda, Argentina, Aruba, The Bahamas, Barbados, Belize, Bolivia, Brazil, British Virgin Islands, Cayman Islands, Chile, Colombia, Costa Rica, Cuba, Curaçao, Dominica, the Dominican Republic, Ecuador, El Salvador, Grenada, Guatemala, Guyana, Haiti, Honduras, Jamaica, Mexico, Nicaragua, Panama, Paraguay, Peru, Puerto Rico, Sint Maarten (Dutch part), St. Kitts and Nevis, St. Lucia, St. Martin (French part), St. Vincent and the Grenadines, Suriname, Trinidad and Tobago, Turks and Caicos Islands, Uruguay, República Bolivariana de Venezuela , and Virgin Islands (U.S.). For the purposes of this report, the countries surveyed for the region may be a smaller subset of the actual regional grouping.

Linkages. The transmission of foreign knowledge and practices that may improve the production capabilities of domestic suppliers, as a result of contractual arrangements between local suppliers and multinational corporations.

Locational incentives. Investment incentives that are intended to influence the location decision of the investors.

Low-income countries. For fiscal year 2017, low-income economies are defined as those with a GNI per capita of $1,025 or less in 2015. For the chapter on OFDI, in 1995, these economies are defined as those with a GNI per capita of $765 or less.

Lower-middle-income countries. For fiscal year 2017, lower-middle-income economies are defined as those with a GNI per capita between $1,026 and $4,035 in 2015. For the chapter on OFDI, in 1995, these economies are defined as those with a GNI per capita between $766 and $3,035.

Manufacturing. Economic sector that produces goods.

Market-seeking FDI. A motivation for FDI in which the investor seeks to access domestic markets by supplying goods and services to the host economy.

Mergers and acquisitions (M&A). Transactions that result in the consolidation of companies or assets. In this report, M&A are FDI by nature, where the purchasing entity is a foreign investor that acquires the assets of a local firm.

Middle East and North Africa (MENA). WBG region that includes the economies of Algeria, Bahrain, Djibouti, the Arab Republic of Egypt, Islamic Republic of Iran, Iraq, Israel, Jordan, Kuwait, Lebanon, Libya, Malta, Morocco, Oman, Qatar, Saudi Arabia, the Syrian Arab Republic, Tunisia, the United Arab Emirates, West Bank and Gaza,and the Republic of Yemen. For the purposes of this report, the countries surveyed for the region may be a smaller subset of the actual regional grouping.

Multinational corporation (MNC). A corporation that has operations in more than one country and usually has a centralized head office which coordinates global management.

Natural resource–seeking FDI. A motivation for FDI in which investors seek to access natural resources—such as oil and gas, mining and minerals, water or solar power—in the host economy.

North America. WBG region that includes the economies of Bermuda, Canada, and the United States.

Outward FDI (OFDI). FDI from the perspective of the home economy. This is in contrast to FDI, which is from the perspective of the host economy. See entry for FDI.

Parent company. Institutional unit that owns enough interest in another firm to manage or operate the firm.

Postconflict countries. For this report, postconflict countries include the subgroup of FCS where conflict has occurred since 1990. In addition to the official list, 11 other countries include Algeria, Colombia, Ethiopia, Guatemala, Mozambique, Nicaragua, Peru, Rwanda, Sri Lanka, Uganda, and Ukraine.

Preferential margin. The difference between the standard corporate income tax rate and the preferential rate granted as an incentive.

Preferential trade agreement. A trading bloc that gives special treatment to participating entities.

Primary. Economic sector that uses natural resources including farming, mining, and fishing.

Reinvested earnings. Net earnings not paid out as dividends but retained by the firm for reinvestment in its business operations in the host country.

Scale effects. Average cost per unit decreases when production increases.

Services. Economic sector that produces nongoods, including financial services and retail services.

South Asia. WBG region that includes the economies of Afghanistan, Bangladesh, Bhutan, India, Maldives, Nepal, Pakistan, and Sri Lanka. For the purposes of this report, the countries surveyed for the region may be a smaller subset of the actual regional grouping.

Strategic asset–seeking FDI. A motivation for FDI in which investors seek to control firm or country-specific asset including brand, distribution network, or supply chain.

Sub-Saharan Africa (SSA). WBG region that includes the economies of Angola, Benin, Botswana, Burkina Faso, Burundi, Cabo Verde, Cameroon, Central African Republic, Chad, Comoros, the Democratic Republic of Congo, the Republic of Congo, Côte d'Ivoire, Equatorial Guinea, Eritrea, Ethiopia, Gabon, The Gambia, Ghana, Guinea, Guinea-Bissau, Kenya, Lesotho, Liberia, Madagascar, Malawi, Mali, Mauritania, Mauritius, Mozambique, Namibia, Niger, Nigeria, Rwanda, São Tomé and Príncipe, Senegal, the Seychelles, Sierra Leone, Somalia, South Africa, South Sudan, Sudan, Swaziland, Tanzania, Togo, Uganda, Zambia, and Zimbabwe. For the purposes of this report, the countries surveyed for the region may be a smaller subset of the actual regional grouping.

Tax holiday. Temporary complete removal of a tax granted to a specific firm or group of firms by a government.

The World Economic Forum's (WEF) Executive Opinion Survey. Conducted by the WEF, this survey captures information on a broad range of socioeconomic topics from executives across the world. In 2016, more than 13,000 responses in more than 130 countries were collected.

Upper-middle-income countries. For fiscal year 2017, upper-middle-income economies are defined as those with a GNI per capita between $4,036 and $12,475 in 2015. For the chapter on OFDI, in 1995, these economies are defined as those with a GNI per capita between $3,036 and $9,385.

Vertical FDI. Investment in an industry that produces inputs for the firms' operations, and is often used to offshore immediate production steps to locations with lower costs.

World Bank Group (WBG). Institutions that constitute the WBG include International Bank for Reconstruction and Development (IBRD), International Development Association (IDA), International Centre for Settlement of Investment Disputes (ICSID), International Finance Corporation (IFC), and Multilateral Investment Guarantee Agency (MIGA).

www.ingramcontent.com/pod-product-compliance
Lightning Source LLC
Chambersburg PA
CBHW041705210326
41598CB00007B/535